LIBRARIES
THE FIRST AMENDMENT AND CYBERSPACE

What

You Need

to Know

ROBERT S. PECK

D0109870

American Library Association
Chicago and London
2000

While extensive effort has gone into ensuring the reliability of information appearing in this book, the publisher makes no warranty, express or implied, on the accuracy or reliability of the information, and does not assume and hereby disclaims any liability to any person for any loss or damage caused by errors or omissions in this publication.

Project editor: Eloise L. Kinney

Text design by Dianne M. Rooney

Composition by the dotted i in Sabon and Avant Garde using QuarkXPress 4.0 on a Macintosh

Printed on 50-pound white offset, a pH-neutral stock, and bound in 10-point coated cover stock by McNaughton & Gunn

The paper used in this publication meets the minimum requirements of American National Standard for Information Sciences—Permanence of Paper for Printed Library Materials, ANSI Z39.48-1992.♾

Library of Congress Cataloging-in-Publication Data

Peck, Robert S.
   Libraries, the First Amendment, and cyberspace : what you need to
know / Robert S. Peck.
      p.   cm.
   ISBN 0-8389-0773-3
   1. Internet access for library users—Law and legislation—United
States. 2. Libraries—Censorship—Law and legislation—United
States. 3. Freedom of speech—United States. I. Title.
KF4315.P43 1999
025.04—dc21   99-39455

Printed in the United States of America.

04 03 02 01 00   5 4 3 2 1

CONTENTS

APPENDIXES

INTRODUCTION

Too often misinformation about free speech is circulated as if it were authoritative. The final straw for me and the inspiration for this book was a panel discussion at a state library association convention. There, as a member of the audience, I was treated to a confidently rendered but distorted description of First Amendment law as it applies to public libraries. As a legal matter, the speaker said, obscenity is something you know when you see it. This was decidedly wrong as a statement of the law, and I was unable to await my own scheduled talk later that day. I stood up during the question period and explained what the U.S. Supreme Court had actually said about obscenity and how the Constitution requires substantial procedural safeguards to be followed before a librarian may adjudge material obscene and take the matter to court. In defense, the panelist, a nonlawyer, justified her statements as based on what her city attorney had told her.

Of course, few city attorneys have much experience with First Amendment law. Their loyalties may not run to civil liberties as much as to whatever powers hold sway locally. In such instances, libraries are stuck with advice that has a more political than legal basis. For too many who provide that advice, the need to avoid controversy overwhelms fidelity to the law. Such political considerations, however, should not be part of the constitutional calculus—for the reasons to knuckle under to would-be censors are infinite and can only expand with each new concession. The result of such a standard operating procedure would then be an abandonment of the library's very purpose and mission: to assist in the diffusion of knowledge.

Neither ignorance of the law nor frustration over its complexity ought to deter compliance with the principles it sets out. Even though the law is filled with subtle touchstones, guidelines, and three-part tests that courts have difficulty applying, there are some basic and unimpeachable tenets that all can understand and act upon. Librarians and library policymakers, dedicated as they are to providing access to information, need an accurate basis upon which to base intelligent and legally appropriate policies about Internet access, as well as the other issues that libraries often face. This book aims to provide that foundation.

The development of constitutionally informed policies can ease some of the conflict that is bound to arise. To be sure, it will not end that conflict because speech, the written word, and pictures have an unquenchable capacity to generate controversy. It is almost a guarantee that whatever policies are eventually adopted will still be matters of great contention, activating factions who object to the materials thus made available or unavailable to the community. It is indisputable that libraries have become the front lines in modern free-speech wars. Still, a well-conceived policy can absorb some of the pain that accompanies that unfortunate reality and make all the difference in the litigation that may well follow.

The role of libraries at the center in the battle over the nation's intellectual freedoms is a familiar and long-running one. Almost from the moment of inception for public libraries, vociferous debates have ensued about material that someone or another has deemed inappropriate for shelving. One of the most enduring controversies over a book in the United States has been over Mark Twain's *Adventures of Huckleberry Finn*. As far back as 1885, the Concord, Massachusetts, Public Library banished the now-classic book as "the veriest trash" and "more suited to the slums than to intelligent, respectable people."[1] The book remains enormously controversial to this day.

As recently as October 19, 1998, the U.S. Court of Appeals for the Ninth Circuit was forced to rule on yet another attempt to remove that book—this time from a mandatory high-school freshman reading list in Tempe, Arizona. The court concluded that assignment of the book did not violate the constitutional right to equal protection of the laws, nor could it be removed because it allegedly contributed to a racially hostile learning environment.[2] *Huckleberry Finn* has endured more than a century of controversy with no sign that the hackles it raises will abate.

Cyberspace now poses additional challenges for libraries. Today's communications revolution, made possible by the "information superhighway," raises all past controversies anew, with some interesting twists on themes that have already played out in the courts. Public concern about cyberspace, especially about unrestricted access, tends to focus largely on the well-worn issues of sexual expression, hate-group material, and unsupervised minors. The contentious access debate echoes the difficult issues that libraries—and other public institutions—have struggled with since the beginning. Pornography and offensive materials always generated calls for censorship that must be rebuffed by the courts. Today, the same issues arise in sometimes difficult and different ways in the context of the Internet. And, in these new controversies, they will force the courts to reexamine the vitality of existing and seemingly bedrock First Amendment doctrine.

This book is intended to be a practical guide to the issues that arise under the First Amendment for libraries that provide public access to cyberspace. Though written in language easily accessible for the layperson, the book provides detailed and authoritative coverage of the legal issues, with citations to cases to assist lawyers who represent libraries in understanding the issues and responding to the demands and pressures that are part of the life of a public or school library. Every attempt was made to convey the law as it currently stands, rather than how the author or even the American Library Association might wish it to be. It will, therefore, pull no punches, indicate where the question is an open one, yet also denote what existing precedent suggests might be the ultimate resolution, at least where that can be determined.

At the same time, this book cannot be treated as a substitute for specific legal advice. However practical this book may be, it is a general discussion of legal issues applied to current national concerns. Each state's laws are different, and courts in different jurisdictions have occasionally reached different conclusions on specific issues. Sometimes a minor factual difference between two seemingly similar events can have a constitutional dimension and dictate a different legal result. The infinite variety of differences that could arise can never be covered in a single volume. And certainly no book can anticipate the precise situation any library might face or the new directions the law might take as a consequence of changing circumstances.

Still, an examination of the way that First Amendment law has developed does give useful and substantial guidance in understanding how it will apply to the powerful new communications medium of cyberspace, which has already lived up to many of its promises. Through access to the World Wide Web, an incredible array of useful information and knowledge is available to both the novice user and the sophisticated researcher. From a seat in front of a computer terminal, whether at home or in a library, a person can receive copies of government documents, court rulings, instantaneous news from many sources around the world, information about a wide variety of organizations and their issues and interests, thoughtful advice on all of life's questions, comparative consumer data about nearly any desired product, and the address and phone number of virtually any person on the planet. Information previously transmitted, if at all, through newspapers, magazines, books, inaccessible government publications, and difficult-to-obtain brochures, pamphlets, and reports is now instantly and widely available in electronic form.

The information explosion we will continue to witness, from front-row seats before a video screen, will have a larger impact on our lives than anything we have yet experienced and possibly a more profound effect than anything since the invention of movable type. Working habits, family relationships, socializing, and much, much more will be transformed. Our ability to obtain rapid, detailed, and specific knowledge about all aspects of the complex world in which we live will be unparalleled. Whatever our interests and whatever our taste in art, literature, and music, we will find it on the Internet, enabling us to travel to far-off lands, museums, events, and, of course, libraries.

It is also undeniable that the Internet has an underbelly that includes some dark and disgusting byways that many of us would rather not confront. That revulsion is, of course, heightened when we consider that our children might be exposed during an early formative period to things that they would never otherwise experience. It is then entirely natural that parents would want to shield their children from sites containing matter they would never permit in their homes—*and* that they would want public officials, including public librarians, to assist in carrying out those wishes.

In that last desire, however, they run into an obstacle that they do not face in their home: the First Amendment's protection of freedom of speech. Neither public librarians nor school officials can make the kinds of subjective decisions about reading matter that parents can. The First Amendment's guarantee of free speech and a free press stands as a broad prohibition against government involvement in constricting the spectrum of communicative materials available to the public. It contains no exception when access is sought by children just because parents object to the materials. Although there is a compelling governmental interest in protecting children from materials that might cause emotional or psychological harm, as will be discussed later in this book, a parent's ad hoc views cannot overcome other First Amendment considerations about guaranteeing adult access and even sometimes children's access despite parental objections. Neither can it set aside legal principles that permit only the most limited and highly specific interference when compelling interests justify government regulation.

Parents can legitimately object to materials because of the ideas those materials promote, whether those ideas reflect contemptible or disrespectful treatment of parents, behavior we recognize as discrimination, or the use of coarse or objectionable language. Parents may also object to treatment of sexuality, violence, or ghoulishness. In the home, a parent's say-so is the only justification needed. Parental decisions about what their minor children can read at home—or access on their computers—are final and unappealable. Not even the government may overrule those parental choices. Parents do not, however, have the authority to require the assistance of government toward their ends. To some, this position may seem unnecessarily and even actively hostile to community values and parental authority. Yet the lessons of history and the theory of our Constitution hold that a free people is better served by free trade in ideas—no matter how despicable—than by authoritative selection by government officials about which ideas are suitable for people, even when in the service of parents.

Once again, libraries are likely to form the front line on this issue as the Internet provides a new medium in which to test the idea of free speech for the next century. A joint survey by the American Library Association and the National Commission on Libraries and Information Science in November 1998 discovered that 73 percent of the nation's public libraries now offer basic Internet access to the public, up from a mere 28 percent only two years earlier.[3] With the advent of the federal E-rate discount to enable more public libraries and schools to connect to the Internet, the public is likely to find libraries a convenient way to access this wondrous electronic world.

Along with the joy this will bring to Mudville, it is likely to bring complaints and protests of the most vociferous nature. In the face of such complaints and requests to limit access to material protected by the Constitution as free speech, it is important to keep in mind the U.S. Supreme Court's declaration that "above all else, the First Amendment means that government has no power to restrict expression because of its message, its ideas, its subject matter, or its content."[4] The explanation for this prohibition lies in one of the major purposes of the First Amendment: to "foreclose public authority from assuming a guardianship of the public mind."[5] Thus, government is generally prohibited from performing a function that every parent performs for his or her children: the exercise of a protective attitude toward the expressive materials available to people and, in many instances, to children. Moreover, librarians may not act as a stand-in for parents, excising from access only those materials that the actual parent had previously designated as unfit for that parent's child.

This is not to say that the First Amendment is an absolute and that it requires an anything-goes attitude by the government and its personnel. There are some narrow and defined exceptions to the First Amendment's protection of speech. These do not, however, amount to a license that enables the exceptions to swallow the rule. Those pressure groups who would have libraries screen material so that no one's sensibilities could ever be offended hark back to an attitude that was rejected on American soil long ago. It is exemplified by the paternalistic declaration of the colonial governor of Virginia, Sir William Berkeley, in 1671:

> I thank God, there are no free schools nor printing [in Virginia], and I hope we shall not have these [for a] hundred years; for learning has brought disobedience, and heresy, and sects into the world, and printing has divulged them, and libels against the best government. God keep us from both.[6]

Today, the overwhelming issue is sexual content—and the Internet has, as it has done with all other subjects, made sex more accessible to all. Moral concerns have long raised the sexual issue as one that libraries must confront. The most brilliant writings in the English language, the plays of William Shakespeare, were considered so risqué that Thomas Bowdler earned his place in history by publishing expurgated versions of these classics. Another morality campaigner, Anthony Comstock, crusaded against vulgar and sexually oriented books that he said seduced men, women, and children into depraved lives, succeeding in getting Congress to pass a law in 1873, which he then zealously enforced. Among the many books that felt the brunt of the Comstock law were such well-known classics as Aristophane's *Lysistrata*, Rabelais's *Gargantua*, Geoffrey Chaucer's *Canterbury Tales*, Boccaccio's *Decameron*, and *The Arabian Nights*.

Comstock also targeted dime novels as "pregnant with mischief," "demoralizing" to youth, and "devil-traps for the young," with their lurid tales of lust, crime, and bloodshed.[7] Yet by the time the law he inspired, which prohibited the sale of these books to minors, came before the U.S. Supreme Court in 1948, the Court had breathed life into the inert constitutional promise of freedom of speech. At issue was whether New York State could enforce such a law against a merchant who had sold true-crime magazines, which contained such titillating articles as "Bargains in Bodies" and "Girl Slave to a Love Cult," to a youngster. Although the Supreme Court saw "nothing of any possible value to society in these magazines, they are as much entitled to the protection of free speech as the best of literature."[8]

The issue never receded after the Comstock era. A national survey taken during the period of the Great Depression found that most children first learned about sex from a number of books in wide circulation, causing a member of Congress to decry easy access to them on the House floor. Perhaps the reason Congress did not pass a law to combat this scourge is that the survey found the books most guilty of conveying sexual information to children, from most frequently cited to least, to be the Bible, the dictionary, the encyclopedia, the novels of Charles Dickens, and the plays of Shakespeare.

Although no one would confuse much of what passes for information on the Internet with these essential works, the underlying question remains the same: can a nation conceived in and dedicated to the idea of intellectual and political freedom restrict access to information that some or even a majority of the people deem untoward in some regard? American history teaches and American jurisprudence generally answers the question in the negative. Still, it is largely in the specifics that the issue becomes more complex.

NOTES

1. Mark I. West, *Children, Culture, and Controversy* (Hamden, Conn.: Archon Books, 1988), 21–22.

2. *Monteiro v. Tempe Union High Sch. Dist.,* 158 F.3d 1022 (9th Cir. 1998).

3. ALA Public Information Office, "New Report Shows More Libraries Connect to the Internet; Access Still Limited" (press release, Nov. 1998).

4. *Police Department v. Mosley,* 408 U.S. 92, 95 (1972).

5. *Thomas* v. *Collins,* 323 U.S. 516, 545 (1945) (Jackson, J., concurring).

6. Robert S. Peck, *The Bill of Rights and the Politics of Interpretation* (St. Paul, Minn.: West Publishing, 1992), 99.

7. West, *supra* note 1, at 12–13; Margaret A. Blanchard, *The American Urge to Censor* 33 William & Mary L. Rev. 741, 757 (1992).

8. *Winters* v. *New York,* 333 U.S. 507, 510 (1948).

CHAPTER 1

Questions and Answers about the First Amendment

Sex, Lies, and Cyberspace

This chapter provides basic information about the First Amendment and its application to libraries in lay terms. Most of the answers are general in nature, but they provide a useful sense of how courts look at key questions. Endnotes provide citations to relevant cases. More detailed explanations of the relevant law are provided in subsequent chapters.

The questions in this chapter are arranged under general topic headings to make it easier for the reader to discover the basic law in the areas that come up most frequently.

First Amendment Basics

1. The First Amendment reads, "Congress shall make no law . . . abridging the freedom of speech, or of the press; or the right of the people peaceably to assemble, and to petition the Government for a redress of grievances." We aren't Congress. Why does this apply to public libraries, public school libraries, or publicly employed librarians?

Although the First Amendment, when first drafted and ratified, was intended to ensure that the federal government would not interfere with free expression rights, its scope was expanded after the addition of the Fourteenth Amendment in 1868. Decisions of the U.S. Supreme Court interpreted Section 1 of that amendment to make the fundamental rights spelled out in the Bill of Rights obligations of the states and their political subdivisions as well. Public libraries and public schools are governmental entities and must comply with the Constitution. When courts indicate that a restriction on local public library materials violates the First Amendment, they are using shorthand to indicate the incorporation of the First Amendment's guarantees by the Fourteenth Amendment.

2. The First Amendment indicates that it prevents the passage of laws restricting freedom of speech. Our library board passes rules, regulations, and guidelines, not laws. Does the First Amendment still apply?

Law is a very broad term that is not just limited to statutes and ordinances. It includes rules, regulations, guidelines, court rulings, and even official actions. If this were not so, government officials could accomplish what the Constitution forbids simply by characterizing the restriction on speech as something other than a law. Were a public employee, acting in his or her official capacity, to remove a book from a library because of disagreement with the ideas expressed in the book, that action would be a violation of the First Amendment, even though no "law" was involved.

3. My state has a constitution of its own. Does it have a First Amendment? If so, where does it fit into the constitutional law?

Every state has a state constitution, which defines the type of government that exists in that state. Each of these constitutions has a declaration of rights, which may go further in protecting the rights guaranteed in the U.S. Constitution. These declarations always include a guarantee of freedom of speech. As a matter of constitutional law, none of these state guarantees of free speech can be *less stringent* than that provided for by the First Amendment, which serves as a floor of the minimal liberties every state must observe. However, through its own constitution, a state *can* further restrict its own authority to interfere with free speech. Thus, the highest courts in several states have held that the state constitutional free-speech analogue to the First Amendment guarantees greater freedom than its federal analogue.

The state that has gone the furthest in this respect is Oregon. Although the U.S. Supreme Court has declared that obscenity falls outside the protection of speech contained in the First Amendment, the Oregon Supreme Court has construed its state constitutional guarantee to protect even obscene speech.[1]

4. What does the constitutional guarantee of freedom of speech mean?

Over the course of more than two centuries, we have developed an understanding of the scope of the constitutional guarantee of freedom of speech. We place great emphasis on freedom of speech because we believe, as Justice Benjamin Cardozo wrote in 1937, that free speech is "the indispensable condition of nearly every other form of freedom."[2] Only through unimpeded access to knowledge and information can we discharge our duties as citizens in a constitutional republic to choose among competing public policies, select political leaders, and call attention to problems and issues otherwise ignored.

At its core, the First Amendment guarantees a freedom of the mind that enables us to think whatever thoughts we want and to convey many of those thoughts to others, without fear of punishment. The Supreme Court has said that the "First Amendment presupposes that the freedom to speak one's mind is not only an aspect of individual liberty—and thus a good unto itself—but also is essential to the common quest for truth and the vitality of society as a whole."[3]

The system of free expression guaranteed by the Constitution enables us to question the official orthodoxy of high authority and attempt to persuade others to our view. And it creates a "marketplace of ideas," in which we are free to sample a broad range of expressions and make our own decisions about the validity, advisability, or attractiveness of the ideas expressed.

In a now-classic description of freedom of speech, the Supreme Court held that the First Amendment constitutes "a profound national commitment to the principle that debate on public issues should be uninhibited, robust, and wide-open, and that it may well include vehement, caustic, and sometimes unpleasantly sharp attacks on government and public officials."[4] Although that declaration by the Court reflected a decision in the area of political speech, the idea of "uninhibited, robust, and wide-open" expression applies to the full range of human thought. "The line between the informing and the entertaining is too elusive" to separate protected speech from unprotected speech.[5]

The Supreme Court has also stated that "above all else, the First Amendment means that government has no power to restrict expression because of its message, its ideas, its subject matter, or its content."[6] Among the bedrock principles that this statement represents is the idea that "under our Constitution the public expression of ideas may not be prohibited merely because the ideas are themselves offensive to some of their hearers."[7]

5. Does the First Amendment include a right of access to information?

The Supreme Court has stated that "the right to receive ideas is a necessary predicate to the recipient's meaningful exercise of his own rights of speech, press, and political freedom."[8] Thus, "the First Amendment protects the public's interest in receiving information."[9]

6. *Do children have lesser First Amendment rights than adults?*

Yes, but those rights remain substantial. The Supreme Court has said that "[s]peech . . . cannot be suppressed solely to protect the young from ideas or images that a legislative body thinks unsuitable for them. In most circumstances, the values protected by the First Amendment are no less applicable when government seeks to control the flow of information to minors."[10]

Still, the Court has "repeatedly recognized the governmental interest in protecting children from harmful materials."[11] These two judicial declarations clearly make a distinction between materials merely deemed unsuitable, which minors have a First Amendment right of access to, and those that have been determined to be harmful, which can be regulated. Generally, materials deemed harmful are those that have been adjudged obscene for minors.

Even though minors' access to harmful materials can be restricted, there are important limitations on this authority as well. First, all minors *cannot* be treated the same. Regulations must be sensitive to the obvious differences in maturity and therefore rights of access for a seventeen-year-old, who will have greater rights, and a five-year-old. As the Court stated, "the government's interest in protecting minors is not equally strong throughout" childhood.[12] A second limitation on the government's authority is that the restrictions cannot be so broad as to adversely affect adults' right of access to material that is protected under the First Amendment for them. Any other result would have the unfortunate and unconstitutional consequence of reducing adult access "to that which would be suitable for a sandbox."[13]

The free-speech rights of minors are somewhat further limited in the context of a public school. Although the Supreme Court has recognized that students do not "shed their constitutional rights to freedom of speech or expression at the schoolhouse gate"[14] and "may not be regarded as closed-circuit recipients of only that which the State chooses to communicate,"[15] the Court has recognized several grounds upon which student rights could be restricted in the school context that have no validity outside of that environment. First, student speech can be suppressed if necessary to avoid a material and substantial interference with schoolwork, discipline, or the rights of others.[16] Such a disturbance must be real and substantial and not merely words that are likely to offend or start an argument.[17] Second, authorities may restrict student speech when "reasonably related to legitimate pedagogical concerns."[18] Finally, a school may restrict student speech thought to bear the school's imprimatur as a function of disassociating itself with the speech.[19]

7. What exceptions are there to the constitutional guarantee of free speech?

The courts have recognized three basic exceptions to the federal Constitution's protection of free speech: obscenity, fighting words, and libel. In addition, the courts have recognized a distinction between conduct and speech.

Several states have taken a different attitude with respect to obscenity. The Oregon Supreme Court found that obscenity was within the free-speech guarantees of the state constitution and may not be punished to impose a uniform vision of how human sexuality should be regarded or portrayed.[20] The Oregon court further said that obscenity may still be regulated in the interests of unwilling viewers, captive audiences, minors, and beleaguered neighbors. Hawaii's Supreme Court has also used its state constitution to invalidate a criminal obscenity law.[21] Five states—Alaska, Maine, New Mexico, South Dakota, and Vermont—do not have laws that punish obscenity.

8. Does the federal constitutional exception for obscenity apply to all displays of nudity?

No. *Obscenity* and *nudity* are not synonymous. Although *obscene materials,* which is a very narrow category of hardcore sexual acts that have a tendency to excite lustful thoughts, can be made illegal, a law that prohibited the circulation or exposure of materials that contained nudity would not be constitutional. In fact, in 1975, the U.S. Supreme Court struck down a law that banned nudity in movies shown in drive-in theaters when the screen was visible from the street.[22]

The Court's decisions recognize that there are innocent displays of nudity, such as a baby's buttocks, as well as other nude displays that do not appeal to prurient interests and are thus not obscene. Moreover, nude paintings, for example, have long been considered a high art form that the Court determined should remain within the First Amendment's protections. For this reason, even those forms of sexual expression that meet the levels of prurience and patent offensiveness that otherwise would constitute obscenity may not be deemed obscene if the material has serious value.

9. *Does the exception for obscenity mean that all pornography can be banned?*

No. In legal terms, *obscenity* and *pornography* are not synonyms. Pornography is a form of protected speech. The U.S. Supreme Court has recognized that erotic messages are within the First Amendment's protections.[23] The Court's obscenity decisions comprehend that sex is a subject in well-regarded literature and art and a mysterious force that commands great human attention. It therefore decided that society's concerns about obscenity should not be a vehicle to interfere with serious artistic or scientific endeavors.

10. *Does the exception for obscenity apply to indecent words?*

The U.S. Supreme Court has unambiguously said that "[s]exual expression which is indecent but not obscene is protected by the First Amendment."[24] However, in the context of the public schools and broadcasting, there is greater governmental authority to restrict indecent expression than there is elsewhere, such as in public protests or publishing.

11. *How is* obscenity *defined by the courts?*

To be obscene, a court or jury must determine that

1. "the average person, applying contemporary community standards," would find that the work, taken as a whole, appeals to the prurient interest;
2. the work depicts or describes, in a patently offensive way, sexual conduct specifically defined by the applicable law; and
3. the work, taken as a whole, lacks serious literary, artistic, political, or scientific value.[25]

12. *If someone accuses material in our library of being obscene and we believe it comes close to the line, can we simply remove it?*

People often mistakenly quote Justice Potter Stewart's statement that "I know it when I see it" as an appropriate way for public officials to judge obscenity. The statement merely reflected Stewart's frustration in attempting to come up with a definition for obscenity. Stewart was wondering out loud, and alone on the Court, whether obscenity might be entirely resistant to legal definition. Constitutional principles, however, hold that freedom of speech is endangered when public officials make ad hoc decisions about what is protected and what is prohibited. If materials are determined to violate state obscenity law, due process demands a prompt hearing in a court of law, where the officials bear the burden of showing that the materials are, in fact, obscene and where the distributor or originator of the materials may defend them. The judicial process alone has the authority to determine whether the materials are obscene and thus removable.[26]

A requirement that there be a finding of obscenity before books may be removed from a school library appears to be unnecessary, under existing judicial precedent. Generally, there is greater authority in school officials to maintain an environment conducive to learning the selected curriculum. In finding the removal of certain school library books that were said to be "anti-American, anti-Christian, anti-Semitic, and just plain filthy" unconstitutional because it represented a school board's disagreement with the ideas presented in those books, the U.S. Supreme Court suggested that there would have been no constitutional problem if the board's removal of the books were based on pervasive vulgarity or educational unsuitability under unbiased regular procedures.[27]

13. Can we remove it temporarily, pending a more formal determination?

Although constitutional decisions look with disfavor upon any temporary breach of First Amendment rights, a temporary block followed promptly by formal proceedings has been deemed permissible in some instances.[28]

14. Isn't there special treatment in the law for child pornography?

Child pornography is a special category of sexual material that the U.S. Supreme Court has said can be prohibited in the interests of preventing commerce in the abusive use of children as subjects of pornography.[29]

15. Where do "harmful-to-minors" laws fit into the obscenity/ pornography issue?

"Harmful-to-minors" is a category of obscenity that uses children as its reference point. Thus, the standard definition of obscenity is revised to determine if the material appeals to the prurient interests of children, is patently offensive to children, and has no social, literary, scientific, or political value for children.

Fighting Words

16. How do the courts define the exception for "fighting words"?

"Fighting words" are those words "which by their very utterance inflict injury or tend to incite an immediate breach of the peace."[30] Such words must be uttered as a direct personal insult in a face-to-face confrontation and calculated or highly likely to result in an immediate violent physical reaction.

17. Does the exception for fighting words mean that hate speech can be prohibited?

No. Because the government cannot prescribe which thoughts we can think or which political philosophies we can advocate, hate speech receives considerable constitutional protection. As a result, the "fighting words" doctrine only applies to a narrow class of speech that constitutes a clear and present danger of responsive violence to personally insulting utterances. It is not, the U.S. Supreme Court has said, a tool to cleanse public debate or regulate words that give offense.[31]

Libel

18. How do the courts define the exception for "libel"?

A written libel or an oral slander defames an individual and has the effect of ruining that person's reputation, standing in the community, or ability to associate with others. Because of the adverse economic consequences that false accusations can have, the courts can award damages to compensate an individual injured by those false accusations. By contrast, truthful yet hurtful accusations incur no similar damage and are not actionable.

19. Are there special categories of libel that have more or less constitutional protection than others?

The U.S. Supreme Court has recognized a different standard with respect to public officials. Because the right to question government actions and policy is central to a democratic republic, the Court has said that a "rule compelling the critic of official conduct to guarantee the truth of all his factual assertions—and to do so on pain of libel judgments virtually unlimited in amount—leads to . . . self-censorship."[32] As a result, the Court requires public officials claiming to have been libeled to demonstrate that the publisher of the alleged libel knew that the statement was false or recklessly disregarded the truth or falsity of it.

A standard similar to that established for public officials was also established for public figures, who, the Court reasoned, have ready access to the mass media to counter criticism of their views and activities.

Other Categories of Speech: Harassment

20. Aren't laws restricting racial or sexual harassment a restriction on freedom of speech?

Generally, anti-harassment laws reach conduct that goes beyond speech. Therefore, the "mere utterance of an . . . epithet which engenders offensive feelings in a employee" cannot constitute illegal harassment.[33]

Racial and sexual harassment are forms of discrimination that violate federal and state civil rights laws. Verbal harassment generally occurs when it is personally directed at someone because of his or her race or gender and has the purpose or effect of unreasonably interfering with the individual's job or student performance or creates a severe or pervasively intimidating, hostile, or offensive environment. To constitute such a hostile environment, a court considers "the frequency of the discriminatory conduct; its severity; whether it is physically threatening or humiliating, or a mere offensive utterance; and whether it unreasonably interferes with an employee's work performance."[34]

The high threshold that must be established to demonstrate a hostile environment ensures that no violation of anti-harassment laws occurs when the language or pictures in question merely offend or express a political philosophy that one finds repugnant on racial or sexual grounds. Instead, an objective standard is utilized to supplement the subjective view of the alleged victim or victims and takes into account the whole record and the totality of circumstances.[35] Conduct that is not severe or pervasive enough to create an objectively hostile or abusive work environment—an environment that a reasonable person would find hostile or abusive—is not a civil rights violation.

21. Can what a patron reads at a desk or views on a computer screen constitute harassment of library employees?

Precedents suggest that what a library patron reads or views can, under some circumstances, constitute harassment of a library employee. Generally, to be harassment, the conduct must be extensive and repetitive in a manner that so pervades the work environment that it becomes hostile *and* with the employer taking no steps to ameliorate the situation once notified of its existence. Some qualifications, though, are in order. First, conduct that is isolated or occasional cannot be considered sufficient to change the work environment and render it hostile.[36] The occasional use of library Internet access by a patron that some find offensive seems to fall within this limitation, especially because employees can look away. Where that is not the case and the patron keeps calling the employee over, a change in work assignments to an employee not offended by the material accessed would be in order.

Second, there generally appears to be a requirement that offensive pictures be accompanied by other sexually discriminatory conduct.[37] Finally, where the complained-of material is related to the employer's business, courts have found that the employee's harassment claim cannot override First Amendment rights to sell, distribute, or provide access to First Amendment–protected material.[38]

To be safe from liability, however, steps to accommodate a complaining employee are advisable, such as the installation of privacy screens that would reduce a complaining employee's exposure to offensive material and reduce the chances that such material could pervasively affect the library environment.[39] In addition, every library should have a written anti-harassment policy and clear notice to fellow employees and patrons of the policy.

22. What do the courts mean by "commercial speech"?

"Commercial speech" comprises messages that "propose a commercial transaction," such as advertising.[40] Where commercial and noncommercial speech are "inextricably intertwined," the entire communication is classified as noncommercial.[41] Commercial speech receives a slightly lesser degree of First Amendment protection, largely to permit the government to regulate commerce and engage in consumer protection.

Basically, commercial speech is entitled to First Amendment protection if it concerns lawful activity and is not misleading.

Other Government Authority over Speech

23. We know that the First Amendment is not an absolute, even where the type of speech is considered protected. What kinds of restrictions can government place on free speech? Does government have any further authority to restrict speech?

To override the constitutional guarantee of the First Amendment and regulate protected speech, the government must demonstrate that it is operating in furtherance of a compelling interest and has chosen the least restrictive means to further that articulated interest.[42] This is an extremely stringent test that is not easily met and must be used to further an overriding and legitimate government concern.

In addition, when speech can be uttered in a public place, the government is permitted to impose "time, place or manner" restrictions. This kind of governmental authority exists to enable government "to keep the peace and to protect other interests of a civilized society."[43]

24. What constitutes a compelling interest sufficient for government to restrict free speech?

National security, the prevention of violence, and the physical and psychological well-being of minors are examples of compelling state interests sufficient to provide a justification for overriding free-speech considerations. Still, the existence of a compelling interest does not constitute a constitutional blank check that enables the government to step in with impunity. The assertion of national security interests did not prevent publication of the *Pentagon Papers* by the *New York Times* and *Washington Post*.[44] The assertion of an interest in preventing violence did not justify imposing a fee to help finance additional law enforcement costs for a white supremacist group's march.[45] And the assertion of interest in the well-being of children was insufficient to justify a ban on "dial-a-porn" telephone messages.[46]

Even where the government meets its burden of demonstrating a compelling interest, it must further prove that it is utilizing the least restrictive means of furthering that interest.

25. What is meant by "the least restrictive means"?

When the government attempts to regulate a fundamental right, "it must do so by narrowly drawn regulations designed to serve those interests without unnecessarily interfering with First Amendment freedoms."[47] Where less drastic means are available to achieve the same basic purpose, even if the result would be less complete from the viewpoint of the government's asserted interest, that less restrictive alternative must be utilized. For example, when the U.S. Supreme Court invalidated the ban on "dial-a-porn," it noted that requiring customers to produce credit cards or receive access codes to overcome scrambling would limit youthful access while preserving adult rights. Although some minors might still evade these obstacles, this alternative solution to protecting the well-being of children was more sensitive than a flat ban was to constitutional considerations of free speech and thus a less restrictive alternative.[48]

26. What is meant by "time, place, or manner restrictions"?

These restrictions limit the times, locations, or means used to convey a message. For example, a law might legitimately limit the volume used by speakers when in a school or hospital zone, to prevent interference with the work going on in those locations. Time, place, or manner regulations will be upheld if they "are content-neutral, are narrowly tailored to serve a significant government interest, and leave open ample alternative channels of communication."[49] Another example of such a restriction would be a regulation that only permits one traffic-disrupting parade permit to be used on any given day.

27. What is meant by a regulation being "content-neutral"?

A "content-neutral" regulation is one that applies to all speech equally, regardless of the subject matter or viewpoint being expressed. A regulation that discriminated between speech on the basis of the topic or a viewpoint discussed would not be neutral and could not be subjected to time, place, or manner restrictions without meeting the "compelling interest test." The reason that content neutrality is important is because "the First Amendment forbids the government to regulate speech in ways that favor some viewpoints or ideas at the expense of others."[50] One important test of whether the government has breached its obligation to content-neutral regulation is "whether the government has adopted a regulation of speech because of disagreement with the message [the regulated expression] conveys."[51]

28. What constitutes a secondary effect that enables government to enact other restrictions?

The concept of secondary effects refers to legitimate objects of government regulation that "happen to be associated with a particular type of speech [but] have nothing to do with [the] content" of that speech.[52] For example, Indiana's law against public nudity was upheld in its application to an establishment that wanted to feature nude barroom dancing, to prevent a criminal element from being attracted to the area surrounding the bar.[53] The Court acknowledged that nude dancing was a form of expression that conveyed "eroticism and sexuality" but held that requiring a G-string and pasties "simply makes the message slightly less graphic."[54] Thus, the permissible scope of a secondary-effect regulation is not to ban an expressive activity altogether, but to lessen its undesirable effect (in this case, attracting a criminal element) while permitting it to still get its message across.

29. Free speech is at its pinnacle in a traditional public forum. What is meant by a "public forum"?

The best description of what is meant by a traditional public forum was written in a 1939 U.S. Supreme Court case: "Wherever the title of streets and parks may rest, they have immemorially been held in trust for the use of the public and, time out of mind, have been used for purposes of assembly, communicating thoughts between citizens, and discussing public questions."[55] In such places where public speech has traditionally taken place or that have been designated as a location for that purpose by the government, government may only regulate (1) to serve a compelling state interest utilizing a regulation that is narrowly drawn to achieve that end; or, (2) to serve a significant, though not compelling, state interest using a content-neutral time, place, or manner regulation that is narrowly tailored to serve the asserted interest and still leaves ample alternative channels of communication.[56]

One of the most sacrosanct rules governing use of public forums is that the "government may not grant the use of a forum to people whose views it finds acceptable, but deny use to those wishing to express less favored or more controversial views."[57]

Not all government property is automatically considered a traditional public forum. Government property may also be classified as a "limited" or "designated" public forum or as a nonpublic forum.

30. What is a "limited" or "designated" public forum?

Where public property has not traditionally been used for public speech, the government may affirmatively open the property as a place for the public's expressive activity. The same constitutional rules apply to the "limited" or "designated" public forum as apply to the traditional public forum, as long as the government continues to designate it for the expressive activities of the public. A municipal auditorium, available for public rental, is an example of a "limited" or "designated" public forum. The government has no authority to deny use of the auditorium to groups whose views it abhors or to entertainment that it views as antisocial.

The government does, however, maintain the authority to withdraw the designation of such a facility as a public forum but cannot exercise that authority solely to withhold use of the forum from disfavored messages or speakers.

31. Is there any right to free speech in a nonpublic forum?

Yes. A nonpublic forum is one that is neither a traditional venue of public expressive activity nor designated as such by the government. A nonpublic forum is a place where communicative activity takes place but is reserved and limited to a specific use, "as long as the regulation on speech is reasonable and not an effort to suppress expression merely because public officials oppose the speaker's view."[58] Within those limitations, qualified speakers may communicate freely. One example of a nonpublic forum would be a school's internal mail system, which could be restricted to communications of official business.

32. What is meant when a restriction is "overbroad"?

Because of the fundamental importance that our constitutional system places on First Amendment freedoms, even where the government retains regulatory authority, it must do so "only with narrow specificity."[59] This means that it must act with care to separate protected speech, not subject to regulation, from speech it may properly regulate.[60] An overbroad restriction violates these constitutional rules by being overinclusive and affecting a substantial amount of other protected speech.

33. What is meant when a restriction is "vague"?

It is a fundamental principle that "laws give the person of ordinary intelligence a reasonable opportunity to know what is prohibited, so that he may act accordingly."[61] This principle, which bars vague laws, is stringently applied when freedom of speech is at stake because ambiguity tends to have a chilling effect on speech, causing speakers to "steer far wider of the unlawful zone" than if the boundaries were clearly marked.[62] That lack of precision in defining the speech that transgresses the regulation or law will unconstitutionally force people to conform their speech to "that which is unquestionably safe."[63] Such a result would be anathema to a system of free speech.

34. What is the constitutional status of libraries?

There is no constitutional obligation on the part of cities or counties to provide public libraries, even though we have learned that libraries discharge an essential function in our society. However, the importance of libraries has been recognized by the courts. For example, in 1966, the U.S. Supreme Court noted that a public library is "a place dedicated to quiet, to knowledge, and to beauty."[64] Although many would find comfort in this reverie, another court accurately described the public library as a "unique sanctuary of the widest possible spectrum of ideas."[65]

Still, like any other governmental undertaking, once the government establishes a service or activity, it is obligated to pursue it in a manner that comports with the requirements of the Constitution. An influential ruling by the federal Third Circuit held a public library to be a limited public forum, where the public's exercise of free-speech rights, including the right to receive information, must be observed so long as the rights are exercised in a manner "consistent with the nature of the Library and consistent with the government's intent in designating the Library as a public forum."[66]

Finally, note that school libraries have been described in terms similar to public libraries. The Supreme Court has called the school library a place where students may "test or expand upon ideas presented . . . in or out of the classroom" and a venue for "self-education and individual enrichment that is wholly optional" and without the restraints that may be placed on students in the "compulsory environment of the classroom."[67]

35. Can materials be removed or restricted if they offend patrons, the community served, or particular groups?

The Supreme Court has declared that "under our Constitution the public expression of ideas may not be prohibited merely because the ideas are themselves offensive to some of their hearers."[68] Furthermore, government authorities may not "as guardians of public morality remove [an] offensive word [or image] from the public vocabulary."[69] A library cannot cordon off "the mere dissemination of ideas—no matter how offensive to good taste— . . . in the name alone of 'conventions of decency.'"[70] To do otherwise on behalf of objecting parties is to exercise a forbidden power of censorship.

36. Does freedom of religion give special constitutional status to religious objections to library materials?

Although the Constitution guarantees that government will not unduly interfere with the "free exercise of religion," religious objections cannot be the basis for government policies, which must remain "neutral in matters of religious theory, doctrine, and practice."[71] To permit religious objections to prevail over neutral government policies and programs, the Supreme Court has said, would be to allow any religious objection "to be a law unto itself."[72]

37. Because religious holiday displays are said to raise issues of separation of church and state, does the Constitution really require such separation?

Yes. Since 1879, and relying on declarations that were contemporaneous to the writing of the First Amendment, as well as shortly thereafter, the U.S. Supreme Court has regarded the use of "separation between church and state" to be essentially "an authoritative declaration of the scope and effect of the amendment thus secured."[73] While the separation language does not appear in the First Amendment, neither does the phrase "separation of powers," which is similarly used as shorthand to describe what the Constitution provides. The Establishment Clause prohibits government from taking an active role that either advances or inhibits religion and was intended to prevent the instrumentalities of government from becoming a battleground for religious advantage.

As to religious holiday displays, this means that libraries may not celebrate or commemorate the religious events. Libraries may, however, have educational displays about comparative religious studies or about holiday seasons that are not exclusively religious in nature.

38. Does that separation mean anything with respect to religious group use of library meeting space?

Although the courts have not ruled definitively on whether meeting space could be used for religious services and have indicated that such a use could be constitutionally problematic, the availability of library meeting space to community groups cannot be denied to a group merely because of its religious character or the religious perspective that its meeting or event might have. Instead, such meeting space should be granted on the same basis that any other private group might obtain permission to use the space. Key to such a grant of meeting space is clear notice that the meetings that take place are instances of private speech that have no endorsement or other support from the public library.

39. Does the Constitution or the law protect the confidentiality of library records?

Although there is a viable argument that the First Amendment establishes some type of confidentiality privilege in library records, no judicial decision establishes such a construction of free-speech rights. Still, legislatures have recognized the potentially chilling effect on free inquiry if one's library-use records could be disclosed. Nearly every state has enacted laws that protect the confidentiality of library records, either in the form of a confidentiality law or an exception to the state's freedom of information act. Under these laws, there are very limited circumstances, usually pursuant to the patron's grant of permission or a court order, when such records can be disclosed.

In addition, there is a federal Video Privacy Act that similarly protects borrowing or rental records for videotapes.

40. Do children have reduced First Amendment rights?

The First Amendment rights of children are not coterminous with those of adults. There is a compelling governmental interest "in protecting the physical and psychological well-being of minors."[74] Even so, government does not have carte blanche to regulate the speech of children or the expressions that they may access. Minors are still accorded "a significant measure of First Amendment protection"[75] and may not be shielded solely to protect them "from ideas or images that a legislative body thinks unsuitable for them."[76] Finally, the Supreme Court has recognized that regulations about materials available to minors should draw appropriate distinctions between younger children and near adults that respect the rights and maturity of the older group.[77]

41. What rights do parents have with respect to the materials that children view in libraries?

Unlike the home, where parents have undiluted authority to determine and enforce their own views about the material that is appropriate for their children, public libraries need not cater to parental preferences. When they do, the libraries run some substantial risks of violating the First Amendment if they elect to restrict materials that parents find offensive.[78] In the end, libraries cannot sit in the place of parents. If parents wish their children to stay away from material they find problematic, they need to instruct their children to stay away or directly engage in the supervision of their children while at the library. Parents cannot expect the library to serve as a day-care center for their children while the parents are elsewhere.

42. Does freedom of speech apply equally to all forms of communication?

The Supreme Court has said that "[e]ach medium of expression, of course, must be assessed for First Amendment purposes by standards suited to it, for each may present its own problems."[79] The statement represents an understanding that the general principles of free speech, which prevent government from insisting on orderliness, sometimes have to give way to other interests because of the form that speech takes. For example, government may not insist that a public park be reserved for a period of seven years for the speech activities of a single private speaker or that those who wish to speak in the park obtain a license to do so. Yet, when broadcasting appeared on the scene, it found that licensing and the assignment of specific frequencies to individuals was the only way to ensure that the medium would not be turned into a cacophony of sound. Thus, broadcasting is said to receive a lesser, even though still substantial, level of First Amendment protection than more direct and pure forms of speech. As a result, it is subject to greater government regulation than other forms of speech.

Under this analysis, simple speech, books, newspapers, and other printed materials are accorded the highest levels of First Amendment protection. Intrusions on these forms of speech are evaluated under the "strict-scrutiny" test, which requires the regulations to be in furtherance of a compelling government interest and the least-restrictive means of accomplishing those goals. When the communication is conveyed in the form of symbolic conduct, such as the burning of a flag or the formation of a human blockade, a sufficiently important, even if not compelling, government interest in regulating the nonspeech element of the conduct can justify incidental limits on freedom of speech.[80] Although an anti-flag-burning statute was struck down by the Supreme Court because it was aimed at the point of view being expressed, the interest in ensuring the ability of customers to pass peaceably into and out of a store that is the subject of picketing would permit the government to arrest those who form an impassable blockade.[81]

Cable television, on the other hand, receives somewhat greater free-speech protection than broadcasting because of its unique characteristics, though the extent of the difference remains undefined.[82] Unlike broadcasting, where all programming is immediately available to anyone with a television set or radio, cable television is a premium service for which lockboxes and other devices are available to allow consumers to control the channels they receive. In addition, because the narrowness of the broadcast spectrum is not an issue for cable, there is less need for regulatory controls on entry into the medium. The smaller regulatory role necessary translates into greater expressive freedom in that medium.

With the advent of the Internet, the level of First Amendment protection to be afforded became a key question. In 1997, the Supreme Court answered that question by finding that the Internet receives the highest level of First Amendment protection available.[83]

Cyberspace

43. What has the Supreme Court said about the First Amendment's treatment of the Internet?

The Supreme Court has held that the Internet is not comparable to broadcasting and instead receives the highest level of First Amendment protection.[84]

44. Does a public library have to provide Internet access?

Just as there are no obligations to establish public libraries, there is no obligation to provide Internet access. However, once a service or activity is established, whether that service consists of traditional library services or Internet access, an obligation to comply with the requirements of the First Amendment comes into play.

45. If a public library does provide Internet access, must it provide e-mail and access to chat rooms?

No. A public library is legally free to select the level and degree of Internet access it will provide to its patrons. Although it may not discriminate in the access it provides between Web sites on the basis of their content, a library may well elect only to provide access to pages available on the World Wide Web, for example. As a practical matter, however, it may be difficult to limit access in that manner. Many e-mail accounts and chat rooms are accessible from a Web page, and some sites provide free e-mail accounts and links to chat rooms.

46. How should a library respond to a complaint about what another patron is viewing on a computer terminal?

No patron's objections to the constitutionally protected material that another accesses through the Internet can provide a justification for censoring or otherwise restricting Internet access. To permit otherwise would allow patrons with a particular ideological or other agenda to post themselves near the terminals and exercise a "heckler's veto" over the exercise of First Amendment rights. The Supreme Court condemned such a result in striking down the Communications Decency Act as unconstitutional.[85] A better solution for accommodating the sensibilities of other patrons is to install privacy screens that shield other patrons from having one patron's Internet choices imposed upon them.[86]

47. Can a library require parental permission before permitting a minor to use unfiltered computer access to the Internet?

Requiring parental permission to use unfiltered Internet access is constitutionally problematic and could conceivably subject a library to liability when a child uses a library terminal without a parent's permission. As noted above, children have substantial First Amendment rights, even if there is a less heightened protection of such rights. Filtering software is woefully imprecise, often blocking out utterly benign sites along with those the programmer actually intended to block. By restricting minors in this fashion, a library would effectively be burdening the minor's free-speech rights with respect to information that a minor has a constitutional right to receive. Thus, a student who is researching a school report might find access blocked. For purposes of the constitutional analysis, it would not matter that the student might obtain a permission slip, return home for a parent's signature, and then turn the slip in at the library to use an unfiltered terminal. Such delay and requiring permission to exercise First Amendment rights cannot be mandated by a public institution.

A library that undertook such a program would also stand in danger of being regarded as having entered a form of contract with the parents of the community that it would not permit minors to make unfiltered access of the Internet without the parents' written permission. When a child, as will inevitably happen, makes unfiltered use of library equipment to his or her parent's dismay, a parent might be able to sue on a legal theory of promissory estoppel for the library's breach of promise that children would not be permitted such access without parental permission. The better course of conduct is for libraries to post notices indicating that it has a policy of permitting anyone to make use of its unfiltered Internet access.

Most libraries require a parent, upon signing their child up for a library card, to take responsibility for the child's reading materials. This disclaimer of responsibility puts parents on notice that the library staff does not act in loco parentis, essentially in the parent's place, while the child is at the library. The disclaimer should be applied equally to Internet usage.

48. Would it be constitutional to provide filtered Internet access in the children's reading room, while permitting anyone, including minors, to make use of unfiltered access in the main reading room?

There appears to be no constitutional problem with this solution, even though American Library Association (ALA) policy would prohibit it. Libraries are used to selecting material on the basis of age appropriateness and other factors for a children's room. At the same time, there are no restrictions on children utilizing other portions of the library, where they might confront stronger stuff and material that would never be selected for a children's room. The approach outlined by this question merely reflects the reality that libraries now accomplish with books, magazines, and other materials in its collection.

By providing filtered access in the children's room, the library is attempting to accommodate some parents' concerns and provide younger children with a friendly environment in which to explore the Internet. The constitutional objections that would otherwise be leveled at filtering restrictions on minors' access to the Internet would be blunted by the unimpeded availability of unfiltered access elsewhere in the library.

Thus, minors who need information that the filters block would still be able to pursue their rights to receive information, while parents who desire their children to have more limited access may steer their children to those terminals.

49. Can a site be manually blocked by a public librarian because of a suspicion that it contains obscene or child pornographic material?

Obscenity and child pornography on the Internet are *illegal*. When a library has notice that such a site exists and could be accessed from its computer terminals, the library should follow previously established guidelines that provide for the temporary blocking of such sites with quick review and adjudication of the likelihood that such sites contain illegal content.

NOTES

1. *State* v. *Henry,* 302 Or. 510, 732 P.2d 9 (1987).

2. *Palko* v. *Connecticut,* 302 U.S. 319, 327 (1937).

3. *Bose Corp.* v. *Consumers Union,* 466 U.S. 485, 503 (1984).

4. *New York Times* v. *Sullivan,* 376 U.S. 254, 270 (1964).

5. *Winters* v. *New York,* 333 U.S. 507, 508 (1948).

6. *Police Department* v. *Mosley,* 408 U.S. 92, 95 (1972).

7. *Street* v. *New York,* 394 U.S. 576, 592 (1969).

8. *Island Trees Union Free School District No. 26* v. *Pico,* 457 U.S. 853, 867 (1982).

9. *Pacific Gas & Electric* v. *Public Utilities Comm'n,* 475 U.S. 1, 8 (1986).

10. *Erznoznik* v. *City of Jacksonville,* 422 U.S. 205, 211 (1975).

11. *Reno* v. *ACLU,* 117 S.Ct. 2329, 2346 (1997).

12. *Id.* at 2348.

13. *Bolger* v. *Youngs Drug Products Corp.,* 463 U.S. 60, 74 (1983).

14. *Tinker* v. *Des Moines Independent Community School Dist.,* 393 U.S. 503, 507 (1969).

15. *Id.* at 511.

16. *Id.* at 508.

17. *Id.*

18. *Hazelwood School Dist.* v. *Kuhlmeier,* 484 U.S. 260, 273 (1988).

19. *Id.*

20. *State* v. *Henry,* 302 Or. 510, 732 P.2d 9 (1987).

21. *State* v. *Kam,* 748 P.2d 372 (Ha. 1988).

22. *Erznoznik* v. *City of Jacksonville,* 422 U.S. 205 (1975).

23. *Barnes* v. *Glen Theatre, Inc.,* 501 U.S. 560 (1991).

24. *Sable Communications* v. *FCC,* 492 U.S. 115, 126 (1989).

25. *Miller* v. *California,* 413 U.S. 15, 24 (1973).

26. *See Freedman* v. *Maryland,* 380 U.S. 51 (1965).

27. *Island Trees Union Free School District No. 26* v. *Pico,* 457 U.S. 853, 871, 874 (plurality op.).

28. *See Elrod* v. *Burns,* 427 U.S. 347, 373–74 (1976).

29. *See New York* v. *Ferber,* 458 U.S. 747 (1982).

30. *Chaplinsky* v. *New Hampshire,* 315 U.S. 568, 572 (1942).

31. *See Cohen* v. *California,* 403 U.S. 15, 25 (1971).

32. *New York Times* v. *Sullivan,* 376 U.S. 254, 279 (1964).

33. *Harris* v. *Forklift Systems, Inc.,* 510 U.S. 17, 22 (1993).

34. *Id.* at 24.

35. *See id.* at 21, 69.

36. *Baskerville* v. *Culligan Int'l Co.,* 50 F.3d 428, 430–31 (7th Cir. 1995).

37. *See, e.g., Robinson* v. *Jacksonville Shipyards, Inc.,* 760 F. Supp. 1486 (M.D. Fla. 1991).

38. *Stanley* v. *The Lawson Co.,* 993 F. Supp. 1084 (N.D. Ohio 1997).

39. *See Mainstream Loudoun* v. *Board of Trustees,* 24 F. Supp.2d 552 (E.D. Va. 1998).

40. *Virginia Pharmacy Bd.* v. *Virginia Citizens Consumer Council, Inc.,* 425 U.S. 748, 762 (1976).

41. *Riley* v. *National Federation of the Blind of North Carolina, Inc.,* 487 U.S. 781, 796 (1988).

42. *Sable Communications* v. *FCC,* 492 U.S. 115, 126 (1989).

43. *Niemotko* v. *Maryland,* 340 U.S. 268, 273–74 (1951) (Frankfurter, J., concurring).

44. *New York Times* v. *United States,* 403 U.S. 713 (1971).

45. *Forsyth County* v. *Nationalist Movement,* 505 U.S. 123 (1992).

46. *Sable Communications* v. *FCC,* 492 U.S. 115 (1989).

47. *Schaumburg* v. *Citizens for a Better Environment,* 444 U.S. 620, 637 (1980).

48. *Sable Communications* v. *FCC,* 492 U.S. 115 (1989).

49. *United States* v. *Grace,* 461 U.S. 171, 177 (1983) (citation omitted).

50. *City Council of Los Angeles* v. *Taxpayers for Vincent,* 466 U.S. 789, 804 (1984).

51. *Ward* v. *Rock Against Racism,* 491 U.S. 781, 791 (1989).

52. *Boos* v. *Barry,* 485 U.S. 312, 320 (1988).

53. *Barnes v. Glen Theatre, Inc.*, 501 U.S. 560 (1991).

54. *Id.* at 571.

55. *Hague v. CIO*, 307 U.S. 496, 515 (1939) (Roberts, J., concurring).

56. *Perry Educational Ass'n v. Perry Local Educators' Ass'n*, 460 U.S. 37, 45 (1983).

57. *Police Dep't v. Mosley*, 408 U.S. 92, 95 (1972).

58. *Perry Educational Ass'n v. Perry Local Educators' Ass'n*, 460 U.S. 37, 46 (1983).

59. *NAACP v. Button*, 371 U.S. 415, 433 (1963) (citations omitted).

60. *Blount v. Rizzi*, 400 U.S. 410, 417 (1971).

61. *Grayned v. City of Rockford*, 408 U.S. 104, 108 (1972).

62. *Speiser v. Randall*, 357 U.S. 513, 526 (1958).

63. *Baggett v. Bullitt*, 377 U.S. 360, 372 (1964).

64. *Brown v. Louisiana*, 383 U.S. 131, 142 (1966).

65. *In the Matter of Quad/Graphics, Inc. v. Southern Adirondack Library System*, 664 N.Y.S.2d 225, 227 (Super. Ct. Saratoga Cty. 1997).

66. *Kreimer v. Bureau of Police*, 958 F.2d 1242, 1262 (3d Cir. 1992).

67. *Island Trees Union Free School District No. 26 v. Pico*, 457 U.S. 853, 869 (1982).

68. *Street v. New York*, 394 U.S. 576, 592 (1969).

69. *Cohen v. California*, 403 U.S. 15, 25 (1971).

70. *Papish v. Board of Curators of the University of Missouri*, 410 U.S. 667, 670 (1973).

71. *Epperson v. Arkansas*, 393 U.S. 97, 103–04 (1968).

72. *Employment Division v. Smith*, 494 U.S. 872, 890 (1990).

73. *Reynolds v. United States*, 98 U.S. 145, 164 (1879).

74. *Sable Communications, Inc. v. FCC*, 492 U.S. 115, 126 (1989).

75. *Erznoznik v. City of Jacksonville*, 422 U.S. 205, 212 (1975).

76. *Id.* at 213–14.

77. *See, e.g., Reno v. ACLU*, 117 S.Ct. 2329, 2348 (1997).

78. *See Island Trees Union Free School District No. 26 v. Pico*, 457 U.S. 853 (1982).

79. *Southeastern Promotions, Ltd. v. Conrad*, 420 U.S. 546, 557 (1975) (citing *Joseph Burstyn, Inc. v. Wilson*, 343 U.S. 495, 503 (1952)).

80. *United States v. O'Brien*, 391 U.S. 367, 376 (1968).

81. *Texas v. Johnson*, 491 U.S. 397 (1989).

82. *See Denver Area Educational Telecommunications Consortium, Inc. v. FCC*, 116 S.Ct. 2374 (1996).

83. *Reno v. ACLU*, 117 S.Ct. 2329, 2343 (1997).

84. *Id.*

85. *Id.* at 2349.

86. *Mainstream Loudon v. Board of Trustees*, 24 F. Supp.2d 552 (E.D. Va. 1998).

CHAPTER 2

Basic First Amendment Principles and Their Application to Libraries

When the United States enshrined the concept of free speech in the Constitution in 1791, it embarked on a potentially dangerous and unprecedented experiment in self-government and individual empowerment. No longer would government be in control of the information available to the citizenry, nor would the government be able to dictate what would be orthodox in politics, religion, art, literature, culture, or matters of opinion. Viewpoints, reasoned or otherwise, could be freely expressed. The First Amendment left decisions about what viewpoints would be in ascendency to popular sentiment and, as Justice Robert Jackson once wrote, was designed to "foreclose public authority from assuming a guardianship of the public mind."[1]

That limitation on the government's authority over the thoughts we express is extraordinarily broad. It overrides governmental and public determinations that speech ought to be limited because "it is thought unwise, unfair, false, or dangerous."[2] "To many," this bar against a paternalistic and "authoritative selection" of what is permissible public discourse "is, and always will be a folly; but we have staked upon it our all."[3] It is dangerous to the status quo and for those in power to allow people to exchange information and ideas unmediated by the government, but that is an essential feature of our democracy. As long as the people exercise their rights of free expression, avoid complacency, and maintain a healthy skepticism about the assertions of those who hold power, they remain in charge and solidify their claim to being a truly free people.

The U.S. Supreme Court has explained the guarantee of free expression embodied in the First Amendment in a number of different but illuminating phrases. "The First Amendment presupposes," it once declared, "that the freedom to speak one's mind is not only an aspect of individual liberty—and thus a good unto itself—but also is essential to the common quest for truth and the vitality of society as a whole."[4] It was fashioned, the Court reminds us, "to assure unfettered interchange of ideas for the bringing about of political and social changes desired by the people."[5] As such, free expression forms "the matrix, the indispensable condition of nearly every other form of freedom."[6]

Justice Felix Frankfurter elaborated on the rationale behind this concept when he characterized the free-speech philosophy of Justice Oliver Wendell Holmes Jr. and wrote: "[T]he progress of civilization is to a considerable extent the displacement of error which once held sway as official truth by beliefs which in turn have yielded to other beliefs. . . . [W]ithout freedom of expression, thought becomes checked and atrophied."[7] For this reason, we deny government the authority to decide what we can and cannot say and what ideas are good or bad for us, for it is a power that cannot be exercised benignly and inevitably "would lead to standardization of ideas either by legislatures, courts, or dominant political or community groups."[8]

It is thus undisputed that "a major purpose of [the First] Amendment was to protect the free discussion of governmental affairs."[9] Still, it would be a grave error to limit our free-expression rights to so narrow a realm. As Justice William Brennan once noted, "[T]he line between ideological and nonideological speech is impossible to draw with accuracy."[10] As a result, "[e]ntertainment, as well as political and ideological speech, is protected; motion pictures, programs broadcast by radio and television, and live entertainment, such as musical and dramatic works, fall within the First Amendment guarantee."[11] After all, "one man's amusement, teaches another's doctrine."[12]

By guaranteeing such a broad freedom of the mind, capable of assisting in the process of self-governance, self-realization, and self-fulfillment, the First Amendment has contributed to the creation of a "marketplace of ideas," in which we are free to sample a wide variety of expressed thoughts, determine for ourselves their validity, and accept or reject them according to our own judgments. The "marketplace" analogy is derived from a formulation written by Justice Oliver Wendell Holmes

Jr.: "[T]he ultimate good desired is better reached by free trade in ideas—that the best test of truth is the power of the thought to get itself accepted in the competition of the market."[13]

To make such a "marketplace of ideas" work, Holmes realized that deep-seated fears about the consequences of uninhibited speech had to be overcome. He wrote, "[W]e should be eternally vigilant against attempts to check the expression of opinions that we loathe and believe to be fraught with death, unless they so imminently threaten immediate interference with the lawful and pressing purposes of the law that an immediate check is required to save the country."[14] His ally in shaping modern First Amendment understandings, Justice Louis Brandeis, put it this way:

> Those who won our independence . . . knew that order cannot be secured merely through fear of punishment for its infraction; that it is hazardous to discourage thought, hope and imagination; that fear breeds repression; that repression breeds hate; that hate menaces stable government; that the path of safety lies in the opportunity to discuss freely supposed grievances and proposed remedies; and that the fitting remedy for evil counsels is good ones. . . .
>
> Fear of serious injury cannot alone justify suppression of free speech and assembly. Men feared witches and burned women.[15]

Development of the First Amendment

The First Amendment was intended as a confirmation of rights thought already to exist as an inherent or natural right. The original Constitution drafted in Philadelphia contained no guarantee of free speech or a free press, because the delegates deemed it unnecessary. No power over speech had been granted to the new federal government. Still, public concern over the rights that had inspired the fight for independence was so great that the new Constitution could not be ratified without the promise that a bill of rights would be added. During the First Congress, James Madison made good on this promise by proposing, in 1789, a bill of rights that included broad guarantees of free expression against the new, more powerful national government created by the Constitution. By 1791, ten amendments, now known as the Bill of Rights, had been ratified by the necessary three-quarters of the states to become part of the federal Constitution. The first of these amendments was designed to ensure that the new national government did not attempt to exercise power over people's speech or matters of conscience, their publications, or their means of influencing fellow citizens or the government itself.

Because legislative power, which remains the primary power of government, resided in the Congress, the First Amendment reads as a limitation on Congress ("Congress shall make no law . . ."). Neither of the other branches of government, the executive or the judiciary, it was thought, has any plenary authority that might be used against free speech, except where authorized by a statute enacted by Congress. When that statutory authority is invoked, it, too, falls within the prohibition of the First Amendment because of the congressional origins of that power. Even without congressional intervention, acts of presidents, the executive branch more generally, or judges must still comply with the First Amendment.

In 1868, as a consequence of the Civil War, the Fourteenth Amendment was added to the Constitution. Along with a guarantee of citizenship in the United States and the state of residence for persons born or naturalized in this country, Section 1 of that amendment provides: "No State shall make or enforce any law which shall abridge the privileges or immunities of citizens of the United States; nor shall any State deprive any person of life, liberty, or property, without due process of law; nor deny to any person within its jurisdiction the equal protection of the laws."

After a number of U.S. Supreme Court cases had suggested that the Constitution's guarantee of due process against actions of a state might also safeguard some of the same rights spelled out in the Bill of Rights, the Court made this speculation part of the law of the land in a 1925 case called *Gitlow* v. *New York*.[16] There, the Court held: "For present purposes we may and do assume that freedom of speech and of the press—which are protected by the First Amendment from abridgment by Congress—are among the fundamental personal rights and liberties protected by the due process clause of the Fourteenth Amendment from impairment by the States."[17] This concept is known as the Incorporation Doctrine, because it holds that the Fourteenth Amendment's due process clause incorporated the most basic and fundamental rights guaranteed in the Bill of Rights.

Because city governments and other public units, including public libraries and public schools, within a state are creatures of that state, the prohibition against abridgment of free speech applies with equal force to them as well.

State Constitutions Also Guarantee Free Speech

Separate and apart from the federal Constitution's guarantee of free speech, every state has a constitution with its own declaration of rights that invariably includes a free-speech provision. Because these constitutions define the powers and limitations of state governments, they may provide greater, though not lesser, protections against interference with speech. In a number of instances, the highest courts in various states have construed their state free-speech provision to afford greater freedom of speech than does its federal analogue.

For example, the California Supreme Court has held that the state constitutional guarantees of free speech and the right to petition enable people to exercise those rights in private shopping centers despite the owners' objections, even though the U.S. Supreme Court has reached a contrary view under the First Amendment.[18] The U.S. Supreme Court's decision, that the First Amendment does not apply on private property, does not overrule California's approach or the several states that have followed California's approach. State constitutional decisions are not affected by federal ones, unless the state decision affords a lesser constitutional protection of rights.

The state that has gone the furthest in this respect is Oregon. Although the U.S. Supreme Court has declared that obscenity falls outside the protection of speech contained in the First Amendment, the Oregon Supreme Court has construed its state constitutional guarantee to protect even obscene speech.[19] Similarly, Hawaii has used free-speech principles to invalidate a criminal obscenity law.[20]

The Scope of Free Speech

Generally, the federal guarantee of free speech means "the public expression of ideas may not be prohibited merely because the ideas are themselves offensive to some of their hearers."[21] It further means that government cannot act as the "taste police," attempting to regulate the choice of words or images even while allowing the speaker the choice of ideas to express. The Court has recognized that granting the government authority to insist upon civility or prohibit the use of swear words would constitute an unlimited license to censor. Instead, it has held that because "government officials cannot make principled distinctions in [the arena of expression], the Constitution leaves matters of taste and style so largely to the individual."[22] The result of this commitment is that, as a constitutional matter, we "must tolerate insulting, and even outrageous, speech in order to provide 'adequate breathing space' to the freedoms protected by the First Amendment."[23]

Our commitment to free speech, in one of the Court's most classic formulations, anticipates "uninhibited, robust, and wide-open" debate that "may well include vehement, caustic, and sometimes unpleasantly sharp" language.[24] It embraces the notion that "above all else, the First Amendment means that government has no power to restrict expression because of its message, its ideas, its subject matter, or its content."[25] It recognizes the concept's importance is not to protect "free thought for those who agree with us, but freedom for the thought that we hate."[26] And it extends to the notion that "the right to receive ideas is a necessary predicate to the recipient's meaningful exercise of his own rights of speech, press, and political freedom."[27] Thus, in addition to protecting the rights of speakers, "the First Amendment protects the public's interest in receiving information."[28]

Exceptions to Free Speech

Nevertheless, freedom of speech is not an absolute—that is, not every thought or word uttered is protected under the U.S. Constitution. Falling within the narrow category of "unprotected" speech are *obscenity, fighting words,* and *libel. Obscenity* is a very narrow category that embraces essentially hardcore sexual acts that have a tendency to excite lustful thoughts. As a legal proposition, *obscenity,* which is explained in some detail in the following chapter, is not a synonym for *nudity, pornography,* or *indecency,* although *child pornography* is a related concept.

Another free-speech exception, *fighting words,* is comprised of those words "which by their very utterance inflict injury or tend to incite an immediate breach of the peace."[29] Such words must be uttered as a direct personal insult in a face-to-face confrontation and calculated or highly likely to result in an immediate violent physical reaction.[30] Since declaring the "fighting words" doctrine in 1942, the Supreme Court has not ruled any specific words or expressive conduct to fall within the exception that would place it beyond the First Amendment's purview. For that reason, it is generally regarded as a dormant concept, although incitement to violence is a similar category of speech that is not protected by the Constitution's free-speech guarantee.

The last unprotected speech form, *libel,* consists of defamatory communications that have the effect of ruining a person's reputation, standing in the community, or ability to associate with others. Because of the adverse economic consequences that false accusations can have, courts can award damages to compensate an individual injured by those reputational slurs. By contrast, truthful yet hurtful accusations incur no similar injury and are therefore not actionable.

To prevent government officers from inhibiting public criticism of their actions, the U.S. Supreme Court has recognized that a different libel standard applies to public officials. Because the right to question government actions and policy is central to a democratic republic, the Court has said that a "rule compelling the critic of official conduct to guarantee the truth of all his factual assertions—and to do so on pain of libel judgments virtually unlimited in amount—leads to . . . self-censorship."[31] As a result, the Court requires public officials claiming to have been libeled to demonstrate that the publisher of the alleged libel knew that the statement was false or recklessly disregarded the truth or falsity of it. For these purposes, the "publisher" of an oral libel, usually known as *slander,* is the speaker.

A standard similar to that established for public officials was also created to cover public figures, who, the Court reasoned, have, by virtue of their newsworthiness, ready access to the mass media to counter criticism of their views and activities.[32] However, neither the receipt of government funds nor the appearance of a person's name in the newspapers necessarily makes a person a public figure.[33] Finally, matters of public concern receive heightened First Amendment protections against accusations of libel.[34]

Special Speech Categories

Other forms of speech receive specialized treatment, as well. Commercial speech, for example, receives First Amendment protection, though to a more moderate degree than other forms of speech, to permit the government to regulate commerce and protect against consumer fraud. Commercial speech consists solely of those messages that "propose a commercial transaction," such as advertising or solicitation.[35] Under Supreme Court precedent, commercial speech must concern a lawful activity and not be misleading to qualify for constitutional protection.[36] On the other hand, noncommercial speech retains its First Amendment shield even if it advocates illegal activity or exaggerates or misleads about the truth.[37]

For the government to exercise legitimate authority over commercial speech, the regulation must promote an important government interest in a manner that directly advances that interest and cannot be substantially more extensive than necessary in its regulation of speech to serve that interest.[38] Where commercial and noncommercial speech are "inextricably intertwined," the entire communication is classified as noncommercial and receives full First Amendment protection.[39]

Child pornography is another special category for First Amendment purposes. The Supreme Court has said that images of children in sexually suggestive poses or engaged in sexual activity can be prohibited in the interests of preventing commerce in the abusive use of children as subjects of pornography.[40] Even though the Court has found that the private, noncommercial possession of obscene materials in one's home cannot be outlawed, the need to prevent abuse of children through their use in the making of child pornography is sufficient to permit the criminalization of the private possession of such materials.[41]

Yet another separate category consists of materials that are deemed "harmful to minors." "Harmful to minors" is a subclassification of obscenity that uses children as the reference point for determining whether the material is subject to regulation. Thus, the traditional definition of *obscenity* is revised to determine if the material appeals to the prurient interests *of children,* is patently offensive *to children,* and has no social, literary, scientific, or political value *for any children,* including those who are nearly adults.

Although some forms of speech fall outside the protective field of the First Amendment, the Court has stated that due process requires that procedural safeguards be in place when regulations are directed against speech, whether protected or unprotected. Thus, those who would censor have the obligation to institute timely judicial proceedings to prove that the material is unprotected. If the material is being made unavailable pending a court determination, the First Amendment requires that the temporary withdrawal of the material be brief and be utilized only to preserve the status quo while prompt judicial review of the censorious action occurs.[42]

Constitutional Tests for the Regulation of Speech

Even speech that is at the core of the First Amendment's protections—and thus undeniably within the "protected" category—is not entirely immunized from government regulation. To determine whether the regulation is constitutional, courts generally apply what is called the "strict-scrutiny" test. Such government interference with speech can come in a variety of forms, ranging from strict censorship or prohibitions to delays in being able to communicate the disputed speech. It can include burdens or obstacles to speaking in the manner desired, such as requirements that the speaker's identity be revealed, that special permission be sought, or that some fee be paid before the right is exercised. To meet the requirements of strict scrutiny, however, the government must demonstrate that it is operating in furtherance of a compelling interest and has chosen the least restrictive means to further that articulated interest.[43] This is an extremely stringent test that is not easily met. As a result, many attempted forms of regulations fail to pass constitutional muster.

A useful example of this form of analysis is the Supreme Court's decision in *Sable Communications* v. *FCC*.[44] There, the Court invalidated a 1988 congressional enactment that prohibited the interstate transmission of indecent commercial telephone messages, or "dial-a-porn." Because the law targeted nonobscene speech, it had to be evaluated under the strict-scrutiny test that applies to protected speech, adult access to which generally cannot be banned. Congressional sponsors of the statute justified the law as a means of protecting the well-being of minors. The Court did not question the compelling nature of this asserted interest. Nevertheless, the law was invalidated because it did not employ the least restrictive means to accomplish its legitimate goal.

The least-restrictive-means requirement connotes that government must only utilize "narrowly drawn regulations designed to serve [its compelling] interests without unnecessarily interfering with First Amendment freedoms."[45] Where less drastic means are available to achieve the same basic purpose, even if the result would be less complete

from the viewpoint of the government's asserted interest, that less restrictive alternative must be pursued. Among the alternatives the Court
found sufficiently workable in the dial-a-porn case were requirements
that customers produce credit cards or receive access codes to unscram-
ble the messages, which would have significantly limited child access
while preserving adult rights. It did not matter, in the Court's analysis,
that, short of a total ban, some children may have found inventive ways
to access the pornographic telephone messages. Solicitude for the rights
of adults overrode such a more complete solution to the problem.

Another of the ways that the Court measures whether a restriction
impermissibly strikes at core protected speech is by examining whether
the law discriminates between otherwise similar speech on the basis of
its content or viewpoint. A "content-neutral" regulation is one that applies to all speech equally, regardless of the subject matter or viewpoint
being expressed. The reason that content neutrality is important is because "the First Amendment forbids the government to regulate speech
in ways that favor some viewpoints or ideas at the expense of others."[46]
One important test of whether the government has breached its obligation of content-neutral regulation is "whether the government has
adopted a regulation of speech because of disagreement with the message [the regulated expression] conveys."[47]

The restriction on content-discriminatory regulations is taken so seriously that a regulation that does discriminate on the basis of content is
subjected to strict scrutiny. As the Court has put it, "above all else, the
First Amendment means that government has no power to restrict expression because of its message, its ideas, its subject matter, or its content."[48]
In the case in which that statement was made, the Court overturned a city
ordinance that prohibited peaceful picketing near a school except when it
was related to a labor dispute involving that school. Although the law attempted to be mindful of employee rights, it still discriminated on the
basis of content. A teacher could carry a sign protesting the school board's
decision against a pay increase, but a student or parent could not carry a
sign protesting a curricular or other policy decision. The lack of even-
handedness was sufficient to invalidate the entire law.

Similarly, the Court later invalidated a congressional ban on public
television editorials as a form of content discrimination. In enacting
the prohibition, Congress had reasoned that editorial opinion from a
government-subsidized broadcaster might give certain views unfair ad-
vantages with the public. The Court, however, held that the "'First

Amendment's hostility to content-based regulation extends not only to restrictions on particular viewpoints, but also to prohibition of an entire topic,'" in this instance, opinion.[49]

Permissible Speech Regulations

One form of regulation that the government generally can implement is a "time, place or manner" restriction. This kind of governmental authority exists to prevent free speech from becoming little more than a desultory form of noise and permits the government to exercise a "traffic-cop" role that is actually encouraging of freedom, rather than restrictive. It enables people to speak without being drowned out by other speakers, much as a schoolteacher who asks students to speak one at a time so all can be heard. Under this authority, traffic-disrupting parades, for example, can be restricted to one a day and one group at a time. Broadcasters can be assigned exclusive rights to use specific frequencies. To accommodate the special needs for quiet by certain enterprises, hospitals and school zones—and residential neighborhoods late at night—can be made off-limits to speech activities that rise above a specified decibel level.

These restrictions limit the times, locations, or means used to convey a message. Time, place, or manner regulations will be upheld by the courts only if they "are content-neutral, are narrowly tailored to serve a significant [though not necessarily compelling] government interest, and leave open ample alternative channels of communication."[50] They must also permit expression at adequate alternative times, places, and manners for the speech restricted.

In one 1984 case, the Supreme Court found a National Park Service regulation that forbid late night use of the parks in Washington, D.C., to be an appropriate use of time, place, or manner authority.[51] A protest group had wanted to set up a "tent city" in Lafayette Park, across from the White House, to call attention to the plight of the poor and homeless. The Court determined that the regulation was evenhanded in its application to all subjects and viewpoints and left the protesters sufficient alternative means of pursuing their protest in that park during daylight hours.

A critical element in valid time, place, or manner regulations is that public officials not be invested with unbridled discretion to implement the restrictions. Judicial rulings recognize the potential for abuse in the exercise of that discretion. It is too easy for an official to favor popular speakers or strictly implement the restriction against those disliked by authorities or by the community itself.[52] The rule, however, does not obliterate all grants of discretion to public officers. To be considered an unconstitutional allocation of discretion, there must be "a close enough nexus to expression or to conduct associated with expression, to pose a real and substantial threat of the identified censorship risks."[53]

Similarly, government has authority to regulate what are called "secondary effects," as long as the real purpose of the regulation is not the suppression of speech. The object of secondary-effects restrictions must be activities that the government already has authority to regulate, which "happen to be associated with a particular type of speech [but] have nothing to do with [the] content" of that speech.[54]

For example, Indiana's law against public nudity was upheld in its application to an establishment that wanted to feature nude barroom dancing. The state, the Court opined, had a legitimate objective in mind: to prevent the area from becoming a magnet for criminals and criminal activity in the area surrounding the bar.[55] The Court still acknowledged that nude dancing was a form of expression that conveyed "eroticism and sexuality" but held that the minimum swatches of clothing required to comply with the ban on nudity "simply makes the message slightly less graphic."[56] The Court did not examine the effectiveness of requiring the erotic dancers to wear G-strings and pasties to deter criminal activity but took the state's assertion that it would at face value. The case demonstrates that a secondary-effect regulation should not attempt to ban an expressive activity altogether but can aim to lessen its undesirable effect. When it does that, courts will not second-guess the legislature on whether the regulation furthers the asserted interest.

Public Forum Doctrine

The kinds of speech activities that can be engaged in on government property, such as public libraries, is governed by the *public forum doctrine*. There are three types of forums recognized under this doctrine: *traditional public, designated public,* and *nonpublic.* In the key modern case on public forums, *Perry Educational Association* v. *Perry Local Educators' Association,* the Supreme Court described the doctrine:

> In places which by long tradition or by government fiat have been devoted to assembly and debate, the rights of the state to limit expressive activity are

sharply circumscribed. At one end of the spectrum are streets and parks which "have immemoriably been held in trust for the use of the public, and time out of mind, have been used for purposes of assembly, communicating thoughts between citizens, and discussing public questions." In these quintessential public forums, the government may not prohibit all communicative activity. . . .

A second category consists of public property which the state has opened for use by the public as a place for expressive activity. . . . Although a state is not required to indefinitely retain the open character of the facility, as long as it does so it is bound by the same standards as apply in a traditional public forum. . . .

Public property which is not by tradition or designation a forum for public communication is governed by different standards. . . . [T]he state may reserve [this property] for its intended purposes, communicative or otherwise, as long as the regulation on speech is reasonable and not an effort to suppress expression merely because public officials oppose the speaker's view.[57]

A street corner at which a person might mount a soapbox and opine about political affairs without impeding traffic or the plaza in front of the state assembly where a group might picket with signs protesting the consideration of some piece of legislation are examples of people using a traditional public forum. A municipal auditorium, available for public rental, is an example of a "limited" or "designated" public forum. In such a forum, the government has no authority to deny use of the auditorium to groups whose views it abhors or to entertainment that it views as antisocial. A limited or designated forum need not be a physical location.

In one recent case, the U.S. Supreme Court determined that when a state university made funds available for student extracurricular activities, it had established a limited public forum and could not deny such funds to a student newspaper that examined issues of student life from a Christian perspective. The refusal to fund the newspaper, based on the university's concern that providing financing would violate the Constitution's requirement of neutrality toward religion, was found to be a form of viewpoint discrimination. Any publication funded through this program was free to write about religion, except that funding was withheld from those that professed to do so from a particular religious viewpoint. The Court found that the Christian newspaper was entitled to student activity funds on the same basis as any other student publication.[58]

In both traditional and designated public forums, government may only regulate (1) to serve a compelling state interest with a regulation that is narrowly drawn to achieve that end; or (2) to serve a significant, though not compelling, state interest with a content-neutral time, place, or manner regulation that is narrowly tailored to serve the asserted interest and still leaves ample alternative channels of communication.[59]

One example of a nonpublic forum is a jail. In 1966, the Supreme Court reviewed the First Amendment claims of student civil rights protesters who had staged a sit-in at a Florida jail to protest racial segregation behind bars. Contrary to public forums, traditional or designated, jails, the Court held, are built for security purposes and not speech.[60] Similar reasoning has made military bases off-limits for political protests.[61]

That does not mean that nonpublic forums are entirely freed from First Amendment requirements. It does mean, however, that the government could impose viewpoint-neutral limits on expressive activities appropriate to that forum. For example, postal mailboxes are a means by which a great variety of communications can be conveyed; however, there is no First Amendment problem in prohibiting "mailable matter" that does not have a valid postal stamp to be deposited in a designated mailbox, which is another form of nonpublic forum.[62] In *Perry*, a rival teachers' union sought access to the internal school mailing system and mailboxes, which the existing union, under its collective bargaining agreement, had been awarded exclusive use of in connection with union activities. The Court reasoned that there was no viewpoint discrimination in this restriction on rival unions; it was merely a distinction based on status, which was considered permissible.

Public libraries are considered *designated public forums* for the purposes for which a library exists.[63] For this reason, libraries cannot discriminate against books eligible for placement on the shelves because of the ideas expressed or patrons eligible to use the library facilities, provided that both comply with viewpoint-neutral rules that have been put into place.

Applying this principle to a religious women's organization that had sought to use a library's auditorium for a meeting on the same basis as Navy recruiters, a swim club, an association for retired federal employees, and a veterans group, a federal court held that the library had created a public forum out of its auditorium and could not restrict access because of the religious or political content of the proposed meeting.[64] The library's policy of excluding religious or political groups was intended to avoid controversy. The court's decision that the library policy was invalid treated the exclusion as a form of content and viewpoint discrimination. Moreover, the court recognized that the First Amendment does not shy away from controversy.

Vagueness and Overbreadth

Two other tests are important in evaluating First Amendment issues: *vagueness* and *overbreadth*. It is a general principle of law that "laws give the person of ordinary intelligence a reasonable opportunity to know what is prohibited, so that he may act accordingly."[65] When a law interferes with the right of free speech, the courts apply a more stringent variation of the vagueness test.[66] Behind this requirement is a recognition that First Amendment "freedoms are delicate and vulnerable, as well as supremely precious in our society. The threat of sanctions may deter their exercise almost as potently as the actual application of sanctions. Because First Amendment freedoms need breathing space to survive, government may regulate in the area only with narrow specificity."[67]

For government to exercise otherwise valid authority over speech, the law or regulation itself "must provide explicit standards for those who apply them. A vague law impermissibly delegates basic policy matters to policemen, judges, and juries for resolution on an ad hoc and subjective basis, with the attendant dangers of arbitrary and discriminatory application."[68] Thus, it must be evident from the law in question that there is an "ascertainable standard for inclusion and exclusion."[69] When that is missing, the law unconstitutionally produces a chilling effect on speech, inducing speakers to "steer far wider of the unlawful zone" than if the boundaries were clearly marked,[70] and forces people to conform their speech to "that which is unquestionably safe."[71]

For example, several years ago, both Missouri and Tennessee enacted prohibitions against the distribution of "violent" videotapes to minors, to stem any influences that might lead to youthful violence. Both laws were struck down because of the inherent vagueness of the term *violence* to define the speech that was the object of the laws.[72] In both instances, the courts relied on a 1948 U.S. Supreme Court precedent, *Winters* v. *New York,* which found unconstitutional a similar ban on the distribution to minors of publications "principally made up of . . . accounts of criminal deeds, or pictures, or stories of deeds of bloodshed, lust or crime."[73] Among the difficulties such a law faces is the likelihood that it would cover as diverse a set of materials as the Bible, historical documentaries, news, and classical literature. In fact, one scholar has estimated that 80 percent of the world's literature, from the beginning of time, centers around evil or violence. To ask a distributor to determine which of these publications or videotapes contained the kind of violence that the legislature was concerned with and which could lawfully be turned over to a minor was to ask too much.

Overbreadth is a related test that is used when an otherwise legitimate regulation also affects speech that may not be lawfully restricted. In *Erznoznik v. City of Jacksonville,* the issue was a city ordinance that banned nudity in motion pictures displayed at drive-in theaters.[74] Although the measure had been enacted to protect children from inappropriate movie material, it treated all nudity as inherently harmful. The Court was not willing to make that leap. It pointed out that some forms of nudity were palpably harmless, such as a "baby's buttocks, the nude body of a war victim, or scenes from a culture in which nudity is indigenous."[75] By banning this harmless protected speech, the ordinance was fatally overbroad and had to be struck down.

The Library Context

These First Amendment principles have ready applicability in the context of the public library. In essence, libraries must establish neutral criteria for the selection and removal of materials in the collection. The public library may not base its decisions on political or ideological considerations, nor on agreement or disagreement with the point of view expressed. Moreover, it may not limit or deny adults access to materials that are unfit for children out of a concern for the welfare of children.

A 1992 ruling by the U.S. Court of Appeals for the Third Circuit (governing Pennsylvania, New Jersey, and Delaware) found that a public library is not a traditional public forum, but a *limited public forum.*[76] The ruling, likely to be influential with other jurisdictions, was based on the establishment of the Morristown libraries for maximum use by the public for "communication of the written word."[77] Still, the court held that, as a limited public forum, the library's obligation is "only to permit the public to exercise rights that are consistent with the nature of the Library and consistent with the government's intent in designating the Library as a public forum. Other activities need not be tolerated."[78]

To the extent a library makes its facilities available to the public for non-library-sponsored functions, the First Amendment requires that it do so evenhandedly. Although the U.S. Supreme Court has left open the question of whether religious groups can make use of a designated public forum for religious ceremonies or prayer services without violating the

First Amendment's prohibition on the "establishment of religion," groups motivated by religious values that are engaged in activities palpably similar to other community groups cannot be denied access to the forum.[79]

Conclusion

Although some speech may teach lessons that society would overwhelmingly abhor and other speech makes some uncomfortable, the lessons of history teach that censorship will not achieve any long-term benefits. Instead, it is our responsibility to meet speech we consider likely to lead to bad tendencies with counterspeech; that is, speech that argues with evil advocacy and instead suggests better paths. For this reason, the First Amendment accords incredibly broad freedom in our expressive choices. It is only thus, the Supreme Court has said, that we "will ultimately produce a more capable citizenry and more perfect polity."[80]

Libraries are repositories of many of these purposes served by the First Amendment. It is inevitable that speech will be controversial and that libraries will become embroiled in those controversies. It is critical that libraries recognize their custodianship of intellectual freedom and remain vigilant of these liberties even in the face of severe criticism for the books, materials, and access they provide.

NOTES

1. *Thomas v. Collins,* 323 U.S. 516, 545 (1945) (Jackson, J., concurring).

2. *Home Box Office, Inc. v. FCC,* 567 F.2d 9, 47 (D.C. Cir. 1977) (citations omitted).

3. *United States v. Associated Press,* 52 F. Supp. 362, 372 (S.D. N.Y. 1943) (Hand, L., J.), *aff'd,* 326 U.S. 1 (1945).

4. *Bose Corp. v. Consumers Union,* 466 U.S. 485, 503 (1984).

5. *Roth v. United States,* 354 U.S. 476, 484 (1957).

6. *Palko v. Connecticut,* 302 U.S. 319, 327 (1937).

7. *Kovacs v. Cooper,* 336 U.S. 77, 95 (1949) (Frankfurter, J., concurring).

8. *Terminello v. Chicago,* 337 U.S. 1, 4 (1949).

9. *Mills v. Alabama,* 384 U.S. 214, 219 (1966).

10. *Lehman v. City of Shaker Heights,* 418 U.S. 298, 319 (1974) (Brennan, J., dissenting).

11. *Schad* v. *Borough of Mount Ephraim,* 452 U.S. 61, 65 (1985) (citations omitted).

12. *Winters* v. *New York,* 333 U.S. 507, 510 (1948).

13. *Abrams* v. *United States,* 250 U.S. 616, 630 (1919) (Holmes, J., dissenting).

14. *Id.*

15. *Whitney* v. *California,* 274 U.S. 357, 375–76 (1927) (Brandeis, J., concurring).

16. *Gitlow* v. *New York,* 268 U.S. 652 (1925).

17. *Id.* at 666.

18. *Robins* v. *Pruneyard Shopping Center,* 592 P.2d 341 (1979), *aff'd sub nom. Pruneyard Shopping Center* v. *Robins,* 447 U.S. 74 (1980); *Lloyd* v. *Tanner,* 407 U.S. 551 (1972).

19. *State* v. *Henry,* 302 Or. 510, 732 P.2d 9 (1987).

20. *State* v. *Kam,* 748 P.2d 377 (Ha. 1988).

21. *Street* v. *New York,* 394 U.S. 576, 592 (1969).

22. *Cohen* v. *California,* 403 U.S. 15, 25 (1971).

23. *Boos* v. *Barry,* 485 U.S. 312, 322 (1988) (citation omitted).

24. *New York Times* v. *Sullivan,* 376 U.S. 254, 270 (1964).

25. *Police Department* v. *Mosley,* 408 U.S. 92, 95 (1972).

26. *United States* v. *Schwimmer,* 279 U.S. 644, 655 (1929) (Holmes, J., dissenting).

27. *Island Trees Union Free School District No. 26* v. *Pico,* 457 U.S. 853, 867 (1982) (plurality op.).

28. *Pacific Gas & Electric* v. *Public Utilities Comm'n,* 475 U.S. 1, 8 (1986).

29. *Chaplinsky* v. *New Hampshire,* 315 U.S. 568, 572 (1942).

30. *See Gooding* v. *Wilson,* 405 U.S. 518, 528 (1972).

31. *New York Times* v. *Sullivan,* 376 U.S. 254, 279 (1964).

32. *Curtis Publishing Co.* v. *Butts,* 388 U.S. 130 (1966); *Gertz* v. *Robert Welch, Inc.,* 418 U.S. 323 (1974).

33. *Hutchinson* v. *Proxmire,* 443 U.S. 111 (1979); *Wolston* v. *Reader's Digest Ass'n,* 443 U.S. 157 (1979).

34. *Dun & Bradstreet* v. *Greenmoss Builders, Inc.,* 472 U.S. 749 (1985) (plurality op.).

35. *Virginia Pharmacy Board* v. *Virginia Citizens Consumer Council, Inc.,* 425 U.S. 748, 762 (1976).

36. *Central Hudson Gas & Electric Corp.* v. *Public Service Commission,* 447 U.S. 557, 566 (1980).

37. *Brandenburg* v. *Ohio,* 395 U.S. 447 (1969); *New York Times* v. *Sullivan,* 376 U.S. 254, 271–72 (1964) (quoting *NAACP* v. *Button,* 371 U.S. 415, 433 (1963) (recognizing that "erroneous statement is inevitable in free debate and that it must be protected if the freedoms of expression are to have the 'breathing space' that they 'need . . . to survive'")).

38. *Board of Trustees of the State University of New York v. Fox*, 492 U.S. 469, 479 (1989).

39. *Riley* v. *National Federation of the Blind of North Carolina, Inc.* 487 U.S. 781, 796 (1988).

40. *See New York* v. *Ferber*, 458 U.S. 747 (1982).

41. *Compare Stanley* v. *Georgia*, 394 U.S. 557 (1969) with *Osborne* v. *Ohio*, 495 U.S. 103 (1990).

42. *Southeastern Promotions, Ltd.* v. *Conrad*, 420 U.S. 546, 560 (1975).

43. *Sable Communications* v. *FCC*, 492 U.S. 115, 126 (1989).

44. *Id.*

45. *Schaumburg* v. *Citizens for a Better Environment*, 444 U.S. 620, 637 (1980).

46. *City Council of Los Angeles* v. *Taxpayers for Vincent*, 466 U.S. 789, 804 (1984).

47. *Ward* v. *Rock Against Racism*, 491 U.S. 781, 791 (1989).

48. *Police Department* v. *Mosley*, 408 U.S. 92, 95 (1972).

49. *FCC* v. *League of Women Voters*, 468 U.S. 364, 384 (1984) (quoting *Consolidated Edison Co.* v. *Public Service Comm'n*, 447 U.S. 530, 537 (1980)).

50. *United States* v. *Grace*, 461 U.S. 171, 177 (1983) (citation omitted).

51. *Clark* v. *Community for Creative Non-Violence*, 468 U.S. 288 (1984).

52. *See, e.g., Saia* v. *New York*, 334 U.S. 558 (1948).

53. *Lakewood* v. *Plain Dealer*, 486 U.S. 750, 759 (1988).

54. *Boos* v. *Barry*, 485 U.S. 312, 320 (1988).

55. *Barnes* v. *Glen Theatre, Inc.*, 501 U.S. 560 (1991).

56. *Id.* at 571.

57. *Perry Educational Ass'n* v. *Perry Local Educators' Ass'n*, 460 U.S. 37, 45–46 (1983) (citations omitted).

58. *Rosenberger* v. *University of Virginia*, 515 U.S. 819 (1995).

59. *Perry Educational Ass'n* v. *Perry Local Educators' Ass'n*, 460 U.S. 37, 45 (1983).

60. *Adderley* v. *Florida*, 385 U.S. 39 (1966).

61. *Greer* v. *Spock*, 424 U.S. 828 (1976).

62. *U.S. Postal Service* v. *Council of Greenburgh Civic Ass'n*, 453 U.S. 114, *appeal dismissed*, 453 U.S. 917 (1981).

63. *Kreimer* v. *Bureau of Police*, 958 F.2d 1242 (3d Cir. 1992).

64. *Concerned Women for America* v. *Lafayette County*, 883 F.2d 32 (5th Cir. 1989).

65. *Grayned* v. *City of Rockford*, 408 U.S. 104, 108 (1972).

66. *Village of Hoffman Estates* v. *Flipside, Hoffman Estates, Inc.*, 455 U.S. 489, 499 (1982).

67. *NAACP* v. *Button,* 371 U.S. 415, 433 (1963) (citations omitted).

68. *Grayned* v. *City of Rockford,* 408 U.S. 104, 108–09 (1972).

69. *Smith* v. *Goguen,* 415 U.S. 566, 578 (1974).

70. *Id.*

71. *Baggett* v. *Bullitt,* 377 U.S. 360, 372 (1964).

72. *Video Software Dealers Ass'n* v. *Webster,* 968 F.2d 684 (8th Cir. 1992); *Davis-Kidd Booksellers, Inc.* v. *McWherter,* 866 S.W.2d 520 (Tenn. 1993).

73. *Winters* v. *New York,* 333 U.S. 507 (1948).

74. *Erznoznik* v. *City of Jacksonville,* 422 U.S. 205 (1975).

75. *Id.* at 213.

76. *Kreimer* v. *Bureau of Police,* 958 F.2d 1242 (3d Cir. 1992).

77. *Id.* at 1259.

78. *Id.* at 1262.

79. *See Concerned Women for America* v. *Lafayette County,* 883 F.2d 32 (5th Cir. 1989); *see also Lamb's Chapel* v. *Center Moriches Union Free School Dist.,* 508 U.S. 384 (1993).

80. *Cohen* v. *California,* 403 U.S. 15, 24 (1969).

CHAPTER 3

The Sexual Conundrum

"Sex," the Supreme Court has recognized, is "a great and mysterious motive force in human life, [and] has indisputably been a subject of absorbing interest to mankind through the ages; it is one of the vital problems of human interest and public concern."[1] Amply represented in classical literature, song, and art, and perhaps a dominant theme in modern communicative media, sex is the biggest and most intractable of free-speech issues. And libraries are frequently embroiled in controversy over sexually oriented materials.

The most frequent mistake made when sexual expression is at issue is the treatment of all of its forms as being of equivalent legal status. *Obscenity* is considered by the layperson as synonymous with *pornography, nudity,* or *indecency.* The law, and the courts, do not use the terms interchangeably—and therein lies the source of much confusion.

Under the Constitution, obscenity is a category all its own. Alone among the various forms of sexual expression, obscenity falls outside the First Amendment's protection. The incongruity of having a special "hard-core" category of sexual expression that is not considered protected speech, while more mild, but nonetheless disturbing forms remain protected, has led the Supreme Court to undergo some interesting legal gymnastics in order to draw a discernible line between obscenity and other forms of sexual expression. In *Jacobellis* v. *Ohio,* U.S. Supreme Court Justice Potter Stewart speculated that the concept of obscenity might well be undefinable.[2] Then he wrote, to his later regret and its constant repetition as if it were law, "I know it when I see it."[3] But coming as it did in a concurring rather than majority opinion, it is not law.

At his retirement announcement, Justice Stewart said ruefully that of "all the other thousands of words that I have written, and the late nights I have spent trying to write opinions for the Court or my separate opinions, I regret a little bit that if I am remembered at all, I will be remembered for that particular phrase, which, in my view, is far from deathless." It is also far from an appropriate way to separate constitutionally protected sexual expression from obscene speech.[4]

Crafting an appropriate definition of *obscenity* has long been a problem for the law. At the time of the nation's founding, only Massachusetts banned obscenity, by which it meant *sacrilegious* or *blasphemous* speech. In 1792, within a year of the ratification of the Bill of Rights, all but one of the fourteen states had enacted laws against blasphemy or profanity.

It did not take long, however, for the concept of obscenity to migrate from the irreverent to the sexual, a realm in which it has steadfastly and exclusively remained. Even though people may sometimes refer to an "obscene" amount of money, consider some form of heresy to be "obscene," or regard barbarous behavior as an "obscenity," the legal sense of the word is restricted to sexual activities or functions. The first American obscenity prosecution of a publication took place in Massachusetts in 1821 over lewd illustrations that were part of the book, *Memoirs of a Woman of Pleasure.*[5] However, although we continue to think of obscenity in terms of imagery, the Supreme Court has said that books that contain no illustrations can still be adjudged obscene.[6]

The first federal obscenity statute was enacted in 1842 and prohibited the importation of obscene pictures, which largely entered the country in the form of "French" postcards. An 1868 English case, *Regina* v. *Hicklin,* profoundly influenced American obscenity prosecutions by defining obscenity as that which had a tendency to deprave or corrupt the morals of the young, as well as those whose minds were open to such improper influences. That version of obscenity dominated American jurisprudence for nearly a century and resulted in the seizure or prosecution of such celebrated works as *Lysistrata, Canterbury Tales, Mrs. Warren's Profession, An American Tragedy, Studs Lonigan, Sanctuary, God's Little Acre,* and *Lady Chatterley's Lover.*

In a famous 1933 decision, a federal court found that *Ulysses* by James Joyce was not obscene when read as a whole.[7] The case marked a departure from the prevailing law, which held that any lewd segment, no matter how minor, was enough to infect an otherwise valuable contribution to literature with corrupting obscenity. It was not until 1942, in a case involving "fighting words," that the Supreme Court took occasion to remark on the issue of obscenity. In *Chaplinsky* v. *New Hampshire,* the Court gratuitously lumped the "lewd and obscene" with other utterances it considered "no essential part of any exposition of ideas" and thus "of such slight social value as a step to truth that any benefit to be derived from them was clearly outweighed by the social interest in order and morality."[8] Although the Court later corrected its error of equating the indecent with the obscene, those who seek removal of library books or wish to limit library Interent access often still treat the two as one.

Defining Obscenity

Finally confronting the issue head-on in 1957 in *Roth* v. *United States,* the Court attempted to find a middle ground that would enable prosecutions to go forward when the objective was to ban gratuitous, hard-core pornography, while still preserving the free-speech rights of those who took a more serious or artistic approach to the subject of sex.[9] Agreeing with the *Chaplinsky* Court that obscenity was "utterly without redeeming social importance," the Court held obscenity to be outside the Constitution's protection. Material that dealt with sex, the Court said, "in a manner appealing to prurient interest" would be considered obscene.[10] That which explored the hold and interest it generated in people, largely as an attempt to delve into human nature, still was well within the First Amendment's protective scope, as long as the originating purpose of the material in question was not "to excite lustful thoughts."[11]

Justice William Brennan, the author of the Court's opinion, quickly realized the dilemma he had created in distinguishing between the lustful and the more detached and artful by later noting that "constitutionally protected expression . . . is often separated from obscenity only by a dim and uncertain line."[12] He soon abandoned altogether the obscenity doctrine he had helped fashion but never won majority support for his revisionist view.[13]

Even though no majority on the Court agreed with him, the Court struggled for years to find a definition that separated the obscene from that which was merely pornographic. The majority of justices, including even Justice John Harlan after blindness had afflicted him, would dutifully screen the films accused of obscenity to determine whether any redeeming social value could be discerned. During this period, several refinements of the definition for obscenity were advanced, all of which tended to move in a more libertarian direction. Finally, in 1973, the Court adopted the definition that still holds sway today. To be obscene, a jury (or the judge in a case tried without a jury) must determine that

1. "the average person, applying contemporary community standards" would find that the work, taken as a whole, appeals to the prurient interest;
2. the work depicts or describes, in a patently offensive way, sexual conduct specifically defined by the applicable state law; and
3. the work, taken as a whole, lacks serious literary, artistic, political, or scientific value.[14]

Only by meeting all three elements of this test, referred to as the *Miller* test for the case in which it was announced, can a work be adjudged obscene. Each element requires that the work be viewed as a whole to avoid the standard that prevailed earlier in the century when a single lustful passage was sufficient to invoke censorship authority over an entire work.

The "community standards" aspect of the test has led to considerable confusion. Although the First Amendment should not mean one thing in a conservative Bible Belt town and another in Hollywood, resulting in different constitutional treatment of the same work depending on where the case is tried, the *Miller* Court adopted the position that the greater explicitness that might be tolerated in New York or Las Vegas should not dictate the standard in Mississippi or Maine, to use the Court's own examples.[15]

Still, there are distinct limits on the level of restrictiveness that a community can impose on sexual expression; otherwise, a puritanical community might apply the label of illegal obscenity to a "depiction of a woman with a bare midriff," a result that is clearly beyond the pale of what the First Amendment can tolerate.[16] Only the prurience element, the first of the three parts of the *Miller* test, is subject to measurement by community standards.[17] The Court assumed that a jury drawn from the community would apply its own general knowledge of the prevailing standards. That determination by the jurors may not be interfered with by some type of legislative attempt to define community standards.[18]

On the other hand, the legislature does have the dominant role in defining what sexual conduct is patently offensive. Such a statute must be written with considerable detail to give fair notice of what crosses the line and cannot leave the issue for determination according to the personal tastes of the community. Finally, the literary, artistic, political, or scientific value found in the third element of the test must be determined by an objective, national standard and not treated as a matter of contemporary community standards or legislative fiat.[19]

In one of the first examinations under the new *Miller* test, the Supreme Court was called upon to decide whether the critically acclaimed movie, *Carnal Knowledge,* could be found obscene in Georgia. The 1971 film had received an *R,* or restricted, rating from the Motion Picture Association of America and made many critics' top-ten lists for the year. Ann-Margret received an Academy Award nomination for her role. Future Oscar laureate Jack Nicholson also starred in the Mike Nichols film, along with Candace Bergen, Rita Moreno, and singer/actor Art Garfunkel. Even though this obviously mainstream release about sexual obsessions had played without incident in twenty-nine other Georgia towns, an Albany, Georgia, jury had found the film to be obscene; and the state's courts had gone along under a state law that treated movies as obscene if they portrayed acts that would constitute "public indecency" if performed in public. All but the tamest of bedroom scenes would qualify a film as obscene under the Georgia law.

The U.S. Supreme Court, however, disagreed with the Georgia courts. It observed that some objective standards, not dependent on a jury's sensibilities, do exist. "While the subject matter of the picture is, in a broad sense, sex," the Court said, "and there are scenes in which sexual conduct including 'ultimate sexual acts' is to be understood to be taking place, the camera does not focus on the bodies of the actors at such times. There is no exhibition whatever of the actors' genitals, lewd or otherwise, during these scenes. There are occasional scenes of nudity, but nudity alone is not enough to make material legally obscene under the Miller standards."[20]

Carnal Knowledge was not obscene, the Court concluded, because it was a serious artistic effort and "not the 'public portrayal of hard core sexual conduct for its own sake, and for the ensuing commercial gain' which we [previously] said was punishable."[21] A library that loaned videotapes of *Carnal Knowledge* could be secure in the knowledge that the film, regardless of the community standard employed, is not obscene. The Supreme Court's judgment on the film is binding on all jurisdictions.

Although it is often said that obscenity is outside the First Amendment's protection, the general rule against content and viewpoint discrimination applies to the regulation or criminalization of obscenity. Thus, for example, a law or regulation could not prohibit obscene depictions of public officials while permitting others to be so portrayed, for that would be to enact a law that favors or disfavors a particular political viewpoint.[22] The Court has also declared that the mere private possession of obscene materials, such as in a person's home, cannot be criminalized.[23] However, there is no legal justification for obscene materials in a public or school library. If the materials have potential use as a subject of study or scholarship, then they have the type of serious value that renders them nonobscene.

Protecting Sexual Expression

It is equally important to understand, as the Court has unambiguously stated, that "[s]exual expression which is indecent but not obscene is protected by the First Amendment."[24] In one case exemplifying this principle, a man protesting the war in Vietnam was arrested for entering a Los Angeles courthouse while wearing a jacket emblazoned with the words, "Fuck the Draft." He was charged with a breach of the peace. The Supreme Court overturned his conviction, noting that "no substantial privacy interests [were] invaded in an essentially intolerable manner" because those offended could easily avert their eyes.[25] The use of the expletive to dramatize the wearer's political opposition to the military draft was obviously not without some social value and could not rob the statement of its status as a form of political dissent. The Court's opinion noted, "one man's vulgarity is another's lyric."[26]

Furthermore, in another case, the Court said that nude dancing, which was being performed solely as a means of entertainment, conveys an erotic message that is within the scope of the First Amendment's coverage.[27] Neither mere nudity nor the depiction of sexual activity qualifies a work as a form of obscenity.

Despite the federal Constitution's approach to obscenity and federal laws that criminalize obscenity, some states have taken a different view. In 1987, the Oregon Supreme Court found that excluding obscenity from the protections of free speech could not be justified with any consistent theory of free expression under the state constitution and may not be punished in the interest of a uniform vision of how human sexuality should be regarded or portrayed.[28] Still, it held that obscenity may be regulated to the extent that the restrictive law focuses on the interests of unwilling viewers, captive audiences, minors, and beleaguered neighbors

Hawaii's Supreme Court has also used its constitution to invalidate a criminal obscenity law, reasoning that the purchase of obscene material must be protected if the private possession of obscenity cannot be criminalized.[29] Some five additional states do not have anti-obscenity statutes on the books.

Guaranteeing Procedural Safeguards

Because the First Amendment looks with extreme disfavor on any attempt to restrain access to speech prior to publication, the Court has recognized that substantial procedural safeguards must be followed before material may be considered obscene. In *Miller*, the Court ensured that "no one will be subject to prosecution for the sale or exposure of obscene materials" without rigorous safeguards against capricious or standardless prosecutions.[30] Under the concept of due process, those who exercise a censorious power over allegedly obscene materials must

> provide a prompt hearing under clear, preexisting standardized guidelines;
>
> bear the burden of proving that the material is obscene;
>
> bear the responsibility for bringing an action in a court of law to affirm any finding that it made that the material is obscene; and
>
> defer to judicial proceedings for the final disposition of whatever restraint may be placed on the material.[31]

A library that takes it upon itself to remove materials because of suspected obscenity has an obligation to follow its existing policies to confirm that suspicion and then must initiate a lawsuit to prove in a court of law that the materials are indeed obscene. These safeguards exist to ensure that sexual expression that is unpopular or personally offensive is not removed unless the legal standards for obscenity are met.

Harmful-to-Minors Standards

The standard for obscenity changes when distribution to minors is at issue. Here, the *Miller* obscenity test is adjusted using minors, rather than adults, as its reference points.[32] Thus, the first element requires that the material must appeal to the prurient interest *of minors*. The second provides a legislature with somewhat more leeway to specify the kind of sexual conduct depicted or described that would be patently offensive *for minors.* These statutes are often called "harmful-to-minor" laws, which is a synonym for "obscene for minors." Finally, the last element must be evaluated in light of whether, taken as a whole, the work lacks serious literary, artistic, political, or scientific value *for minors.* That value for minors must be examined in light of whether the material holds serious value for "any reasonable minor, including a seventeen-year-old."[33] If it does, then it cannot be restricted as harmful to minors.

The justification for greater restrictions on the availability of material to minors is a recognition that the state has a compelling interest in protecting the psychological and emotional well-being of children that does not exist when the state attempts to take a similarly paternalistic attitude toward adults. If the government could make authoritative decisions about what thoughts were acceptable for adults and which were not, the entire purpose of the First Amendment would be eviscerated.

However, what a parent might regard as inappropriate fare for his or her children does not define the state's more-limited authority here. Although one parent might decide that his or her child will not watch or read about the *Power Rangers,* others clearly will. The government could not logically enforce the judgments about access of the most restrictive parent; otherwise, it would be ignoring the same judgments of less restrictive parents, who might well constitute a majority of the community. Even a majority vote, if it were possible, cannot delineate the scope of the government's restrictive authority. *Our right to free speech is not subject to any vote; it will not yield to community sentiment.*

It is clear, for example, from the Court's own declarations that nudity cannot be regarded to be harmful to minors per se, even though many parents—perhaps a substantial majority—would draw the line there. "Rather, to be obscene 'such expression must be, in some significant way, erotic,'" according to the Court.[34]

The Library Context

Some harmful-to-minors laws exempt public libraries from their coverage. The exemptions assume that some of the materials that a library acquires for its adult patrons may fit the definition. The legislators nonetheless do not want librarians to guess at which of those materials might be obscene for children and deny access to adults. A harmful-to-minors controversy did surround the book *Sex,* by pop star Madonna. The book made it onto the *New York Times* best-seller list. For many public libraries, the list serves as one of the selection criteria for new works that will be purchased. Libraries that purchased the book on this basis sometimes found themselves entangled in a high-profile political and cultural battle. The book may well have fit into the definition of a harmful-to-minors statute, causing one judge to acknowledge that it is senseless to enforce such laws against bookstores:

> A bookstore owner would violate the statute by selling to a 17-year-old a copy of Madonna's book, Sex, yet the child could obtain the same book from a library without any impediment. It is hard to see how the bookstore owner could be understood to act to harm or endanger the welfare of the minor, while the librarian would not.[35]

The library exemption is, in part, a recognition that the line between the harmful and the benign is often difficult to draw. A harmful-to-minors law drafted with ambiguity as to the materials covered offends the First Amendment's prohibitions against vagueness and overbreadth. The Court has repeatedly held that "the salutary purpose of protecting children" does not obviate the responsibility of regulators to spell out the specific criteria that renders expression harmful to minors rather than protected speech.[36] Similarly, if the statute adversely affects the right of adults to have access to materials that might be harmful to children, a law or regulation could be found to be fatally overbroad and thus unconstitutional.[37] That aspect of the overbreadth rules seems to advise that a library exemption is wise policy.

The Special Category of Child Pornography

One further way that the law protects children is in the realm of child pornography. Typically, an anti-child-pornography statute prohibits the possession or viewing of material that shows a minor in a state of nudity, when the minor is not related to the person possessing or viewing the material. The child pornography laws usually exempt from coverage bona fide artistic, medical, scientific, educational, religious, governmental, and judicial purposes when performed by a physician, psychologist, sociologist, scientist, teacher, person pursuing bona fide studies or research, librarian, clergy, prosecutor, judge, or other person having a proper interest in the material. The informed consent of a parent can also be a statutory exception for the photographing or use of the minor in a state of nudity.

In *New York* v. *Ferber,* the Supreme Court found that protecting the physical and psychological well-being of minors was a sufficiently compelling governmental interest to prohibit child pornography, which was found to have nearly nonexistent countervailing value.[38] Holding that this form of expression causes permanent harm to the children exploited and that the harm is continuous by virtue of the ongoing circulation of the materials, the Court concluded that child pornography was sufficiently akin to obscenity, which is likewise outside the Constitution's protection. Still, the Court required that child pornography laws specifically define the conduct prohibited and that criminalization "be limited to works that *visually* depict conduct by children below a specified age."[39] Vladimir Nabokov's novel *Lolita,* about a man with a sexual passion for young girls who seduces and is seduced by a twelve-year-old girl, is not child pornography, even though it was banned in France shortly after its 1955 publication and subsequently in parts of the United States. However, an illustrated or filmed version of the book using a child actress in explicit scenes could be child pornography.

In the case of child pornography, the *Miller* obscenity test is adjusted: "A trier of fact need not find that the material appeals to the prurient interest of the average person; it is not required that sexual conduct portrayed be done so in a patently offensive manner; and the material at issue need not be considered as a whole."[40] In other words, the threshhold for what constitutes child pornography is considerably lower than that of obscenity. Still, as with obscenity laws, the Court requires a criminal intent or knowledge of the activities that constitute the crime before a person could be convicted of child pornography.[41]

In 1990, the Court declined to permit the private possession of child pornography to be protected against criminal laws in the same manner as it had protected the private possession of obscenity. The difference, the Court said, is that child pornography laws are not a paternalistic exercise over the thoughts that an adult may have but an attempt "to destroy a market for the exploitative use of children."[42] For that reason, along with its *de minimis* value as a form of expression, the private possession of illegal child pornography can be prohibited entirely.

Pornography and Women

Although the Court has recognized the need to protect children from exploitation through the making and possessing of pornography featuring minors, an attempt to use the same arguments on behalf of women has not overcome the prevailing First Amendment norms. Indianapolis enacted an ordinance that defined pornography as the "graphic, sexually explicit subordination of women, whether in pictures or in words" and further described it as "a discriminatory practice based on sex which denies women equal opportunities in society." The American Booksellers Association successfully challenged the ordinance in court. The trial court found that the special protections afforded children in *Ferber* were not "readily transferable to adult women as a class."[43]

The court's opinion, authored by a woman judge, went on to note that women had more to lose from laws that limit free-speech rights, for supporters of the law should remember that, "in terms of altering sociological patterns, much as alteration may be necessary and desirable, free speech, rather than being the enemy, is a long-tested and worthy ally."[44] In approving the decision in the case, the Seventh Circuit Court of Appeals was even more emphatic, finding that the ordinance discriminated on the basis of the viewpoint expressed:

> Speech treating women in the approved way—in sexual encounters "premised on equality"—is lawful no matter how sexually explicit. Speech treating women in the disapproved way—as submissive in matters sexual or as enjoying humiliation—is unlawful no matter how significant the literary, artistic, or political qualities of the work taken as a whole. The state may not ordain preferred viewpoints in this way. The Constitution forbids the state to declare one perspective right and silence opponents.[45]

The U.S. Supreme Court affirmed the Seventh Circuit decision without comment. For libraries, the decision means that books and other materials *cannot be removed* from availability because they depict women—or any other group other than children—in a sexually exploitive manner.

The Rights of Adults

Although the Court has been most emphatic in its protection of children from being exploited in sexual pictures, it has been equally determined not to allow concerns about exposing children to sexually oriented materials to have the effect of restricting adult access to those otherwise legal materials. As already explained, one example of the Court's reasoning on this issue comes in the context of a federal law that prohibited both obscene and indecent interstate commercial telephone messages, often referred to as "dial-a-porn." In a challenge to the law, the Court had no difficulty upholding the ban on obscene commercial telephone messages. The First Amendment's protections simply do not extend to obscenity.

It did, however, strike down the ban on indecent messages. Although conceding that the state did have a compelling interest in preventing minors from beings exposed to sexual expression that is indecent even if not obscene, the Court emphasized the requirement that a law passed pursuant to that authority must be narrowly drawn to serve that purpose and not intrude on adult rights. To permit any other result, the government would "'reduce the adult population . . . to . . . only what is fit for children.'"[46]

In support of the total ban, the federal government argued that no lesser step could prevent children from gaining access to the indecent messages. The Court was unpersuaded, noting that hearings held by the Federal Communications Commission (FCC) demonstrated that credit card requirements, access through special codes, and scrambling rules were a sufficient solution to the problem of keeping indecent dial-a-porn messages out of the reach of minors. The Court went on to suggest that even if "a few of the most enterprising and disobedient young people would manage to secure access to such messages" if a less restrictive regulation were enacted, such a result must be tolerated so that the content of adult telephone conversations are not limited to that which is suitable for children.[47]

The Communications Decency Act (CDA), which is discussed at greater length in chapter 9 and which attempted to cleanse the Internet of indecent images available to children, was also struck down by the Supreme Court as an interference with adult rights.[48] The act was successfully challenged by the American Library Association and the Freedom to Read Foundation, among others, because of its potentially devastating effect on Internet access at public libraries.

The Rights of Children

Not only must a regulator be mindful of adult rights, it must also be mindful of children's rights. The Court, for example, has held that even limited restrictions enacted out of a concern for youthful well-being must be restricted to harmful material that is "virtually obscene."[49] One federal appellate court combed U.S. Supreme Court decisions and concluded that they teach "that if any reasonable minor, including a seventeen-year-old, would find serious value, the material is not 'harmful to minors.'"[50] Citing and quoting other courts with approval, the court continued: "'[I]f a work is found to have serious literary, artistic, political or scientific value for a legitimate minority of normal, older adolescents, then it cannot be said to lack such value for the entire class of juveniles taken as a whole.'"[51]

In one case applying this principle, a Georgia law that prohibited the sale or display to minors of material containing nude figures was found to be substantially overbroad and thus unconstitutional on several grounds, including its effect of barring high-school seniors and college freshmen from having access to publications merely containing some nudity.[52] By broadly prohibiting access to these near-adults, the state had overstepped its legitimate interests in the well-being of youngsters.

In a case involving a municipal ordinance that prohibited movies containing nudity at drive-in theaters, the U.S. Supreme Court defined some of the rights of minors that are at stake. Enacted as a measure to protect children from what the Jacksonville, Florida, city council deemed inappropriate movie material, the ordinance was struck down as unconstitutional by the Court.[53] Once again, the Court acknowledged that there were some instances in which the government may "adopt more stringent controls on communicative materials available to youths than on those available to adults."[54] Still, it ruled, "[s]peech . . . cannot be suppressed solely to protect the young from ideas or images that a legislative body thinks unsuitable for them. In most circumstances, the values protected by the First Amendment are no less applicable when government seeks to control the flow of information to minors."[55]

In this instance, the ordinance was doubly flawed. It restricted adult access to movies that adults had a right to view, and it was unconstitutionally overbroad. Its overbreadth problem was the result of the ordinance's irrational treatment of all nudity as harmful, including a "baby's buttocks, the nude body of a war victim, or scenes from a culture in which nudity is indigenous."[56] Nudity, in and of itself, is not prohibitable. The Court held that an ordinance burdening expression may not sweep so broadly that it curbs speech that does not have the harmful effects that the government seeks to remedy.

The decision has considerable significance for public libraries. First, in the most analogous circumstances, it holds that a library cannot enforce a rule that prohibits the viewing of nudity in public areas of the library. Although one could imagine such a rule being enacted to inhibit readers from openly looking at nude pictures in full view of others or "surfers" from accessing certain sexually oriented sites on the Internet, such a rule that focuses on nudity, in and of itself, is too broad a term for such regulations. Further, it would improperly limit and restrict adults.

In addition, the Court recognized that children have a right of access to ideas, even ideas that some official body thinks inappropriate for children. Library regulations that attempt to discourage access to ideas would violate those rights. For example, if a recent and notorious instance of youth violence captures attention across the nation and is tied to some form of expression—music, books, videos, or Web sites—that appears to glorify violence, community leaders may well wish to know whether the accused expressive work is available to children in the public library and, if so, limit the access of minors. The Supreme Court's decision, along with other cases described in subsequent chapters, defines such actions as a violation of youth rights.

Sex and the Public Library

Library collections house many materials containing forms of sexual expression. Medical and health books, classic works of literature, dictionaries and encyclopedias, and the latest best-sellers ensure that sex is a constant on the open shelves of public libraries. Any attempt to exclude these materials would substantially impair a library's ability to serve its community. For this reason, many statutes that forbid the display or open access of sexually oriented materials out of a concern for minors exempt libraries from the law.

Public bodies will often be uncomfortable with these materials, purchased and maintained at public expense. Still, the First Amendment has important application here. That application is well-represented by a dispute that involved the Library of Congress and *Playboy* magazine. Under a federal program, the Library of Congress had been reproducing books and magazines in braille and recorded editions for blind and visually impaired individuals. From 1973 to 1985, articles, though not the photographs or cartoons, from *Playboy* had been produced in braille and proved to be one of the most popular magazines in the program. A member of Congress, alarmed at this use of taxpayer funds, succeeded in getting the program's appropriation reduced by the exact amount being spent annually on *Playboy*. In response, the Librarian of Congress announced that braille editions of *Playboy* were being discontinued to abide by the direction the library received from the Congress by its reduction of available monies.

In ruling the exclusion of *Playboy* a violation of the First Amendment, a federal court found that the braille program constituted a form of non-public forum for the communication of ideas.[57] Under such an analysis, the elimination of *Playboy* because of its sexual content amounted to a form of viewpoint discrimination that is inconsistent with the authority the government has over nonpublic forums.[58] What is significant about the decision is its indication that the elimination of materials from a collection or an ongoing program because of its constitutionally protected sexual content will be viewed as a First Amendment violation.

Conclusion

Every library collection is likely to have a considerable amount of material that is sexually oriented in some way or another. However, the mere treatment of sex or the revelation of nudity is not the measure of whether the material is obscene and thus not protected by the First Amendment. Neither nudity nor sex are per se inappropriate for minors. Except for a narrow category of materials that qualify as obscene or child pornography, sexual expression is broadly protected by the Constitution.

Still, government is not completely without authority over sexual expression. Several basic rules must be remembered. To regulate nonobscene sexual expression, government must only act

1. in furtherance of a compelling governmental interest;
2. utilizing the least restrictive means of accomplishing that overriding goal;
3. with specificity under preexisting guidelines, rather than with vague or ambiguous language that permits authorities to exercise ad hoc judgments;
4. in a manner that preserves adult rights of access;
5. in a manner that recognizes and considers the access rights of older minors; and
6. in accordance with written guidelines that afford adequate procedural safeguards to the expression at issue.

As the case law reviewed in this chapter indicates, this is a heavy burden that is not easily met.

NOTES

1. *Roth* v. *United States,* 354 U.S. 476, 487 (1957).

2. *Jacobellis* v. *Ohio,* 378 U.S. 184, 197 (1964) (Stewart, J., concurring).

3. *Id.*

4. *See, e.g., Miller* v. *California,* 413 U.S. 15, 23–24 (1973) ("statutes designed to regulate obscene materials must be carefully limited").

5. *Commonwealth* v. *Holmes,* 17 Mass. 336 (1821).

6. *Kaplan* v. *California,* 413 U.S. 115 (1973).

7. *United States* v. *One Book called Ulysses,* 5 F. Supp. 182 (S.D. N.Y. 1933), *aff'd,* 72 F.2d 705 (2d Cir. 1934).

8. *Chaplinsky* v. *New Hampshire,* 315 U.S. 568, 572 (1942).

9. *Roth* v. *United States,* 354 U.S. 476 (1957).

10. *Id.* at 487 (footnote omitted).

11. *Id.* at 487 n. 20.

12. *Bantam Books* v. *Sullivan,* 372 U.S. 58, 66 (1963).

13. *Paris Adult Theatre I* v. *Slaton,* 413 U.S. 49, 98, 113 (1973) (Brennan, J., dissenting).

14. *Miller* v. *California,* 413 U.S. 15, 24 (1973).

15. *Id.* at 32.

16. *Jenkins* v. *Georgia,* 418 U.S. 153, 161 (1974).

17. *Id.* at 160.

18. *Smith* v. *United States,* 431 U.S. 291, 302–03 (1977).

19. *Pope* v. *Illinois,* 481 U.S. 497 (1987).

20. *Jenkins* v. *Georgia,* 418 U.S. 153, 161 (1974).

21. *Id.* (citation omitted).

22. *R.A.V.* v. *City of St. Paul,* 505 U.S. 377, 384 (1992).

23. *Stanley* v. *Georgia,* 394 U.S. 557 (1969).

24. *Sable Communications* v. *FCC,* 492 U.S. 115, 126 (1989).

25. *Cohen* v. *California,* 403 U.S. 15, 21, 22 (1971).

26. *Id.* at 25.

27. *Barnes* v. *Glen Theatre, Inc.,* 501 U.S. 560 (1991).

28. *State* v. *Henry,* 732 P.2d 9 (Or. 1987).

29. *State* v. *Kam,* 748 P.2d 372 (Ha. 1988).

30. *Miller* v. *California,* 413 U.S. 15, 28 (1973).

31. *Freedman* v. *Maryland,* 380 U.S. 51 (1965); *see also Vance* v. *Universal Amusement Co., Inc.,* 445 U.S. 308 (1980).

32. *See Ginsberg* v. *New York,* 390 U.S. 629 (1968).

33. *American Booksellers Ass'n* v. *Webb,* 919 F.2d 1493, 1504–05 (11th Cir. 1990), *cert. denied,* 500 U.S. 942 (1991) (relying on *Pope* v. *Illinois,* 481 U.S. 497 (1987)).

34. *Erznoznik* v. *City of Jacksonville,* 422 U.S. 205, 214 n. 10 (1975) (quoting *Cohen* v. *California,* 403 U.S. 15, 20 (1971)).

35. *State* v. *Maynard,* 910 P.2d 1115, 1123 (Or. App. 1996), *vacated on other grounds,* 327 P.2d 264 (Or. 1998).

36. *See, e.g., Interstate Circuit, Inc.* v. *Dallas,* 390 U.S. 676, 689 (1968).

37. *See, e.g., ACLU* v. *Reno,* 521 U.S. 844 (1997).

38. *New York* v. *Ferber,* 458 U.S. 747 (1982).

39. *Id.* at 764 (emphasis in original).

40. *Id.*

41. *Id.* at 765.

42. *Osborne* v. *Ohio,* 495 U.S. 103, 109 (1990).

43. *American Booksellers Association, Inc.* v. *Hudnut,* 598 F. Supp. 1316 (S.D. Ind. 1984), *aff'd,* 771 F.2d 323 (7th Cir. 1985), *aff'd summarily,* 475 U.S. 1001 (1986).

44. *Id.* at 1137.

45. 771 F.2d at 325 (citation omitted).

46. *Sable Communications* v. *FCC,* 492 U.S. 115, 128 (1989) (quoting *Butler* v. *Michigan,* 352 U.S. 380, 383 (1957)).

47. *Id.* at 130.

48. *ACLU* v. *Reno,* 521 U.S. 844 (1997).

49. *See Virginia* v. *American Booksellers Ass'n,* 484 U.S. 383, 395 (1988).

50. *American Booksellers Ass'n* v. *Webb,* 919 F.2d 1493, 1504–05 (11th Cir. 1990), *cert. denied,* 500 U.S. 942 (1991) (footnote omitted).

51. *Id.* at 1505 (citations omitted).

52. *American Booksellers Ass'n* v. *McAuliffe,* 533 F. Supp. 50 (N.D. Ga. 1981).

53. *Erznoznik* v. *City of Jacksonville,* 422 U.S. 205 (1975).

54. *Id.* at 211.

55. *Id.*

56. *Id.* at 213.

57. *American Council for the Blind* v. *Boorstin,* 644 F. Supp. 811, 815 (D.D.C. 1986).

58. *Id.* at 816.

CHAPTER 4

The Right to Offend

Every library attempts to tailor its collection to the interests of the community it serves. Books about Idaho history, for example, are more likely to be found in the Boise Public Library than in those of Cincinnati. A children's library will more likely feature Dr. Seuss rather than Dr. Ruth. Nonetheless, such wise tailoring cannot provide a legally defensible excuse for excluding certain materials from a library on the basis of some determination that it is "offensive to the community."

Resisting the impulse to exclude materials palpably offensive is difficult. Everyone, even the most committed First Amendment advocate, will find that some utterance, some publication, some set of images simply goes beyond all imaginable propriety for him or her. For some, the expression of racial or religious hatred should find no sanction in the law. For others, it may be an expression of a particular form of sexuality or the description of sexual conduct. Still others may recoil at the depiction of violence. Each, according to personal sensibilities or experiences, would draw the line somewhat differently.

Our constitutional commitment to free speech, however, does not permit such subjective and ad hoc decisions. It establishes the public library as one of the places where majority sentiment or majority vote about offensiveness is irrelevant. A library attempts to serve all members and all interests in the community. Except in the narrow category of sexual obscenity, discussed in chapter 3, the law does not recognize a First Amendment exception based on subjective degrees of offensiveness. As the Supreme Court has stated, "It is firmly settled that under our Constitution the public expression of ideas may not be prohibited merely because the ideas are themselves offensive to some of their hearers."[1] It has further added offensiveness is "classically not [a] justificatio[n] validating the suppression of expression protected by the First Amendment. At least where obscenity is not involved, we have consistently held that the fact that protected speech may be offensive to some does not justify its suppression."[2] Although it would be much more pleasant if people spoke and wrote with civility and avoided noxious language and ideas, it remains "a prized American privilege to speak one's mind, [even though] not always with perfect good taste."[3]

Any other approach to the principle of free speech, particularly in a forum such as a public library, would render the concept meaningless. Speech, even of the most seemingly benign variety, has an enormously notorious capacity to offend. As this book was being written, the city government in Washington, D.C., was reeling from a controversy in which a mayoral aide used the word *niggardly* and had to resign after a large number of people misinterpreted the word as a form of racial slur. It is often not enough that no offense or ill will was meant or was even within the speaker's contemplation. When offensiveness is the measure, only the audience's reaction—no matter how wrongheaded—counts.

One of the most enduring controversies over a book, now more than a century old, concerns Mark Twain's *Adventures of Huckleberry Finn*. Derided as trash in 1885 to prevent its shelving at the Concord (Massachusetts) Public Library, the book remains controversial to this day among some segments of the African American community for its use of racial epithets and the consequences that it holds for the esteem of African American children by the circulation of that slur among children. The mirror image of that controversy can be found in Anne Arundel and St. Mary's counties in Maryland, where complaints from some segments of the white community caused school superintendents to remove from the curriculum Maya Angelou's *I Know Why the Caged Bird Sings* and Toni Morrison's *Song of Solomon,* modern classics by African American authors. The complaining parents called the books trash, just as *Huckleberry Finn* was, as well as "anti-white." Despite the heated debate, the books were eventually restored.

Similarly, and to the bewilderment of many, parents have also complained about such well-accepted children's reading fare as *The Wizard of Oz, The Diary of Anne Frank,* and *Grimm's Fairy Tales.* To protect access to books like these, however, we must act on principle and protect access to books containing stronger stuff and admittedly more problematic stories. As one federal appellate court ruled recently, even in instances when works are accused of being racist, in whole or in part, books and other literary works may not be banned from school curricula.[4] If this is true for children, who are generally regarded as having more plastic minds that are especially susceptible to outside influences, then it is even more the case with respect to adults, where the government's interest in preventing emotional or psychological harm is far less compelling.

No False Ideas

In the free-speech battles that have received the greatest amount of attention, we have learned that the danger to freedom of speech is almost never the result of censorship of material that we as a society universally value. Popular sentiment is enough to keep those expressions secure and defrock the would-be censors of their authority. Instead, the danger is always to speech that does not have wide support or obvious merit. As a result, free-speech cases and issues often involve dubious forms of speech, less than commendable individuals, and speech that many would find offensive.

Justice Oliver Wendell Holmes Jr. captured the essence of this concept when he wrote in 1929 that "if there is any principle of the Constitution that more imperatively calls for attachment than any other it is the principle of free thought—not free thought for those who agree with us but freedom for the thought that we hate."[5] On several occasions in the last few years, the Court again reaffirmed this touchstone by noting that "in public debate our own citizens must tolerate insulting, and even outrageous, speech in order to provide 'adequate breathing space' to the freedoms protected by the First Amendment."[6]

In reaching that conclusion, the Court is cognizant of the way that a grant of authority to censor caustic and extreme expression can quickly and logically mutate into authority to censor all but the most innocuous pablum. If we were to reach that point, freedom of speech would be entirely eviscerated, so far removed from the nation's foundational principles that it would be emptied of all meaning, even as an aspirational goal of society.

One of the principal reasons that the Constitution does not tolerate authoritative selection of appropriate thoughts by government authority is that we still believe it essential for the people—and not just those who hold office—to govern. To do so knowledgeably, people must be free to sample ideas from every source, consider them, and decide which have merit and which should be tossed into the dustbin. But even majority sentiment that some thoughts are too gruesome or dangerous to hold cannot overcome our constitutional commitment to free trade in ideas. Justice Thurgood Marshall recognized this necessary truism for democratic government when he wrote for the Court that "[o]ur whole constitutional heritage rebels at the thought of giving government the power to control men's minds."[7] Any other rule surely "would lead to standardization of ideas either by legislatures, courts, or dominant political or community groups."[8] Instead, we adhere to the notion that "[u]nder the First Amendment there is no such thing as a false idea. However pernicious an opinion may seem, we depend for its correction . . . on the competition of other ideas."[9]

For this reason, a library cannot discriminate against ideas that challenge all that we hold dear—whether in the selection and retention of books, in the access to Web sites that some deem problematic, or in the use of its meeting rooms. To enable library authorities to act as the "taste police" would be to give unbridled discretion about what speech is to be permitted and what speech excluded. Such a notion is wholly inconsistent with the concepts of intellectual freedom and individual liberty. And such a notion would have banished from the nation's libraries many of the works we now consider classic and essential.

One of the reasons that untoward speech is protected and tolerated is because that speech is often a form of dissent—dissent against political authority, dissent against conformity, and dissent against a pervasive culture. Just as political dissent is protected, no matter how displeasing to those in government, the protection of other ideas that a democratic majority might wish to suppress is a theme that recurs throughout our First Amendment jurisprudence. The reason to protect dissident views is obvious: our form of government is built upon the premise that

> every citizen shall have the right to engage in political expression and association. . . . History has amply proved the virtue of political activity by minority, dissident groups, who innumerable times have been in the vanguard of democratic thought and whose programs were ultimately accepted. Mere unorthodoxy or dissent from the prevailing mores is not to be condemned. The absence of such voices would be a symptom of grave illness in our society.[10]

Speech as a Safety Valve and Early Warning System

Such a constitutional policy does not merely have the advantage of consistency across the spectrum of viewpoints. It also advances important societal goals, performing a sort of safety-valve function. It allows people to blow off steam through the expression of untoward thoughts. It permits people to experiment with notions that, upon mature reflection, they, too, freely choose to abhor. In choosing not to suppress such expressions, we prevent those condemnable thoughts from gaining a special kind of hold on people's minds, much as the forbidden apple did with Adam and Eve.

This constitutional policy reflects a sort of maturity of thinking. With so much of the world's literature devoted to violence and crime, it would be easy to condemn all of it for the tragedy and evil visited upon the world. Possibly, there are books that appeal to people of such disaffection and alienation that they resort to vengeful and unspeakable acts in imitation. Mysteries often feature criminal deeds that seem to suggest that a slightly more clever person could get away with it. We do not restrict access to such books in the library. We do not—and could not—require a psychological profile to ensure that every library patron who wants to read these books will not use them as a blueprint for criminal violence. Instead, we know that the overwhelming majority will not be adversely affected by such reading fare. If we were to act otherwise, literature would be the poorer indeed.

This laissez-faire approach also enables others to spot potentially cancerous ideas and prevent them from spreading out of view and without opposition. And it empowers people with the knowledge that comes from study to understand how such ideas take hold and proliferate, that they might benefit from the lessons of history and prevent the spread of an ideological strain that carries disastrous consequences. If we were instead to suppress such hateful opinions, we would enjoy no safety. The thoughts would still exist and would merely move underground, where they could neither be monitored nor counteracted. The resentment of the adherents, forced into darkness, would build and might well emerge stronger, more widespread, and in more virulent form on a population unaware of its existence and ill-prepared for the onslaught.

For these reasons, as well as the law's need to follow neutral principles and ensure free trade in ideas, "the First Amendment forbids the government to regulate speech in ways that favor some viewpoints or ideas at the expense of others."[11] Government, the Supreme Court has said, "may not prohibit the expression of an idea simply because society finds the idea itself offensive or disagreeable."[12] Instead, speech regulations must be neutral as to the subject matter discussed or the viewpoint expressed. Contrary to arguments that have been made in some quarters, the Supreme Court has ruled that a concern for the emotive impact that speech might have is a content-based interest that must be subjected to rigorous scrutiny of the sort that usually invalidates a measure.[13]

No segment of society ought to be able to use the power of government to silence another. Such a power can only stifle debate and dialogue. Instead, we hold to the belief enshrined in the First Amendment that suppression would operate to the detriment of society, no matter how disagreeable or hateful the message. Such a power cannot be exercised as library policy.

No Civility Police

Even untoward and outrageous language in expressing ideas that could be conveyed more civilly falls within constitutional protections. In one famous case already mentioned, a protester against the Vietnam War wore a jacket emblazoned with the words, "Fuck the Draft," to express his dissent. The Supreme Court overturned his arrest and conviction, noting that "one man's vulgarity is another's lyric."[14] The protestor was arrested for maliciously and willfully disturbing the peace through the use of untoward language on his jacket. In reversing his conviction, the Court noted that the protestor's message could not be read as a direct personal insult to any particular person and that the state had no authority to protect "the sensitive" in a public place "from otherwise unavoidable exposure to appellant's crude form of protest."[15] Government authorities may not act "as guardians of public morality [to] remove this offensive word from the public vocabulary."[16]

"Surely," the Court continued, "the State has no right to cleanse public debate to the point where it is grammatically palatable to the most squeamish among us" for that is a right that cannot be contained and would likely produce great mischief.[17] Finally, the Court concluded that it could not "sanction the view that the Constitution, while solicitous of the cognitive content of individual speech, has little or no regard for that emotive function which, practically speaking, may often be the more important element of the overall message sought to be communicated."[18] It then quoted Justice Felix Frankfurter for the proposition that "[o]ne of the prerogatives of American citizenship is the right to criticize public men and measures—and that means not only informed and responsible criticism but the freedom to speak foolishly and without moderation."[19]

Thus, as the Court has said, "the First Amendment recognizes, wisely we think, that a certain amount of expressive disorder not only is inevitable in a society committed to individual freedom, but must itself be protected if that freedom would survive."[20] The general rule adopted holds that "so long as the means are peaceful, the communication need not meet standards of acceptability."[21]

One important case dealing with the idea of offensiveness, *Terminello* v. *Chicago,* decided in 1949, involved a breach-of-the-peace prosecution against an ex-Catholic priest who had delivered a racist and anti-Semitic diatribe before a protesting and "howling" crowd.[22] Writing for the majority, Justice William O. Douglas noted that free speech "may indeed best serve its high purpose when it induces a condition of unrest, creates dissatisfaction with conditions as they are, or even stirs people to anger."[23] To rob speech of the ability to be "provocative and challenging" would take away the very reason the First Amendment secures its liberty.[24]

A celebrated autobiographical novel provides a case in point. Claude Brown wrote *Manchild in the Promised Land* in 1965. It received immediate critical acclaim and widespread controversy for its frequent use of expletives. Libraries were advised by community leaders not to carry the book. However, the expletives were a necessary part of the story, giving a very real picture of the Harlem ghetto in a manner that was both pleasurable reminiscence and sharp social criticism.

Although many instances of provocative speech may not seem to further society's progress, there are also many instances where it has exposed prejudices and preconceptions that have required repair. Indeed, in the 1960s and 1970s, *Terminello,* based on protecting hate speech, was the precedent relied upon to guarantee the free-speech rights of civil rights protesters at demonstrations, sit-ins, and marches, where their protests were viewed as hostile and destructive of the mainstream culture. Experience teaches that we cannot protect the rights of any group within our society unless we protect the rights of all.

This lesson has had to be learned again and again—in recent years on college campuses where schools have adopted "speech codes" that amount to little more than political correctness run amok. In *Doe* v. *University of Michigan*, a federal court struck down a campus speech code that, among other things, prohibited stigmatizing verbal behavior as unconstitutionally vague and overbroad.[25] The court found that administrators at Michigan had used the code in a manner that showed little solicitude for free-speech interests and punished constitutionally protected expression. It is interesting to note that during the eighteen months the code was in effect, at least twenty African American students were charged by white students with using offensive speech, including a reference to one student as "white trash." As another court said in yet another university-based case, "[T]he First Amendment does not recognize exceptions for bigotry, racism, and religious intolerance on ideas or matters some may deem trivial, vulgar or profane."[26] These speech codes are but another well-meaning effort to protect certain segments of society from detestable speech, but, in the end, the codes both violate the Constitution and ill serve its intended beneficiaries.

Libraries as Marketplaces of Ideas

As with a state university, a public library cannot shut off "the mere dissemination of ideas—no matter how offensive to good taste—... in the name alone of 'conventions of decency.'"[27] To do so impinges upon free inquiry and open debate, the very hallmarks of the search for knowledge. In *Sweezy* v. *New Hampshire*, Chief Justice Earl Warren, writing for the Court, recognized the peril to our nation of any attempt to impose a straitjacket on intellectual freedom.[28] He wrote: "Teachers and students must always remain free to inquire, to study and to evaluate, to gain new maturity and understanding; otherwise our civilization will stagnate and die."[29]

Ten years later, Justice William Brennan returned to this important theme for the majority in the context of schools but with equal significance for libraries:

> Our Nation is deeply committed to safeguarding academic freedom, which is of transcendent value to all of us and not merely to the teachers concerned. That freedom is therefore a special concern of the First Amendment, which does not tolerate laws that cast a pall of orthodoxy over the classroom. . . . The classroom is peculiarly the "marketplace of ideas." The Nation's future

depends upon leaders trained through wide exposure to that robust exchange of ideas which discovers truth "out of a multitude of tongues, [rather] than through any kind of authoritative selection."[30]

Similarly, a public library is "peculiarly the 'marketplace of ideas.'" It is impossible to conceive how a library could fulfill its mission if it asserts the power to proscribe ideas. Necessarily, those ideas must include those that are widely regarded as offensive or repugnant.

Conclusion

The framers of the First Amendment "knew that novel and unconventional ideas might disturb the complacent, but they chose to encourage a freedom which they believed essential if vigorous enlightenment was ever to triumph over slothful ignorance."[31] Libraries are decidedly on the side of enlightenment. They have no role in hiding ideas, no matter how offensive.

To be meaningful, the right to free speech cannot be subjected to limits based on contemporary public tastes. Sometimes, only expression that shocks will be noticed and usefully convey an idea that would otherwise be ignored. Although some might decry the effect this has had on the public culture, there are ways other than censorship to persuade people that incivility or offensive expression may be counterproductive to the advancement of the ideas they cherish. Certainly, a government that exercises authority over how ideas are expressed has the power to suppress those ideas altogether.

Instead, we rely on people, social pressures, and the concept of self-restraint to define the limits of appropriate expression. "At the heart of the First Amendment lies the principle that each person should decide for him or herself the ideas and beliefs deserving of expression, consideration, and adherence," the Court has said. "Our political system and cultural life rest upon this ideal."[32]

NOTES

1. *Street* v. *New York*, 394 U.S. 576, 592 (1969).

2. *Carey* v. *Population Services International*, 431 U.S. 678, 701 (1977) (plurality op.).

3. *Bridges* v. *California,* 314 U.S. 252, 270 (1941) (footnote omitted).

4. *Monteiro* v. *Tempe Union High Sch. Dist.,* 158 F.3d 1022, 1028 (9th Cir. 1998).

5. *United States* v. *Schwimmer,* 279 U.S. 644, 655 (1929) (Holmes, J., dissenting).

6. *Boos* v. *Barry,* 485 U.S. 312, 322 (1988).

7. *Stanley* v. *Georgia,* 394 U.S. 557, 565–66 (1969).

8. *Terminello* v. *Chicago,* 337 U.S. 1, 4 (1949).

9. *Gertz* v. *Robert Welch, Inc.,* 418 U.S. 323, 339–40 (1974) (footnote omitted).

10. *Sweezy* v. *New Hampshire,* 354 U.S. 234, 250–51 (1957).

11. *City Council of Los Angeles* v. *Taxpayers for Vincent,* 466 U.S. 789, 804 (1984).

12. *United States* v. *Eichman,* 496 U.S. 310, 319 (1990).

13. *Boos* v. *Barry,* 485 U.S. 312, 321 (1988).

14. *Cohen* v. *California,* 403 U.S. 15, 25 (1971).

15. *Id.* at 21.

16. *Id.* at 23.

17. *Id.* at 25.

18. *Id.* at 26.

19. *Id.* (quoting *Baumgartner* v. *United States,* 322 U.S. 665, 673–74 (1944)).

20. *City of Houston* v. *Hill,* 482 U.S. 451, 472 (1987).

21. *Organization for a Better Austin* v. *Keefe,* 402 U.S. 415, 419 (1971).

22. *Terminello* v. *Chicago,* 337 U.S. 1 (1949).

23. *Id.* at 4.

24. *Id.*

25. *Doe* v. *University of Michigan,* 721 F. Supp. 852 (E.D. Mich. 1989).

26. *Iota Xi Chapter of Sigma Chi Fraternity* v. *George Mason University,* 773 F. Supp. 792, 795 (E.D. Va. 1991).

27. *Papish* v. *Board of Curators of the University of Missouri,* 410 U.S. 667, 670 (1973).

28. *Sweezy* v. *New Hampshire,* 354 U.S. 234 (1957).

29. *Id.* at 250.

30. *Keyishian* v. *Board of Regents,* 385 U.S. 589, 603 (1967) (citation omitted).

31. *Martin* v. *City of Struthers,* 319 U.S. 141, 143 (1943).

32. *Turner Broadcasting System, Inc.* v. *FCC,* 512 U.S. 622, 641 (1994).

CHAPTER 5

Religious Motivations and Library Use

Some who challenge library materials and policies are motivated by sincerely held religious beliefs. They may believe that some materials are so evil that only a few, or perhaps no one at all, should have access to them. Or they may be more modestly concerned with materials accessible to their children that appear to contradict tenets of their faith or tear down religious or parental authority. Too often, these challenges are fueled by a significant misunderstanding about the constitutional meaning of the First Amendment's religious clauses. Misleading refrains are heard, such as "the Constitution guarantees 'freedom of religion,' not freedom from religion."

At the same time, some public librarians have a markedly inaccurate view of what the First Amendment requires them to do in response to a request, for example, for a meeting room from a religious group. Although many questions about religious freedom are indeed open to debate, there is also much more clarity on others than many people seem to realize.

The First Amendment literally prohibits governmental "establishment of religion" and protects the "free exercise" of religion. Together, the two clauses ensure that neither government nor religion becomes the handmaiden of the other. Government can neither advance nor inhibit religion. Sometimes these dual requirements create a tension that is not easily reconciled. Somehow, government must ensure that it does not become an arena where rival religious factions vie for official imprimatur or advantage, while also championing and protecting the right of all to pursue the faith of their choice.

The Separation Principle

The first part of the First Amendment, the *Establishment Clause,* is often described as requiring the separation of church and state. Opponents of strict separation often deride the concept, noting that the words "separation of church and state" do not appear anywhere in the Constitution. This, of course, is undoubtedly true, as it is of the constitutional concept of "separation of powers," though no one seriously doubts that the Constitution requires that form of separation to be observed as well. Chief Justice William Rehnquist has criticized the separation phraseology as "a metaphor based on bad history."[1] Still, there is substantial history and analysis behind the concept that makes it useful in understanding what is required.

The idea that the Establishment Clause was intended to erect "a wall of separation between church and state" is usually attributed to Thomas Jefferson, who stated as much in an 1802 letter to the Danbury Baptist Association. The letter was no casual undertaking but was prepared with the assistance of Jefferson's attorney general, Levi Lincoln. In 1879, the Supreme Court held that Jefferson's letter should "be accepted almost as an authoritative declaration of the scope and effect of the amendment thus secured."[2] Ironically, the concept has biblical roots, appearing in St. Mark's Gospel: "Render to Caesar the things that are Caesar's, and to God the things that are God's." James Madison, often called the "Father of the Constitution" for his leading role in drafting both the Constitution and Bill of Rights, cited that biblical passage when he wrote that it was an "aberration from the sacred principle of religious liberty [to] giv[e] to Caesar what belongs to God, or join[] together what God has put asunder."[3]

The authors of the First Amendment also drew heavily on John Locke, who had written that "I esteem it above all things necessary to distinguish exactly the business of civil government from that of religion, and to settle the just bounds that lie between the one and the other."[4] It was also a guiding precept of Roger Williams, who founded Rhode Island as a land of religious tolerance after he had been banished from Massachusetts for preaching religious ideas that the majority found dangerous. To ensure religious liberty, he wrote in 1643 (likely influencing Jefferson's use of the wall metaphor) that there must be a "hedge or wall of separation between the garden of the church and the wilderness of the world."[5]

Moreover, the framers of the Constitution were familiar with English history, where there was ample evidence that the church had been corrupted by the involvement of the State in its affairs. The Anglican Book of Common Prayer, for example, was repeatedly rewritten each time power changed hands in Parliament, with an eye toward advancing a political, rather than a spiritual, agenda.[6] Dissenting ministers were subject to arrest for their failure to bend their wills to that of the king. Surely, the framers concluded, history had taught that when government worked hand in hand with religion, political manipulators would push the alliance toward personal end with the result being that religious liberty would wilt.

A critical event in developing our modern understanding of the necessities of religious liberty, including a hands-off posture on the part of government, was the battle between Patrick Henry and Jefferson over competing religious bills in Virginia before the Constitution was written. Henry sponsored a bill that would have levied a "moderate tax or contribution annually for the support of the Christian religion, or of some Christian church, denomination or communion of Christians, or for some form of Christian worship."[7] All Christian faiths would have been eligible for the taxpayers' largesse under the Henry bill. In opposition, Jefferson authored "A Bill to Establish Religious Freedom," which prohibited compelled support for religious worship, ministry, or places as contrary to rights of conscience and instead guaranteed freedom of religious belief.

When the opposing legislative measures finally received full consideration in the Virginia legislature, Henry was the state's governor, and Jefferson was the American Minister to France. It fell to Madison to drum up support for the underdog Jefferson proposal. Madison argued, in a famous writing called "A Memorial and Remonstrance," that allowing the state to recognize and prefer religion was a violation of "an unalienable right." If a state could establish Christianity as its favored form of religion, he continued, then it could "with the same ease" establish one sect of Christians over all others. The argument proved enormously persuasive, as congregations throughout the state inundated the legislature with petitions urging rejection of the Henry bill and passage of the Jefferson religious-liberty alternative.

As Justice Felix Frankfurter observed, the "battle in Virginia, hardly four years won, . . . was a vital and compelling memory in 1789," when the Bill of Rights was drafted and approved in Congress.[8] That Madison was the force behind both the Jefferson bill and what became the First Amendment speaks to the relevance of the Virginia fight in understanding the Establishment Clause. In fact, during the congressional debate over the Bill of Rights, Madison explained that the Establishment Clause was intended, in part, to quell fears that "one sect might obtain a pre-eminence, or two combine together, and establish a religion to which they would compel others to conform."[9] He later added in explanation that the provision "[s]trongly guarded . . . the separation between Religion and Government."[10]

Although the Establishment Clause operated as a bar against federal support of religion, it had no effect on the states prior to its incorporation under the Fourteenth Amendment. Still, by 1833, each of the states rejected established churches, and the concept of church-state separation became an article of constitutional faith in the United States.[11]

Today, the concept retains considerable vitality despite agitation that the "wall of separation" should be lowered. As the Court put it in 1992 in response to a formulation that would put government-sponsored prayer to a majority vote: "While in some societies the wishes of the majority might prevail, the Establishment Clause of the First Amendment is addressed to this contingency and rejects [it]."[12]

The *Lemon* Test

Though much criticized and not applied uniformly to all Establishment Clause issues, the test most often used to evaluate alleged violations of the separation principle consists of three parts and is called—some would say appropriately—the *Lemon* test, after the case in which it was articulated, *Lemon* v. *Kurtzman*.[13] The *Lemon* test requires that any law, rule, or government practice

1. have a secular purpose,
2. have a primary effect that neither advances nor inhibits religion, and
3. not foster an excessive entanglement with religion.[14]

The first of these requirements ensures that government does not act as if it were a religious body. Although many of our laws are consonant with religious teachings, they also have a clear secular purpose. For example, every religion treats murder as sinful and wrong, but our homicide laws do not seek to implement this religious teaching so much as reflect our societal commitment to the value and dignity of each human life.

In a number of instances, the Supreme Court has struck down laws or practices that failed to have a sufficiently secular purpose. For example, Kentucky's law that required the Ten Commandments be posted in every public-school classroom was found to have no secular purpose.[15] Similarly, Alabama's "moment-of-silence" requirement for public schools was invalidated because the law sought to provide time specifically for students to pray silently, a palpably religious purpose.[16] It may well have been upheld if the law truly attempted to ensure students a moment to contemplate anything they chose to, whether it be prayer and religion or an upcoming math test or sports event.

Similarly, the Court struck down a Louisiana statute that required equal classroom time for "creation science" if evolution was taught, because the purpose of the law was "to endorse a particular religious doctrine."[17] The lesson of these cases for libraries is that selection, retention, and other policy decisions cannot be made to advance, promote, or endorse a religious purpose.

At the same time and to some illogically, the Court has found no religious purpose in Sunday closing laws because legislatures are free to choose a "uniform day of rest for all citizens" or the distribution of secular textbooks to public and parochial schools alike, in the interests of improved education for all.[18]

The second part of the *Lemon* test requires that the law be neutral in its effect. Under this part of the test, a Connecticut law that prohibited employers from requiring employees to work on the Sabbath of their faith was invalidated, because it favored religious objections to work over all other objections.[19]

The bar against excessive entanglement, the third requirement in the *Lemon* test, ensures that government cannot enact a program that would require it to monitor religious activity or to use state resources to ensure that a secular purpose and effect is maintained.

Although some justices of the Court fervently want to inter the *Lemon* test, it has survived the attacks on it to date. Still, in some instances, the Court has avoided use of the *Lemon* test and instead analyzed the issues under a test based on historical practice or on principles of government neutrality.[20]

Religious Displays

One area of continuing dispute has been the placement of religious symbols on public property, which holds important implications for library displays. The Supreme Court has ruled that governmental sponsorship of the display of a crèche in celebration of Christmas violates the Establishment Clause, unless accompanied by other symbols of the season.[21] The idea that a patently religious object can be transformed into a secular display by surrounding it with other items has been derisively termed the "two-reindeer" rule, meaning that a nativity scene on public property probably passes constitutional muster if it is surrounded by a couple of reindeer and a plastic Santa Claus. A recent federal appellate decision seems to confirm this simplistic solution. In a case arising from Jersey City, New Jersey, the Third Circuit found no constitutional violation in a Christmas display of a nativity scene that was surrounded by a four-foot plastic Santa, a ten-inch-tall plastic Frosty the Snowman, a sled, a Christmas tree that also featured Kwanzaa symbols, and two signs celebrating its citizens' "diverse cultural and ethnic heritages."[22]

In a 1989 case, the Court dealt with two separate Christmas and Chanukah displays in Pittsburgh, Pennsylvania. One was a Christian nativity scene, donated by a Roman Catholic group, and placed on the Grand Stairway in the county courthouse. The other stood in front of government building with a sign saluting liberty during the holiday season and featuring a large Christmas tree and a large menorah, donated by a Jewish group. A sharply divided Supreme Court, in which only two justices agreed entirely with the final result, split the baby, ruling the stairway display unconstitutional, while the outdoor one constitutional.[23] As to the crèche, a majority concluded that its placement illegally endorsed a patently Christian message. The Court found that "government may acknowledge Christmas as a cultural phenomenon, but under the First Amendment it may not observe it as a Christian holy day by suggesting that people praise God for the birth of Jesus."[24]

As to the other display, a different coalition of justices constituting a majority concluded that it merely treated Christmas and Chanukah as contemporaneous cultural traditions that have a secular aspect to them, which was furthered by the city sign declaring liberty to be the message of the holiday season.[25] Illogically, the Court declared that because "government may celebrate Christmas as a secular holiday," it "may also acknowledge Chanukah as a secular holiday"; otherwise, it would be engaged in "a form of discrimination against Jews."[26] Although many would say that the hocus-pocus utilized by the Court demeans religion by bending holidays to secular purposes, the two justices who controlled the opinion undoubtedly regarded their conclusion as Solomonic. The decision demonstrates the touchy and difficult terrain in this area of the law.

For public libraries preparing holiday displays, the case stands for the proposition that such displays cannot advance a particular religious dogma but can celebrate the cultural holiday traditions that have become ingrained in the American ethos. It may also use different religious traditions as part of an educational display intended to examine comparative religious traditions.

Religious Use of Public Forums

A separate and much easier question is presented when public institutions endeavor to make bulletin boards or other public space—in essence, a public forum—available to community groups, an issue recently explored in *Capitol Square Review Board* v. *Pinette*.[27] The dispute began when the Ku Klux Klan sought to erect a large temporary Latin cross during the 1993 Christmas season on the grounds of the Statehouse Plaza in Columbus, Ohio. The state had designated the plaza as a public forum for the discussion of public questions and for public activities. The Capitol Square Review and Advisory Board was the state agency that reviews applications to use the plaza, and the board rejected this one. The U.S. Supreme Court concluded that the Klan had the right to erect the cross as a manifestation of private religious speech in a traditional public forum and that no Establishment Clause violation would occur because the State did not sponsor the religious expression, the expression was made on government property that had been opened to the public for speech purposes, and permission was requested through the same application process and on the same terms required of other private groups. Instead, the Court found the denial of the Klan's application to be a violation of their free-speech rights.

The case means that libraries that establish a community bulletin board must make it available on an equivalent basis to all comers who qualify under neutral criteria. It is also clear that it is advisable in such circumstances to erect a sign informing patrons that this is a bulletin board for the private expression of community groups and *does not* indicate any support or endorsement of its content by the library.

The principles applicable here also have implications for the use of meeting rooms in public libraries. The issue reached the Supreme Court when a Long Island, New York, school district denied the use of a school auditorium to a church group for an after-school-hours film series on family issues from a Christian perspective. The Court ruled that the denial constituted a violation of the free-speech rights of the church group.[28] By opening the after-hours use of the auditorium to community groups, the school had established a designated public forum. Its refusal to permit this film series amounted to a form of unconstitutional viewpoint discrimination. The Court found that there was no danger that the school would have been viewed as endorsing religion because the film series would not have been shown during school hours, would not have been sponsored by the school, and would have been open to the public with a clear indication of the sponsoring organization. Still, the Court took no position on whether the church could have conducted a religious service in that auditorium instead of showing the film series. This issue remains an open question that more closely implicates the Establishment Clause than a public discussion of a secular issue that focuses on a religious viewpoint.

The Free Exercise of Religion

At the same time as it prohibits the establishment of religion, the First Amendment guarantees the "free exercise of religion," which is basically synonymous with the idea of freedom of religion. Here, too, history supports a broad view that religious liberty is a fundamental right. It is schoolbook history that many who helped settle this continent did so to escape religious persecution in the Old World. Logically, this should mean that, like freedom of speech, freedom of religion should receive the highest level of constitutional protection, namely strict scrutiny analysis. That logic was the prevailing opinion among constitutional scholars until 1991, when the Supreme Court changed the standard it applied in evaluating claims that religious liberty had been abridged.

In *Employment Division* v. *Smith,* the Court held that laws that are neutral about religion and not intended to affect religious practices adversely are constitutionally valid, even if those laws have a discriminatory impact.[29] In other words, only if the law were intended to persecute a religion or religious adherents generally would it run afoul of the Free Exercise Clause. One example of a law that would still be unconstitutional was enacted by the city of Hialeah, Florida.

A new city ordinance prohibited the sacrifice or other ritual killing of animals, unless by a licensed food establishment in a manner that accorded with health laws. The ordinance was enacted shortly after followers of the Santeria religion, which engages in animal sacrifice, purchased a Hialeah building that they intended to transform into a church. The clear anti-religious intent behind the law caused the Supreme Court to declare it unconstitutional.[30]

Yet, because of the *Smith* decision, a seemingly neutral and not blatantly discriminatory law could have pernicious results that would be immune from constitutional challenge. Thus, for example, a law that prohibited changes to buildings designated as historical landmarks would, for example, override the right of a church to change the position of its altar, something it might be required to do to conform with the ruling in Vatican II. The First Amendment would provide no relief for the church. This example, in fact, was the situation of the Immaculate Conception Church in Boston. Luckily, the state's Supreme Judicial Court found that the Massachusetts Constitution afforded greater free exercise protection than the U.S. Constitution did and concluded that the church could reposition its altar.[31] Other states have similarly found greater state constitutional protection for religious exercise than the U.S. Supreme Court has held to exist under the federal Constitution.[32]

Congress attempted to add statutory protection for religious exercise to the existing level of federal constitutional protection through passage of the Religious Freedom Restoration Act.[33] The act required that any substantial governmental burden on religious exercise be justified by a compelling state interest and be effected by the least-restrictive means. The Supreme Court, however, saw the act as an unconstitutional attempt to amend the Free Exercise Clause by legislation and declared it beyond any powers granted Congress by the Constitution.[34] Although the Court's ruling found the act unconstitutional as it applies to state and local government, the act remains in effect against federal intrusions on religious exercise, because the federal government may always voluntarily limit its own authority.

Conclusion

What do the Constitution's religion clauses mean for libraries? The clauses mean that public and public-school libraries must follow the mandate of neutrality on issues of religion. As public institutions, *these libraries can neither advance nor inhibit religion.* Neither may they appear to be in league with any single religion or even all religions against irreligion.

This legal obligation of neutrality does not mean that all aspects of religious study must be removed from the library. Public and school libraries are certainly free to include religious works within their collections. Failure to do so would deny patrons an important source of information, including access to the most widely published book in the English language, the Bible. Another aspect of the guarantee of religious freedom means that a public library should not interfere with a patron who engages in prayer on library property in a manner that is not disruptive and otherwise comports with neutral library rules. And it means that libraries are not free to excise books from their collections because the ideas expressed offend a particular faith or are antagonistic to that faith.[35] Many would say that Salman Rushdie's *Satanic Verses* fits within that rubric. Despite the serious offense with which the Moslem world treats the novel, the First Amendment recognizes no exception that would permit its removal from a public library. Nor would it recognize a similar exception for a book that attacked a particular community's majority religion.

Although the First Amendment prohibits public-school sponsorship of Bible readings, it does not prohibit courses on comparative religion that might include the reading of different holy books.[36] It is for this reason that such books have a rightful place on the shelves of public and school libraries.

By the same token, public libraries must distinguish between sponsorship of religious activities and neutral, informative, comparative religious events. For example, many libraries put together displays for the benefit of their library patrons. Perhaps when the World Series is being played, the display might feature books about baseball. In anticipation of the Fourth of July, books about the American Revolution and the Declaration of Independence might be displayed. But the requirement of separation of church and state means that Christmas may not be celebrated by the library as a religious holiday, though it may be celebrated as a cultural event. A display featuring a manger scene, therefore, would violate the constitutional requirements, but a display that focused on the various events of winter, including Christmas, would likely pass constitutional muster. And a display that featured literature appropriate to the season and did not connote a message of religious exclusion would also likely meet with judicial approval.

Many libraries, as well, make available bulletin boards or meeting rooms for community groups. By doing so, these libraries have established the boards and rooms as designated public fora. They are often made available on a first-come, first-serve basis. The Constitution's religion and speech clauses have an effect on this usage. First, a library may not discriminate against religious groups in their usage. This means that religious groups must be permitted to post on the bulletin board or meet in the community room on the same basis as any other community group. The only additional limitation that the Constitution imposes, the Supreme Court has suggested, is the use of these fora *for religious services* because of the message of endorsement that would flow from such usage.

Libraries are not locations for proselytizing about religion or any matter of opinion. The library's general policy of being hospitable to all ideas is a policy of studied neutrality that coincides completely with the requirements of the First Amendment's religious clauses. Although literature may well advocate a particular form of religious worship or religious viewpoint and that literature should not be excluded from the shelves, the library as an institution has no place in advancing or inhibiting religion.

NOTES

1. *Wallace* v. *Jaffree,* 472 U.S. 38, 108 (1985) (Rehnquist, J., dissenting).

2. *Reynolds* v. *United States,* 98 U.S. 145, 164 (1879).

3. Robert Alley, ed., *James Madison on Religious Liberty* (Buffalo, N.Y.: Prometheus Books, 1985), 90.

4. John Locke, *A Letter Concerning Toleration* 9, in Six Works of Locke (London 1823 and 1963 photo. reprint), *cited in School Dist.* v. *Schempp,* 374 U.S. 203, 231 (1963) (Brennan, J., concurring).

5. Roger Williams, *A Letter to Mr. John Cottons* (1643), quoted in Leonard W. Levy, *The Establishment Clause* (New York: MacMillan, 1986), 184.

6. *Engel* v. *Vitale,* 370 U.S. 421, 425–27 (1962).

7. Levy, *supra* note 5, at 54.

8. *McGowan v. Maryland,* 366 U.S. 420, 464–65 (1961).

9. 1 Annals of Cong. 758 (Aug. 15, 1789).

10. Alley, *supra* note 3, at 90.

11. *See Illinois ex rel. McCollum v. Board of Educ.,* 333 U.S. 203, 215 (1948) (Frankfurter, J., concurring).

12. *Lee v. Weisman,* 505 U.S. 577, 596 (1992).

13. *Lemon v. Kurtzman,* 403 U.S. 602 (1971).

14. *Id.* at 612–13.

15. *Stone v. Graham,* 449 U.S. 39 (1980).

16. *Wallace v. Jaffree,* 472 U.S. 38 (1985).

17. *Edwards v. Aguillard,* 482 U.S. 578, 594 (1987).

18. *McGowan v. Maryland,* 366 U.S. 420, 445 (1961); *Board of Education v. Allen,* 392 U.S. 236 (1968).

19. *Estate of Thornton v. Caldor,* 472 U.S. 703 (1985).

20. *See, e.g., Marsh v. Chambers,* 463 U.S. 783 (1983); *Board of Education of Kiryas Joel Village Sch. Dist. v. Grumet,* 512 U.S. 687 (1994).

21. *Lynch v. Donnelly,* 465 U.S. 668 (1984).

22. *ACLU of New Jersey v. Schundler,* 1999 WL 7766 (3d Cir. Feb. 16, 1999).

23. *Allegheny County v. Greater Pittsburgh ACLU,* 492 U.S. 573 (1989) (plurality op.).

24. *Id.* at 601.

25. *Id.* at 615.

26. *Id.*

27. *Capitol Square Review Bd. v. Pinette,* 515 U.S. 753 (1995).

28. *Lamb's Chapel v. Center Moriches Sch. Dist.,* 508 U.S. 385 (1993).

29. *Employment Division v. Smith,* 494 U.S. 872 (1990).

30. *Church of the Lukumi Babalu Aye v. City of Hialeah,* 508 U.S. 520 (1993).

31. *Society of Jesus v. Boston Landmarks Comm'n,* 564 N.E.2d 571 (Mass. 1990).

32. *See, e.g., Minnesota v. Hershberger,* 462 N.W.2d 393 (Minn. 1990).

33. 42 U.S.C. § 2000bb–2000bb-3.

34. *City of Boerne v. Flores,* 521 U.S. 507 (1997).

35. *See Island Trees Union Free School Dist. No. 26 v. Pico,* 457 U.S. 853 (1982) (plurality op.) (holding that school officials removal of books that were anti-Christian and anti-Semitic violated the free-speech guarantee of the First Amendment).

36. *Abington Township v. Schempp,* 374 U.S. 203 (1963).

CHAPTER 6

Just between You and Your Librarian—Library Confidentiality Laws

James Madison's vision of a free people recognized the central importance of guaranteeing "freedom of the mind."[1] Madison used that notion to urge ratification of the Constitution that he was most responsible for drafting and later embodied the concept in the First Amendment. An aspect of the Supreme Court's recognition of the constitutional solicitude for free thinking is its declaration that a person's "abstract beliefs [and thoughts], however obnoxious to most people, may not be taken into consideration" by government in doling out punishment.[2]

It would also certainly be an invasion of that freedom to permit a wide-ranging investigation into a person's reading habits. That someone might have read *Mein Kampf* means neither that the person subscribes to the odious ideas contained in the book nor that the person has any connection to someone who does. Yet it is easy to see how the circulation of this information could harm a person's reputation. It is also just as likely that foreknowledge of the public disclosure of that kind of information would lead a person to avoid controversial texts altogether.

In today's no-holds-barred version of politics, even at the most petty of levels, it would not take too much imagination to see political opponents exploit the worst possible inferences from the books their counterparts used at a public library. One can easily envision a person mounting the proverbial soapbox to declare of an opponent, "It is a matter of public record that he has read . . ." The same opprobrium found in contests for public office has infected office and academic politics and many other aspects of our social interactions. Similar attempts to embarrass or ridicule people, for no reason at all, require no stretch of the imagination. In such a world, readers would steer clear of unpopular, controversial, or suggestively titled books, a consequence that is significantly at odds with the core principles of the First Amendment and a result to be avoided if intellectual freedom has any meaning or purpose.

The Supreme Court has recognized as much in an important case called *Bantam Books, Inc. v. Sullivan*.[3] The case had its genesis when the Rhode Island Commission to Encourage Morality in Youth began to notify distributors that certain designated books or magazines had been declared by the commission to be "objectionable" for sale, distribution, or display to youths under eighteen years of age. Distributors who did not voluntarily cease carrying the identified publications would be referred to the state's attorney general for prosecution as a purveyor of obscenity, while the commission also notified its correspondents that the list of objectionable publications would be circulated to local police departments.

The Court ruled that this attempt at blacklisting books amounted to "a scheme of state censorship effectuated by extralegal sanctions; [the commission] acted as an agency not to advise but to suppress."[4] The significance of the decision is that it recognizes that the government's use of threats, intimidation, and exposure can chill the exercise of free-speech rights.

No Constitutional Right to Confidentiality in Library Records

Despite this logical consequence, the courts have not as yet declared confidentiality of public records to be within the still-nascent constitutional right to privacy. A First Amendment argument, however, could easily be fashioned that some sort of qualified privilege, perhaps not unlike the priest-penitent privilege, should exist against the disclosure of library records. Without such a recognition of the confidential nature of the information, the potential to chill free-speech rights is palpable in a manner long recognized by the Court. As Justice William O. Douglas once noted:

> A requirement that a publisher disclose the identity of those who buy his books, pamphlets, or papers is indeed the beginning of surveillance of the press. . . . Once the government can demand of a publisher the names of the purchasers of his publications, the free press as we know it disappears.[5]

More recently, the Supreme Court recognized this potential outcome in the context of a governmental request for information about supporters of a nonprofit advocacy group. It noted that without adequate safeguards to protect confidentiality, the "practical effect may be to discourage protected speech" and thus constitute "an infringement on First Amendment activities."[6] Where grand jury subpoenas have sought library or bookselling records, substantial case law exists in which courts have recognized the First Amendment implications of the request and put government to the compelling interest–least restrictive means test.[7] Still, reliance on First Amendment protections in the library context has largely been made unnecessary by statutory protections that have been enacted.

Video Privacy Act

When Judge Robert Bork was nominated to the Supreme Court in 1987, he derided the notion that a right to privacy existed in the Constitution. Although he failed to win Senate approval, his nomination did have an impact on privacy law. To examine whether he practiced what he preached about constitutional issues, one enterprising news outlet, during the hearings on his nomination, obtained a copy of his video-rental records from his neighborhood store. The flap over the exposure of the judge's personal video-rental records provided the impetus for the passage, one year after his nomination, of a federal Video Privacy Act to protect the confidentiality of such records.[8]

The act, which includes public libraries as well as private businesses in its coverage, prohibits any videotape renter or lender from disclosing personally identifiable information about its patrons, except to four specific categories of recipients. First, the information may be disclosed to anyone who has the informed, written consent of the patron identified. By this, the person whose records will be disclosed must grant permission in writing and must have been fully informed about the nature of the records sought and the uses to which it will be put. Obviously, this exception also means that the patron can look at his or her own video-borrowing history.

Second, the information may be disclosed to representatives of a law enforcement agency, provided that they have obtained a valid search warrant. A police officer or other law enforcement official typically obtains a right to conduct a search by applying to a judge or magistrate for the warrant, which is a form of court order. The Fourth Amendment requires that the application be accompanied by proof that there is good reason—known as "probable cause"—to believe that the search will uncover evidence of a crime. One or more affidavits will be attached to the application to establish the basis for the officer's reasonable suspicion that the evidence exists at the place to be searched. The search warrant will be very specific about where the officer is permitted to search and what the officer is permitted to seize. A warrant may be invalidated after the fact—and the evidence obtained from the search excluded from trial—if the warrant is drafted too broadly.

Third, information may be disclosed under the Video Privacy Act to anyone pursuant to a court order, provided that the patron whose information is being sought had notice of the court proceeding and an opportunity to contest the order. Usually, this exception will apply to subpoenas that have been contested and approved by a court. In such instances, a party has demonstrated to a court that the information sought either is evidence or will lead to evidence relevant to an issue in the case. A subpoena can be resisted by a library, permitting a court to determine whether there is a significant enough connection between the information sought and the subject of the litigation.

Fourth, patron information may be disclosed in the form of a mailing list, provided that patrons had a clear and conspicuous opportunity to remove themselves from the list when they originally signed up for the service. This provision permits a video store to sell its mailing list, without anyone's rental history being identified, to others who might market products to video enthusiasts. To be able to sell such a list, a patron would have had to have been informed that the use of personally identifiable information might be sold to others in the form of a mailing list and have permitted the patron to indicate at the time of enrolling in the video service that no such use of his or her name and address is authorized.

Violation of the federal Video Privacy Act can result in a hefty award of damages. The act specifies that a minimum verdict of $2,500 should be awarded when damages are assessed. If actual damages are higher than $2,500, such as might occur if the revelation of the information causes someone to lose a lucrative job, then the amount necessary to compensate the injured party can be awarded.

In addition, the act authorizes the award of punitive damages, which are available when the offending party's conduct was especially egregious.

Punitive damages are sometimes a multiple of the amount of money awarded in actual damages and are intended to punish the offender and deter such conduct in the future by both the offender and others who might similarly be reckless in their custodianship of personal information. Violators of the act may also be ordered to reimburse the person whose personal information was disclosed for any expenses incurred in litigation, including attorneys' fees. Finally, the act authorizes a court to order any further relief, such as an injunction, that it deems appropriate.

Exemption from State Freedom of Information Acts

The federal law, however, only addresses the privacy of video-borrowing records and does not address library-borrowing records more generally. The states have not, however, been idle on this issue, and virtually every state has adopted a law addressing the confidentiality of public-library records. Often, these laws exist as an exception to the state's freedom of information act (FOIA). FOIA generally requires that public records be made available to any member of the requesting public.

The purpose of FOIA is to ensure that government operates in the sunshine. The idea behind this kind of exposure was famously expressed by Justice Louis Brandeis: "Publicity is justly commended as a remedy for social and industrial diseases. Sunlight is said to be the best of disinfectants; electric light the most efficient policeman."[9] As the Brandeis quote makes clear, the idea behind FOIA is that if the people can examine the records of governmental decision makers, decisions are more likely to be premised on the public's interest, rather than the policymakers' interest. When public policy wanders away from the public interest, only exposure can inform the public of the foibles, corruption, or nonfeasance that needs to be corrected. In a governmental system in which power resides in the people, it is essential that the people be able to examine the books and records of their government.

Still, it is undeniable that some government-held information must be maintained as confidential. It is for this reason that many state FOIAs exempt certain public-library records from its disclosure requirements. Typically, the exemption ensures the confidentiality of records that identify the people who have borrowed any books, documents, films, recordings, or other library property. Personnel records are separately exempted from the operation of FOIA. On the other hand, minutes of library board meetings, library policies and procedures, and other administrative and policy records fall squarely within the requirements of FOIA and must be produced under the procedures that the law and implementing library policies set forth.

The effect of such an exemption is evident from a New York case. The case arose after a commercial printer suspected that some of its employees were misusing their business computers to access the Internet through the Saratoga Springs library. The company prohibits employees from using work computers for personal purposes. After receiving a number of exorbitant telephone bills, the company came to believe that employees were using their computers to log onto the company's mainframe computer in Wisconsin and access long-distance lines to call the local library's Internet access, which is available to anyone with a freely available library password.

To assist its investigation into which employees were responsible for some $23,000 in long-distance charges accomplished through this technique, the company made a FOIA request to the Saratoga Springs Public Library. The library rejected the request, because of the FOIA exemption for library records, which specifically included records relating to computer database searches. The New York court noted that the state FOIA was enacted to protect the people's right to read and think, according to a memorandum issued by the state assembly when the law was passed. The court noted that a library was "a unique sanctuary of the widest possible spectrum of ideas [and] must protect the confidentiality of its records in order to insure its readers' right to read anything they wish, free from the fear that someone might see what they read and use this as a way to intimidate them."[10] The court continued, "[R]ecords must be protected from the self-appointed guardians of public and private morality and from officials who might overreach their constitutional prerogatives. Without such protection, there would be a chilling effect on our library users as inquiring minds turn away from exploring varied avenues of thought because they fear the potentiality of others knowing their reading history."[11]

Nonetheless, the court had to determine whether there was a justification for receiving the records that overrode any considerations of confidentiality. The court decided that there was not. Although other rationales might prevail, such as the need for the information as part of a criminal investigation, the court had difficulty seeing the company's request as different from a request "by a parent who wishes to learn what a child is reading or viewing on the 'Internet' . . . or by a spouse to learn what type of information his or her mate is reviewing at the public library." [12] Clearly, the exemption of library records from FOIA covered these requests by parents or spouses. The court held that the legislature spoke "in rather direct and unequivocal fashion, . . . that the confidentiality of a library's records should not be routinely breached." [13]

Library Confidentiality Laws

Another way in which library records are maintained as private is through laws passed especially for the purpose of maintaining the privacy of library records. Usually, these laws prohibit the disclosure of personally identifiable information about the use of or requests for materials from the library. They often contain privacy exceptions when the patron identified by the record has given written permission or a court has ordered the library to release the information. In practice, these laws operate quite similarly to FOIA and its exceptions. Generally, a confidentiality statute will authorize a person whose record has been improperly revealed to sue the library for damages.

In *Brown* v. *Johnston*,[14] the Iowa Supreme Court examined the scope of a library record confidentiality statute when law enforcement officials sought circulation records for books on witchcraft while investigating a series of local cattle mutilations. After being refused such records, the county attorney filed a subpoena, seeking the records. The Iowa Supreme Court decided that the request by a county attorney in the form of a subpoena issued by a court fit within one of the exceptions to the confidentiality law. Moreover, while recognizing that a qualified privilege under the First Amendment exists, the Iowa high court held that the privilege must be subordinated to the "State's interest in well-founded criminal charges and the fair administration of criminal justice."[15] Like the New York court under its FOIA interpretation, the Iowa court found the interests of the criminal justice system can, under appropriate circumstances, override any right to confidentiality.

Conclusion

Public libraries have substantial obligations to protect the confidentiality of library-use records. That obligation overrides a company's interest in its employees' use of libraries and even a parent's or spouse's interests in the reading habits of a child or mate, respectively. A failure to protect these records against disclosure could result in substantial financial liabilities.

Even so, the confidentiality obligations imposed by statute or that arguably exist under the Constitution are not absolute. They must give way to exceptions, which include, among other things, court orders issued pursuant to a criminal investigation. In the face of a request for personal-borrowing information from public officials, a library authority should not make its own judgment as to whether there is an overriding public interest in the release of the records. That decision remains the domain of a court.

NOTES

1. *Federalist* No. 51 (J. Madison).

2. *Wisconsin v. Mitchell,* 508 U.S. 476, 485 (1993) (citing *Dawson v. Delaware,* 503 U.S. 159 (1992)).

3. *Bantam Books, Inc. v. Sullivan,* 372 U.S. 58 (1963).

4. *Id.* at 72.

5. *United States v. Rumely,* 345 U.S. 41, 57 (1953) (Douglas, J., concurring).

6. *FEC v. Massachusetts Citizens for Life, Inc.,* 479 U.S. 238, 255 (1986); *see also Denver Area Educational Telecommunications Consortium, Inc. v. FCC,* 518 U.S. 727, 754 (1996) (recognizing that maintenance of a subscriber list for controversial programming will have a restrictive impact on viewing because patrons will "fear for their reputations should the operator, advertently or inadvertently, disclose the list").

7. *See, e.g., In re Grand Jury Subpoena Duces Tecum,* 78 F.3d 1307, 1312 (8th Cir.), *cert. denied,* 117 S.Ct. 432 (1996).

8. 18 U.S.C. § 2710.

9. *Quoted in Buckley v. Valeo,* 424 U.S. 1, 67 (1976) (citing Louis Brandeis, *Other People's Money* (New York: F. A. Stokes, 1933 ed.), 62).

10. *In the Matter of Quad/Graphics, Inc. v. Southern Adirondack Library System,* 664 N.Y.S.2d 225, 227 (Super. Ct. Saratoga Cty. 1997).

11. *Id.* at 227–28 (citation omitted).

12. *Id.* at 228.

13. *Id.*

14. *Brown v. Johnston,* 328 N.W.2d 510 (Iowa 1983).

15. *Id.* at 512.

CHAPTER 7

Workplace Issues

Employee Free Speech and Harassment

L ibraries are traditional spheres of free expression and places of central importance to a democratic form of government. Within them citizens can access all sorts of information generated by their government, as well as data created independently and sometimes contrary to and critical of that government. People can also find a wealth of information about virtually every topic under the sun—and a considerable number that look beyond the sun. In such an environment, where speech exists in multiple media, it is only natural to anticipate that those who work there might also want to exercise their ability to speak—and might also reflect the same range of reactions to the speech of others that are found in the rest of society.

Employee Free-Speech Rights

In the public-library workplace and while away from the job, then, it is axiomatic that employees do not entirely give up their free-speech rights—or any of the many other rights that are recognized in the law. The government can, however, control or regulate employee speech that bears official imprimatur—in essence, speech that appears to others as though it is the government itself speaking—or is otherwise disruptive of the workplace. Thus, the employee behind the reference desk has no First Amendment right to proselytize on behalf of her political, religious, or social views. Nor does another employee have a First Amendment right to disturb others to express himself.

At other times, though, when speaking as an individual about matters of public concern, public employee speech rights are at their zenith. Such a rule that permits employees, off the job, to criticize library governance or management makes eminent good sense. An employee may well have special insights about issues or appropriate library policies derived from experience and from opportunities to observe the internal operation of the agency. To deprive that employee of an opportunity to advocate operational changes that would advance the public interest would also deprive taxpayers of an expert source of policy advice. In the leading case on public-employee speech, a teacher was fired for writing a letter to the editor that criticized school fund-raising in the district. The Supreme Court vindicated the teacher's "right to speak on issues of public importance" and restored him to his job.[1] This constitutional protection of employee-speech rights also applies to and protects a government contractor from losing a franchise because of activities critical of the government.[2]

To win such a case, the employee must show that the "conduct was constitutionally protected, and that this conduct was a 'substantial factor' or, to put it in other words, that it was a 'motivating factor'" in the employment action taken against the employee.[3] If, however, the negative employment decision was unrelated to the speech issue, the government may defend by proving it would have acted the same way absent the alleged speech issue.[4] For example, a person's record of frequent tardiness despite supervisor warnings may justify a firing; the employee's activism on some public issue would not immunize the person from being let go unless the lateness issue was a mere pretext for a firing that was, in actuality, retaliation for speaking out on a public issue.

It may seem that this rule is open to abuse. A problem employee might become a public activist on problems in the workplace solely to avoid discipline. The ploy, however, is unlikely to work. The courts have recognized this tactic and declared that a person cannot transform his or her employment difficulties into a matter of public concern to obtain the protection that the First Amendment affords. In one case, an assistant district attorney was anxious to forestall her transfer. She attempted to make transfers in the office a policy issue. She surveyed her fellow prosecutors about the office's transfer policy, the impact of transfers on their morale, and their opinions about the usefulness of creating a grievance committee. She was then fired.

In ruling against the attorney in her lawsuit, the Supreme Court found that she had created no issue of public concern.[5] The attorney was not seeking to inform the public about problems in the operation of the district attorney's office, and her activism could not "fairly be considered as relating to any matter of political, social, or other concern to the community."[6]

Although personal grievances rarely rise to the level of public concern, illegal discrimination is a matter of overriding societal importance. If an employee confronts his or her employer in a private conversation about issues of racial discrimination, even though it is not being communicated to the public, it is indisputably a matter of public concern and thus protected under the First Amendment, the Supreme Court has ruled.[7] By the same token, conversations with an employer about violations of law at the workplace also involve matters of public concern and will generally be protected by the First Amendment.

Employee-to-employee conversations are also covered by the public-concern rule. Generally, comments about a public issue made to a coworker cannot be grounds for firing, unless the conversation is capable of adversely affecting relations with the employer's patrons. An important case on this issue arose after President Reagan was shot by John Hinckley. A civilian data-entry clerk in the Harris County, Texas, constable's office was discharged for reacting to a news report of the assassination attempt by telling another employee, "[I]f they go for him again, I hope they get him."[8] The statement was made in private conversation in a room separated from areas accessed by the public.

In an opinion written by Justice Thurgood Marshall, the Court concluded that the "inappropriate or controversial character of a statement is irrelevant to the question whether it deals with a matter of public concern."[9] Here, the statement was undeniably political, a comment reflecting negative views about one president's policies. Once that it was established that the speech was about a matter of public concern, only a further demonstration that it nonetheless interfered with the "effective functioning of the public employer's enterprise" could justify the firing.[10] It was important to the result in this case that the statement supportive of the illegal act of assassination was not made by a person charged with enforcing the law or communicated to the public as if emanating from the constable's office. There was also no evidence that it interfered with the office's efficient functioning. It was thus found to be protected speech, and the employee was restored to her job.

The issue has rarely gone to court in the public- or school-library context. Still, the same principles apply. In one instance, for example, a librarian at West Virginia Northern Community College brought suit, alleging, among other things, that she was fired after receiving consistently high approval ratings when she criticized school administrators' plans for remodeling the school's Learning Resources Center. The gist of her criticism, which was ultimately accepted as valid even as she was fired, was the plan would have directed student traffic between classes directly through the library area. The librarian scored this layout as unreasonably disruptive to library users and likely to pose a security risk for the library's collection.

The West Virginia Supreme Court of Appeals found that the college violated the librarian's rights in firing her over her criticism of the resource center plan.[11] Applying the teachings of the U.S. Supreme Court, it ruled "public employees are entitled to be protected from firings, demotions and other adverse employment consequences resulting from the exercise of their free speech rights, as well as other First Amendment rights."[12] Still, to be protected, such exercises of free-speech rights must be about a matter of public concern, not made with knowledge that the statements are false or reckless about the truthfulness of the allegations, and not made so as to disrupt the discipline or harmony of the workplace or destroy the personal loyalty and confidence of coworkers.[13] In this case, the court found that her criticism of the resource center plan was indeed a matter of public concern, was neither reckless nor disruptive, and was a substantial factor in her dismissal. As a result, her First Amendment rights had been violated.

Harassment

One form of interference with the efficient functioning of the workplace and a violation of civil rights laws as well is *discriminatory conduct*. Despite the considerable progress the country has experienced in civil rights, the scourge of discrimination still finds manifestation in the workplace. Inequality among employees remains unfortunately widespread and a continuing challenge to address.

Although some forms of disparate treatment are easily recognized as discrimination and prohibited by law, others are not. Racial exclusion, for example, quickly becomes apparent and can be addressed by the law. The demand of sexual favors in return for continued employment is another clear act of illegal discrimination, known as *quid pro quo discrimination*.

However, when the issue of harassment arises as a result of the presence of offensive words or images in the workplace, the task of separating protected speech from illegal harassment is a somewhat more challenging endeavor.

Federal and state civil rights laws treat harassment that is based on race, gender, religion, or national origin as an illegal form of discrimination.[14] In some states or localities, additional categories of protected classes, such as sexual orientation, may exist. In evaluating accusations, however, it is important to remember that harassment that is not attributable to the alleged victim's membership in a protected classification is not actionable under Title VII of the Civil Rights Act, which is the principal anti-harassment law.[15] Thus, for example, harassment of someone for being left-handed, no matter how cruel, would not constitute a civil rights violation, even though it could conceivably violate some other law. Under federal law, and the law of most states, illegal workplace discrimination, including harassment, are those acts that adversely affect the "terms, conditions, or privileges of employment."[16]

Understandably, a workplace filled with abuse based on a person's race, gender, or national origin makes good work performance virtually impossible. That kind of hostile environment will constitute a violation of the law and fits squarely within the rubric of an adverse effect on the "terms, conditions, or privileges of employment." The Supreme Court has acknowledged that such abuse rises to the level of a violation of the federal Civil Rights Act "[w]hen the workplace is permeated with 'discriminatory intimidation, ridicule, and insult,' that is 'sufficiently severe or pervasive to alter the conditions of the victim's employment and create an abusive working environment.'"[17]

In examining such allegations, courts will focus upon whether the conduct complained of is so "severe or pervasive enough to create an objectively hostile or abusive work environment—an environment that a reasonable person would find hostile or abusive."[18] By taking this approach, the Supreme Court steered "a middle path between making actionable any conduct that is merely offensive and requiring the conduct to cause a tangible psychological injury."[19] A case of harassment or a hostile work environment will not be made out by proof of a "mere utterance of an . . . epithet which engenders offensive feelings in an employee."[20] The case law requires that the hostility be objectively discernible and sufficiently frequent that work is affected.

To adjudge an environment hostile, a court considers all the circumstances, including "the frequency of the discriminatory conduct; its severity; whether it is physically threatening or humiliating, or a mere offensive utterance; and whether it unreasonably interferes with an employee's work performance."[21] Generally, to make out a claim based on a hostile work environment, a plaintiff must demonstrate

1. the plaintiff belongs to a protected class;
2. the plaintiff was subject to unwelcome harassment;
3. the harassment was based on plaintiff's race, sex, or national origin;
4. the harassment affected a term, condition, or privilege of employment; and
5. the employer knew or should have known about the harassment and failed to take prompt, effective remedial action.

The high threshold that must be met to establish a hostile environment ensures that no violation of anti-harassment laws occurs when the language or pictures in question merely offend or express a political philosophy that one finds repugnant on racial or sexual grounds. Instead, the alleged harassment is objectively analyzed to supplement the subjective view of the alleged victim or victims and takes into account the record as a whole and the totality of circumstances.[22] This way, a case of harassment cannot be made out by the hypersensitive reaction of one individual.

The interplay of these various legal concerns becomes most apparent in specific examples. In one instance, the Los Angeles Fire Department had established an anti-sexual-harassment policy that prohibited sexually oriented magazines, "particularly those containing nude pictures, such as *Playboy, Penthouse* and *Playgirl*," from being brought into the workplace.[23] A federal court invalidated this portion of the policy because it interfered with a firefighter's First Amendment right to the "private possession, reading and consensual sharing of *Playboy*."[24] The court went on to state that it was not enough to allege the need to avoid sexual harassment but that the employer had an affirmative duty to show "that real, not imagined, disruption [to the workplace] is threatened [by the prohibited activity]."[25] It was also not enough that women in the workplace were offended at the sight of nude pictures, because the coworker who challenged the constitutionality of the policy merely sought to read his magazine quietly and in private. On the other hand, the court suggested a different issue might have been raised if he sought to "expose the contents of the magazine to unwitting viewers."[26] Finally, the court rejected the notion that an employer could restrict access to such magazines to prevent employees from entertaining degrading thoughts about women coworkers. Such an "effort to regulate the behavior of male fire fighters by regulating the material which they may read is categorically impermissible. . . . government cannot regulate material in order to prevent the readers from developing certain ideas."[27] In fact, attempts to alter the reader's viewpoint by restricting access to materials "are the most disfavored of all regulations touching upon the First Amendment."[28]

The Equal Employment Opportunity Commission, the federal agency with responsibility over issues of discriminatory harassment, has said that a "workplace in which sexual slurs, displays of 'girlie' pictures, and other offensive conduct abound can constitute a hostile work environment even if many people deem it to be harmless or insignificant."[29] This is certainly true and accepted by the courts. Still, the key judicial inquiries focus on the pervasiveness of the discriminatory expressions and the conduct it engenders.

In one case, a female shipyard worker successfully sued her employer for sexual harassment because a large and pervasive number of pictures of nude and partially nude women had been pasted throughout the workplace by coworkers. The company tolerated the posting of such pictures, even though it prohibited the posting of political and commercial materials. The company had also prohibited workers from bringing newspapers or magazines onto the job but apparently looked the other way when workers read pornographic magazines. Members of management participated in this conduct by reading the same magazines and posting similar pictures or calendars in their offices.

That environment was accompanied as well by frequent lewd and sexual comments and jokes directed or made at the expense of the small number of women working at the shipyard. The result was a "working environment [of sexually harassing behavior that occurred] with both frequency and intensity."[30] Importantly, the court found no First Amendment issue at stake because the employer said it was not seeking to express itself through the sexually oriented pictures or the verbal harassment at the shipyard.[31] An enterprise that had sexual expression as part of its underlying purpose would have received a different analysis from that undertaken by this court.

Here, however, the company could easily have enforced its policy against posting any pictures or other materials at the workplace. The court in this case also went further than any other court in holding that "the pictures and verbal harassment are not protected speech because they act as discriminatory conduct in the form of a hostile work environment."[32]

This second part of the court's free-speech analysis, that the pictures and verbal comments were not protected speech, finds no significant support in other case law and appears to have been refuted by the Supreme Court's own declaration that "a mere offensive utterance" cannot constitute punishable harassment.[33] Other courts have consistently held that "[c]asual or isolated manifestations of discriminatory conduct, such as a few sexual comments or slurs, may not support" a claim of discriminatory conduct.[34] Instead, it is only when such pictures and comments are sufficiently severe and pervasive, such as "a steady stream of vulgar and offensive epithets because of her gender," that the balance in First Amendment analysis changes.[35]

For that reason, a number of cases have found no violation of Title VII when a person has been offended by similar nude imagery in the workplace. In one case involving a male employee, the issue revolved around frequent derogatory comments made by fellow workers and written onto work schedules, calendars, the employee's locker, and the men's restroom walls, as well as numerous posted and photocopied drawings purporting to show the complaining employee variously sodomizing a woman, being sodomized by a deer, and appearing as a fly between a graphic drawing of a woman's spread legs. The court found that even if the incidents could be characterized as discrimination based on sex, which it doubted, "the frequency of the harassment that was explicitly sexual was low and isolated in time."[36] The court then concluded that "these isolated incidents, even if targeted at [the employee] because he was male, were not pervasive or severe enough to constitute an abusive work environment."[37]

In another case, a female police sergeant, the first appointed in that department, sued after she had found herself and women more generally the object of derogatory comments in a pseudonymously written column in the police officer association's newsletter. Specifically, the complaining officer was the subject of four columns, with another six columns more generally, that crudely questioned the propriety of having women on the force. A federal appellate court ruled that "these columns are the equivalent of the 'mere utterance of an . . . epithet which engenders offensive feelings in an employee'" and, as a matter of law, "not severe or pervasive enough to create an objectively hostile or abusive work environment."[38]

Taking an entirely different view of the intersection of free speech and harassment than the court in the shipyard case, the Fifth Circuit in this case said:

> Where pure expression is involved, Title VII steers into the territory of the First Amendment. It is no use to deny or minimize this problem because, when Title VII is applied to sexual harassment claims founded solely on verbal insults, pictorial or literary matter, the statute imposes content-based, viewpoint-discriminatory restrictions on speech.[39]

Even in those instances where the harassing conduct is sufficiently severe and pervasive, liability can be avoided by prompt action under a comprehensive anti-harassment policy. The Supreme Court has advised that such a policy must address harassment specifically as part of an overall nondiscrimination policy and alert employees to the employer's interest in correcting any discrimination.[40] To avoid the difficulty faced when the person to whom the harassment must be reported is the harasser, alternative reporting authorities should be established, and the policy must be designed to encourage victims to come forward.[41]

An example of decisive action that avoided liability was described in *Bennett v. Corroon & Black Corporation*.[42] There, a woman employee discovered that she was the subject of at least four obscene cartoons posted in the men's room that depicted her engaged in "crude and deviant sexual activities." The cartoons were visible during their one-week posting to both male employees, including the chief executive officer of the company, and to the company's male clients.[43] The woman resigned from her post after discovering the cartoons and later sued. In rejecting her claims, the court credited the parent company's actions in firing the CEO, who failed to remove the cartoons; continuing to pay her after her resignation; paying medical bills she incurred for psychiatric counseling arising from the incident; and ensuring her of its good opinion of her and its desire to have her back in its employ.[44] The federal appeals court concluded that Title VII afforded no further relief to a victim of harassment than the company had undertaken voluntarily.

It is quite possible an employer will not have to go quite as far as that one did. Generally, "an employer's legal duty is . . . discharged if it takes reasonable steps to discover and rectify acts of sexual harassment of its employees."[45] Thus, in one case where the employee complained to the human resources department about sexually demeaning comments from her supervisor, sufficient action was taken when the supervisor was told to cease his offensive behavior, was placed on probation, and had a pay increase held up. Because the harassment then ceased and a workable policy had been in place, it was the employee's fault, not the employer's, that the procedure had not been utilized to stop the harassment at an earlier stage.[46] In fact, the Supreme Court has recognized that even if a plaintiff makes out a prima facie case of sexual harassment, the employer can rebut the case by affirmatively demonstrating that its conduct was reasonable in attempting to prevent and correct the harassing behavior and that the plaintiff unreasonably failed to take advantage of the measures the employer had put in place *or* failed to otherwise avoid the harm.[47]

These holdings, in the context of Internet access, strongly suggest that libraries can and should adopt privacy screens at terminals and work to relieve those employees who may be offended by sites accessed by patrons of Internet use. This issue will be discussed further in chapter 9.

Conclusion

Libraries must respect the free-speech and anti-discrimination rights of employees. Generally, library employees have a First Amendment right to speak out on matters of public concern, including library management and policy. For their speech to remain a matter of public concern, the employees must not attempt to transform their own employment complaints into issues of public interest. To exercise this right appropriately and within the protection of the First Amendment, employees must not appear to convey their opinions in a manner that will be taken as the official views of the library, and they cannot use their expressive rights to impair the efficient operation of the library.

Although it is possible that speech or imagery can contribute to a hostile work environment, remember that conduct that is isolated or occasional cannot be considered severe and pervasive enough to change the work environment.[48] Equally important, issues of sexual harassment must be considered in the context of the constitutional right of adults to read and view sexual material that is not obscene.[49] In successful sexual harassment cases that involve images, there is often other discriminatory conduct that pervaded the work environment and rendered it hostile.[50] Finally, because context is critical in these cases where the complained-of material is related to the employer's business, an employee's harassment claim has not been held to override First Amendment rights to sell, distribute, or provide access to First Amendment–protected material.[51] The use of privacy screens also helps avoid the harassment issue.

This last consideration seems particularly important in the context of a public library. If an employee could object to constitutionally protected material as offensive in the library, then each employee would have a certain amount of control over the contents of the library and could accomplish, by a claim of harassment, the removal of materials that the library itself could not under the First Amendment. It is possible that a patron could attempt to harass an employee by demanding constant assistance from a particular librarian as a pretext for displaying racially, religiously, or sexually offensive material. However, a library on notice of such behavior can develop policies that accommodate the employee's position, such as rotating personnel who assist patrons, and recognizing such abuse of available assistance for what it is and denying further help. Clearly, the library's own anti-harassment policy and grievance procedures should anticipate this issue and address it.

NOTES

1. *Pickering* v. *Board of Education*, 391 U.S. 563, 574 (1968).

2. *Board of Comm'rs* v. *Umbher*, 116 S. Ct. 2361 (1996).

3. *Mr. Healthy City Sch. Dist. Bd. of Educ.* v. *Doyle*, 429 U.S. 274, 287 (1977).

4. *Id.*

5. *Connick* v. *Myers*, 461 U.S. 138 (1983).

6. *Id.* at 143.

7. *Givhan* v. *Western Line Consolidated Sch. Dist.*, 439 U.S. 410, 415 (1979).

8. *Rankin* v. *McPherson*, 483 U.S. 378, 380 (1987).

9. *Id.* at 387.

10. *Id.* at 388.

11. *Orr* v. *Crowder*, 315 S.E.2d 593 (W. Va. 1983), *cert. denied*, 469 U.S. 981 (1984).

12. *Id.* at 601 (footnote omitted).

13. *Id.* at 602.

14. *Meritor Savings Bank* v. *Vinson,* 477 U.S. 57, 66 (1986) (citations omitted); *see, e.g.,* 42 U.S.C. § 2000e et seq. (1996).

15. *Gross* v. *Burggraf Construction Co.,* 53 F.3d 1531 (10th Cir. 1995).

16. 42 U.S.C. § 2000e-2(a)(1).

17. *Harris* v. *Forklift Systems, Inc.,* 510 U.S. 17, 22 (1993).

18. *Id.*

19. *Id.*

20. *Id.* at 21 (citation omitted).

21. *Id.* at 24.

22. *See id.* at 21, 69.

23. *Johnson* v. *County of Los Angeles Fire Dep't,* 865 F. Supp. 1430, 1434 (C.D. Cal. 1994).

24. *Id.*

25. *Id.* at 1439 (citing *McKinley* v. *Eloy,* 705 F.2d 1110, 1115 (9th Cir. 1983)).

26. *Id.* at 1440.

27. *Id.* at 1441.

28. *Id.*

29. *EEOC Compliance Manual* (CCH) § 614, ¶ 3114(C)(1), at 3274 (1990).

30. *Robinson* v. *Jacksonville Shipyards, Inc.,* 760 F. Supp. 1486 (M.D. Fla. 1991).

31. *Id.* at 1534.

32. *Id.* at 1535.

33. *Harris* v. *Forklift Systems, Inc.,* 510 U.S. 17, 24 (1993).

34. *Lowe* v. *Angelo's Italian Foods, Inc.,* 87 F.3d 1170, 1175 (10th Cir. 1996).

35. *Gross* v. *Burggraf Construction Co.,* 53 F.3d 1531, 1539 (10th Cir. 1995).

36. *Noble* v. *Monsanto Co.,* 973 F.Supp. 849, 857 (S.D. Iowa 1997).

37. *Id.*

38. *DeAngelis* v. *El Paso Municipal Police Officers Ass'n,* 51 F.3d 591, 595–96 (5th Cir.), *cert. denied,* 516 U.S. 974 (1995) (citations omitted).

39. *Id.* at 596–97.

40. *Meritor Savings Bank* v. *Vinson,* 477 U.S. 57, 72–73 (1986).

41. *Id.*

42. *Bennett* v. *Corroon & Black Corp.,* 845 F.2d 104 (5th Cir. 1988).

43. *Id.* at 105.

44. *Id.* at 106.

45. *Baskerville* v. *Culligan Int'l Co.,* 50 F.3d 428, 432 (7th Cir. 1995).

46. *Id.*

47. *Faragher* v. *City of Boca Raton,* 524 U.S. 775 (1998).

48. *Baskerville* v. *Culligan Int'l Co.,* 50 F.3d 428, 430–31 (7th Cir. 1995).

49. *United States* v. *X-Citement Video, Inc.,* 513 U.S. 64, 72 (1994); *see also ACLU* v. *Reno,* 117 S.Ct. 2329, 2346–47 (1997).

50. *See, e.g., Robinson* v. *Jacksonville Shipyards, Inc.,* 760 F. Supp. 1486 (M.D. Fla. 1991).

51. *Stanley* v. *The Lawson* Co., 993 F. Supp. 1084 (N.D. Ohio 1997).

CHAPTER 8

Children, Schools, and the First Amendment

Adults in the United States enjoy complete freedom from government thought control. Other societies and cultures have attempted to suppress certain ideas as too perilous for society to tolerate, but the First Amendment prevents the U.S. government from exercising a paternalistic oversight over adult access to dangerous or sinful thoughts. As the U.S. Supreme Court noted in a 1959 decision, "the First Amendment's basic guarantee is of freedom to advocate ideas, . . . [including ideas that the State believes are] contrary to the moral standards, the religious precepts, and the legal code of its citizenry." [1]

Minors, however, do not stand in the same shoes as adults when First Amendment rights are at issue. Although minors retain significant free-speech rights of their own, the Supreme Court has long held that the state's authority "to control the conduct of children reaches beyond the scope of its authority over adults." [2] Although there is a distinction between conduct and speech that has a constitutional dimension, the idea that exposure to certain ideas or images may influence juvenile conduct has considerable traction and has sometimes succeeded in justifying a variety of speech restrictions on youth.

Nonetheless, the primary responsibility and decision-making authority for the custody, care, and nurture of children indisputably rests with parents. The government's appropriate role through laws and regulations, the Court has said, is in supporting parental upbringing choices, as well as in advancing, sometimes independently of parents, the well-being of youth. [3] Particularly when government asserts an interest in protecting youth from certain types of speech, government is engaged in a high-wire act that must concede to parents an overriding authority that is sometimes at odds with the government's one-size-fits-all judgments.

Still, in the exercise of its independent interest in children, the government has a certain amount of authority to restrict youth access to materials that remain perfectly legal for adults. This concession of official power rests upon a recognition that there is a compelling state interest "in protecting the physical and psychological well-being of minors."[4] That power has been validly exercised, for example, to shield minors from some materials that are not obscene for adults but are deemed obscene for children.[5] It includes as well the power to safeguard minors from indecent broadcasts.[6] And it embraces the power to screen minors from some instances of vulgarity in school.[7]

This seemingly broad authority, however, is not without limits. Speech regulations enacted in the interests of protecting youth must be narrowly drawn to serve those ends and cannot unnecessarily interfere with the free-speech rights of either adults or children.[8] In one case, frequently cited on this issue, the Court struck down a law that generally made it a crime to sell materials to the general public that could have a potentially harmful effect on children. The law failed the First Amendment's narrow-tailoring requirement by interfering with the right of adults to read what they wished. Instead, greater precision of regulation is required by the Constitution. Justice Felix Frankfurter, writing for a unanimous Court, equated the law to attempting "to burn the house to roast the pig."[9] There is no government authority, the Court added, to "quarantin[e] the general reading public against books not too rugged for grown men and women in order to shield juvenile innocence."[10] It was also largely on this basis—that the law accomplished more than necessary to effectuate its purpose—that the Internet-cleansing Communications Decency Act (CDA) was declared unconstitutional.[11]

Children Have First Amendment Rights, Too

In *Erznoznik* v. *City of Jacksonville,* a city ordinance that attempted to protect children from modern movie portrayals of sex banned nudity in motion pictures shown at drive-in theaters.[12] The U.S. Supreme Court overturned the law as unconstitutionally overbroad for it treated all nudity as harmful. Importantly, the Court stated that "[s]peech . . . cannot be suppressed solely to protect the young from ideas or images that a legislative body thinks unsuitable for them."[13]

In another case, the issue was whether the federal government could ban unsolicited contraceptive advertising from the mail. Although the law was declared invalid as applied to a manufacturer's unsolicited advertising flyers on other constitutional grounds, the Supreme Court thought very little of the government's attempt to justify the ban as a way to help parents prevent outside stimuli from preempting parental initiatives on a sensitive and controversial subject.[14] The law, the Court noted, "quite clearly denies information to minors, who are entitled to 'a significant measure of First Amendment protection.'"[15] One aspect of that protection that the federal statute "ignored" was an older minor's "pressing need for information about contraception."[16] Finally, and memorably, the Court declared that the "level of discourse reaching a mailbox simply cannot be limited to that which would be suitable for a sandbox."[17]

This last declaration, condemning attempts to cleanse speech sufficiently so that it would be appropriate for the sandbox set, is a further guide to the limits on speech regulations aimed at protecting minors from speech beyond their maturity. It is a recognition as well that four-year-olds and sixteen-year-olds are at different levels of development and must be treated accordingly. In the case striking down the CDA, the Supreme Court forthrightly declared "that the strength of the Government's interest in protecting minors is not equally strong throughout [childhood]."[18] It was troubling to the Court that the CDA applied to everyone under the age of eighteeen, thereby including a substantial number of near adults.[19] A seventeen-year-old might be away from home at college, yet the CDA would make it a crime for a parent to e-mail birth-control information to his or her child. To the Court, such a result was unfathomable.[20] It is a function of both the requirement of narrow tailoring—that is, that laws be no more restrictive than necessary to accomplish a compelling government interest—and the growing maturity of older minors that the First Amendment requires more sensitive treatment and greater recognition of minors' free-speech rights.

For similar reasons, courts have held "that if any reasonable minor, including a seventeen-year-old, would find serious value [in allegedly obscene-for-minor materials], the material is not 'harmful-to-minors.'"[21]

Student Expressive Rights in Public Schools

Even in the more structured environment of the public schools, the Court has acknowledged that children retain substantial First Amendment rights. In one landmark case, the Court declared:

> It can hardly be argued that . . . students . . . shed their constitutional rights to freedom of speech or expression at the schoolhouse gate. . . . Students in school as well as out of school are "persons" under our Constitution. They are possessed of fundamental rights which the State must respect, just as they themselves must respect their obligations to the State. In our system, students may not be regarded as closed-circuit recipients of only that which the State chooses to communicate. They may not be confined to the expression of those sentiments that are officially approved.[22]

In that particular case, the Court upheld the rights of students who wore black armbands in silent protest against the Vietnam War, despite a school rule that had been enacted to prevent such protests. Student free-speech rights should be observed, the Court held, unless the minors' use of expressive freedom "materially disrupts classwork or involves substantial disorder or invasion of the rights of others."[23] Such disruption must be real and not be the product of an "undifferentiated fear or apprehension of disturbance."[24] By so stating, the Court prevented school authorities from suppressing controversial speech based on educated guesses that the expression might give rise to unpleasant reactions or heated passions. To hammer the point home, the Court recognized that

> [a]ny word spoken, in class, in the lunchroom, or on the campus, that deviates from the views of another person may start an argument or cause a disturbance. But our Constitution says we must take this risk; and our history says that it is this sort of hazardous freedom—this kind of openness—that is the basis of our national strength and of the independence and vigor of Americans who grow up and live in this relatively permissive, often disputatious, society.[25]

Although students have meaningful rights to engage in nondisruptive speech, they also cannot be denied access to those ideas or images that officials decide are unsuitable for them, as long as the speech is neither obscene for minors nor subject to some other legitimate proscription.[26] Most of the time, the Court said, "the values protected by the First Amendment are no less applicable when government seeks to control the flow of information to minors."[27]

Student Rights and School Library Books

These concepts have been explored further in some cases that are especially relevant to the First Amendment issues that arise in the context of school libraries. Perhaps no case is more important in this regard than

Island Trees Union Free School District No. 26 v. *Pico,* also known as the "Island Trees" case.[28] The lawsuit had its genesis when three school board members attended a conference sponsored by a politically conservative group. They returned to the school district with a blacklist of books that they had been advised should not be in school libraries. Upon further investigation, they learned that ten of the books on the list were found in the district's school libraries. The board then gave an "unofficial direction" that the books be removed for further inspection. In response to adverse publicity about this action, the board put out a press release that concluded the books were "anti-American, anti-Christian, anti-Semitic, and just plain filthy."[29]

Among the volumes removed were such well-regarded books as *Slaughterhouse Five,* by Kurt Vonnegut Jr.; *The Naked Ape,* by Desmond Morris; *Down These Mean Streets,* by Piri Thomas; *Best Short Stories of Negro Writers,* edited by Langston Hughes; the anonymously written *Go Ask Alice; A Hero Ain't Nothin' But a Sandwich,* by Alice Childress; *A Reader for Writers,* edited by Jerome Archer; *The Fixer,* by Bernard Malamud; and *Soul on Ice,* by Eldridge Cleaver.

A review committee concluded that five of the ten removed books should be returned to the shelves, two be placed in restricted circulation, and two be removed permanently. The last book received no recommendation. Nonetheless, the full board voted, without comment, to remove all books but one.

Several students then filed a lawsuit, claiming the removal violated their First Amendment rights. By a 5–4 vote, and featuring seven separate opinions, the Supreme Court upheld the students' claims. The majority agreed that school boards do not have unrestricted authority to select library books and that the removal of books can violate the First Amendment. The plurality opinion held that, although officials possess "significant discretion to determine the content of their school libraries," such "discretion may not be exercised in a narrowly partisan or political manner."[30] In essence, the Court proscribed "the official suppression of ideas."[31] If the board removed the books to deny students "access to ideas with which [the board] disagreed," then a constitutional violation occurred because the action amounted to "the precise sort of officially prescribed orthodoxy unequivocally condemned" in earlier constitutional decisions.[32]

The Court, however, found no constitutional violation would have occurred if the board's motivation for the removals were based on the books' pervasive vulgarity or educational unsuitability.[33] In determining the board's real motivation, it was important to the Court that the board did not have, let alone follow, "established, regular, and facially unbiased procedures for the review of controversial materials."[34] Such well-established procedures would insulate the process, the Court reasoned, from partisan or ideologically motivated book removals.

Writing separately, Justice Harry Blackmun supported the opinion of the Court in stating that there is no authority to "deny access to an idea simply because state officials disapprove of that idea for partisan or political reasons."[35]

Critically, the decision said that a school library is the place where "students must always remain free to inquire, to study and to evaluate, to gain new maturity and understanding."[36] It is there, the Court continued, that a student learns "to test or expand upon ideas presented to him, in or out of the classroom."[37] It is the "unique role of the school library," the Court added, to afford students "an opportunity at self-education and individual enrichment that is wholly optional" and therefore outside the school officials' claims of discretion and control of values that are more likely to be indulged in the "compulsory environment of the classroom."[38]

Using the same analysis as the Supreme Court, a 1995 federal court decision rebuked officials for the removal of two copies of an award-winning novel, *Annie on My Mind,* from school library shelves as a First Amendment violation.[39] The school superintendent had ordered the removal of the book after receiving numerous protests about the novel's noncondemnatory treatment of a budding lesbian relationship between high-school girls. Although school board members defended their action as based on a determination that the book was educationally unsuitable, the Court pierced the veil of this rationalization and concluded that they "removed *Annie on My Mind* largely because they disagreed with ideas expressed in the book."[40]

School Authority over Curricular Material and Activities

In the classroom, the Supreme Court has observed that school officials have significant discretion to determine educational suitability in the use of classroom materials. In *Hazelwood School District* v. *Kuhlmeier,* the removal issue did not involve school library books, but two pages of a newspaper produced by students as part of a high-school journalism class.[41] The pages contained articles on student pregnancies and parental divorce. With the print deadline pressing and no time to have the articles rewritten, the principal decided removal was the only solution available for the problematic material. The pregnancy article, he concluded, might prove embarrassing to the students discussed even though the article used false names. Moreover, he thought the discussions of sexual activity and birth control by students were inappropriate for some of the younger students at the school. The divorce story, the principal contended, might have portrayed some of the parents unfairly and should have sought the parents' consent or responses to their children's characterizations. The principal's decision to delete the articles for these reasons prompted the student editors to sue.

While reaffirming that students retain their First Amendment rights in school, the Court paid particular attention to earlier precedents that held such rights must be "applied in light of the special characteristics of the school environment."[42] One aspect of those special characteristics, the Court forthrightly stated, is that a "school need not tolerate student speech that is inconsistent with its 'basic educational mission,' even though the government could not censor similar speech outside the school."[43] Still, the Court made a distinction between a student's personal speech and speech such as "school-sponsored publications, theatrical productions, and other expressive activities that students, parents, and members of the public might reasonably perceive to bear the imprimatur of the school . . . [and which] may fairly be characterized as part of the school curriculum . . . designed to impart particular knowledge or skills to student participants and audiences."[44] Personal expression receives greater constitutional protection; speech that appears to be that of the school's is subject to greater control.

By treating the removal action as a curricular decision, the Court was able to treat the student-written articles as the school's own speech. Obviously, as the Court said, school officials may control student expression in the curriculum "to assure that participants learn whatever lessons the activity is designed to teach, that readers or listeners are not exposed to material that may be inappropriate for their level of maturity, and that the views of the individual speaker are not erroneously attributed to the school."[45] As the actual speaker at issue, then, the school may not only regulate speech that interferes with those objectives or that impinges on other students' rights, but it may also deal appropriately with speech that is "ungrammatical, poorly written, inadequately re-searched, biased or prejudiced, vulgar or profane, or unsuitable for im-mature audiences."[46]

The authority acceded to school authorities by the Court is in fact so broad that it covers virtually any expression that the school deems inap-propriate, a range, defined by the Court itself, that includes speech from "the existence of Santa Claus in an elementary school setting to the par-ticulars of teenage sexual activity in a high school setting" and even advo-cacy of "conduct otherwise inconsistent with 'the shared values of a civilized social order.' "[47] The key to the exercise of this expansive license over student speech is a requirement that the school officials' "actions are reasonably related to legitimate pedagogical concerns," a difficult stan-dard to challenge when officials use educational rationales as pretexts for actions that arise out of other, less admirable motivations.[48]

Courts traditionally take school officials' protestations of educational justification at face value. Only smoking-gun evidence that a political motive lies behind the censorious action can overcome officials' asser-tions of pedagogical concerns. An example of the extreme use of this li-cense came quickly after the *Hazelwood* decision. At a high school in Columbia County, Florida, the school board decided to discontinue use of a humanities textbook for eleventh- and twelfth-graders based on a single parent's complaint about the textbook's inclusion of *Lysistrata*, by Aristophanes and written around 411 B.C., and *The Miller's Tale*, by Geoffrey Chaucer and written around A.D. 1380–1390. The complaint focused on the selections' sexuality and vulgarity. In response to the par-ent's petition, the books were placed in locked storage, although copies remained available in the school library, along with other adaptations and translations of *Lysistrata* and *The Miller's Tale*.

A group of parents who disagreed with the removal decision sued on behalf of their children. Affirming the federal district court's decision and relying on *Hazelwood*, the Eleventh Circuit upheld the removal of the textbook as a curricular decision that was based on legitimate peda-gogical concerns, even though the judges "seriously question[ed] how young persons just below the age of majority can be harmed by these masterpieces of Western literature."[49]

Schools do not, however, have to exercise the authority that the Supreme Court has determined they have over official school publica-tions. Even the *Hazelwood* Court conceded that First Amendment rights attach more fulsomely when a school has designated the publication as a forum for student expression.[50] A number of schools have done so. Some states reacted to the *Hazelwood* decision by enacting laws that protect the free-speech rights of student journalists except in those instances where the expression will result in disruption or disorder in the school.[51] State constitutions may also be interpreted to provide greater expressive rights for student journalists than the U.S. Supreme Court recognized under the First Amendment.[52]

Sexuality and vulgarity, as in the Florida case involving *Lysistrata* and *The Miller's Tale,* have been well established as the most plausible pedagogical justifications for removing a publication from the curriculum or punishing speech on a public school campus. Thus, for example, in *Seyfried* v. *Walton,* the federal Third Circuit upheld a school superintendent's authority to cancel an expurgated version of the play *Pippin* because it still contained too much sexual content.[53] And the U.S. Supreme Court also upheld the authority of a school to punish a student for a student election nominating speech at a schoolwide assembly that made extensive use of double entendres and lewd references to speak of the candidate's qualifications for office.[54]

Even student speech that could not possibly be thought to bear the school's imprimatur can be subjected to some restrictions based on its sexuality or vulgarity. In one case, a school policy was upheld that permitted officials to ban distribution of underground newspapers if the material was "obscene to minors," "libelous," "pervasively indecent or vulgar," likely to cause "a material and substantial disruption of the proper and orderly operation of the school or school activities," or advertising a "product or service not permitted to minors by law."[55] A different federal appellate court, however, concluded that the First Amendment was violated by school distribution policies that are content-based and are not limited to regulations of time, place, and manner of distribution.[56]

Although indecency, obscenity, and vulgarity have fallen within the authority of school officials to be treated according to standards that consider the maturity of the student population, other objections that similarly claim an educational purpose have not fared as well in court. In *Pratt* v. *Independent School District No. 831,* a federal appeals court found the removal of a film version of the Shirley Jackson story *The Lottery* from the curriculum unconstitutional.[57] The film had been part of the classes for five years when parents and other citizens complained about the story's violence and the critical approach it took to traditional religious and family values. The film tells a story about the stoning of one resident of a small American town each year as a form of sacrifice. The court concluded that the film was eliminated because of its "ideological content" in violation of the First Amendment.[58]

A more protective standard relating to student press rights applies to publications that students bring onto the school campus but are not distributed there. A leading case involved an off-campus newspaper called *Hard Times* that was a satirical and sexually blunt publication. Students bought the newspaper off-campus for a quarter. After an incident in which a teacher confiscated a student's copy of the newspaper, the school board, overruling the principal's decision not to take action, suspended the student publishers of the paper and exacted additional sanctions against them. In vindicating the students' rights, the court found that this was not an instance where the school was punishing and prohibiting speech "out of regard for fellow students who constitute a captive audience [or] . . . in avoiding the impression that it has authorized a specific expression."[59] Instead, the court held that "school officials have ventured out of the school yard and into the general community where the freedom accorded expression is at its zenith . . . [and] must be evaluated by the principles that bind government officials in the public arena."[60]

Religion and Curriculum

Although schools exist to inculcate young people with the "fundamental values necessary to the maintenance of a democratic political system"[61] and the social and moral outlooks that comprise "community values,"[62] there are still limits on those choices. One limit is the First Amendment requirement of viewpoint neutrality. The Establishment Clause and its emphasis on government neutrality toward religion provides a further limitation on this authority. Comparative religion can be taught as a legitimate school subject, but Bible readings, which are designed to advance a particular theology, cannot.[63] It is a difference between teaching about religion and teaching religion. The issue has also reached the U.S. Supreme Court twice in the guise of the debate over evolution versus the biblical story of creation.

The first time the Court decided the issue, in 1968, it had been asked to judge the constitutionality of a 1928 Arkansas law, based on the 1925 statute that had famously been the issue in the Scopes "Monkey Trial." The Arkansas law made it unlawful for any teacher in a public school or university to teach or to use a textbook that teaches "that mankind ascended or descended from a lower order of animals."[64] After the Little Rock school district adopted a textbook that would have violated the law, a new teacher in the school sought a court order declaring the law unconstitutional so that she could use the assigned textbook without fear of subsequent criminal prosecution or dismissal. She won at the trial court level, but the Arkansas Supreme Court reversed, finding that the law merely reflected state authority to set school curriculum.

In the U.S. Supreme Court, that state authority was trumped by competing constitutional considerations. In the 1982 school-library-book case, school authority had to yield, in the Court's words, to the "transcendent imperatives of the First Amendment."[65] The Court noted that neither it nor the lower courts had "failed to apply the First Amendment's mandate in our educational system where essential to safeguard the fundamental values of freedom of speech and inquiry and of belief."[66] Most importantly, within the public schools, the First Amendment "does not tolerate laws that cast a pall of orthodoxy over the classroom."[67]

Here, the Court found that the "Arkansas law selects from the body of knowledge a particular segment which it proscribes for the sole reason that it is deemed to conflict with a particular religious doctrine; that is, with a particular interpretation of the Book of Genesis by a particular religious group."[68] Such a result, the Court continued, conflicts with the First Amendment's requirement that government "must be neutral in matters of religious theory, doctrine, and practice."[69] Thus, government's "undoubted right to prescribe the curriculum for its public schools does not carry with it the right to prohibit, on pain of criminal penalty, the teaching of a scientific theory or doctrine where that prohibition is based upon reasons that violate the First Amendment."[70] Support for religious doctrine is just such an impermissible reason, which was the underlying purpose of the Arkansas statute at issue in this case. The Court concluded, "[T]here can be no doubt that Arkansas has sought to prevent its teachers from discussing the theory of evolution because it is contrary to the belief of some that the Book of Genesis must be the exclusive source of doctrine as to the origin of man."[71]

Although the Court's decision appeared definitive, the issue returned to the Court nearly two decades later. This time, the law being challenged was a Louisiana statute that mandated the teaching of evolution or "creationism," whichever had been excluded, if the school chose to teach one of the theories. The state defended this "equal time" law as a means of promoting academic freedom. That explanation, however, proved puzzling to the Court, because it could not understand how the goal of academic freedom could be advanced by outlawing the teaching of evolution unless creationism is also taught.[72] The Court instead unmasked the real aim of the law: "[T]he purpose of the Creationism Act was to restructure the science curriculum to conform with a particular religious viewpoint. Out of many possible science subjects taught in the public schools, the legislature chose to affect the teaching of the one scientific theory that historically has been opposed by certain religious sects."[73]

While invalidating the Louisiana law as unconstitutional, the Court said that "teaching a variety of scientific theories about the origins of humankind to schoolchildren might be validly done with the clear secular intent of enhancing the effectiveness of science instruction."[74] That sort of survey of competing scientific approaches was not what Louisiana had attempted. Instead, the "Louisiana Creationism Act advance[d] a religious doctrine by requiring either the banishment of the theory of evolution from public school classrooms or the presentation of a religious viewpoint that rejects evolution in its entirety."[75]

Although the evolution cases establish that school authorities cannot promote religious doctrine through curricular choices, it is equally clear that parents and students cannot exercise similar control over the classroom. Two federal appellate cases decided in 1987 emphatically deny parents the authority to force removal of books or alterations in curriculum to satisfy their religious objections. In *Smith* v. *Board of School Commissioners,* spurred on by a federal judge who took exception to the Supreme Court's school prayer decisions, the plaintiffs, 624 Christian Evangelicals, initially succeeded in winning the court-ordered removal of forty-four elementary and secondary school history, social studies, and home economics textbooks because they taught the "religion" of humanism.[76] The parents claimed that humanism was an anti-religion religion being promoted in the public schools to the detriment of theistic faiths and in violation of the principle of separation of church and state.

In reversing the removal decision, the federal appeals court found that "use of the challenged textbooks has the primary effect of conveying information that is essentially neutral in its religious content to the school children who utilize the books; none of these books convey a message of governmental approval of secular humanism or governmental disapproval of theism."[77] Instead, "the message conveyed is one of a governmental attempt to instill in Alabama public school children such values as independent thought, tolerance of diverse views, self-respect, maturity, self-reliance and logical decision-making."[78] The First Amendment cannot and does not forbid that objective. The books were restored to the Mobile public school system.

About the same time, in a different case, another group of fundamentalist parents sought to have their children exempted from the basic reading series that served grades one through eight because they believed them to be inconsistent with the parents' religious beliefs. For example, in the eighth-grade reader, a poem, "The Blind Men and the Elephant," told of six blind men, each feeling a different part of an elephant, who come to different conclusions about what the creature must look like. The poem states as a moral that as is "so oft in theologic wars" the men "rail on in utter ignorance" about an elephant none has actually seen. The parents complained that the poem taught that each religion described God from a limited vantage point and that all are only partly right. To the parents, this was heresy because their Fundamentalist beliefs held that the Bible was the literal truth and all other religions false.

Similarly, they complained about a passage from *The Diary of Anne Frank,* the much-admired writings of a young Jewish girl in hiding, who died in a Nazi concentration camp. In the passage, she tells a boy that it doesn't matter what religious belief one has—it is simply important to have some religious belief. But to the complaining parents, it does matter what religious belief one has, and they did not want their children taught otherwise.

Other selections were scored for similar reasons: *The Wizard of Oz* for its treatment of the supernatural and the concept of a "good" witch; a description of Leonardo da Vinci as the human with a creative mind that "came closest to the divine touch"; a poem, "Look at Anything," that suggested a child can become a part of anything and understand it better with the use of imagination, which was criticized as an "occult practice"; a science fiction tale that featured the use of mental telepathy, a process the parents found religiously objectionable and claimed would be understood by the students as a scientific concept; and twenty-four passages said to have evolution as a theme, which the parents believed taught their children that there is no God. Further, parents objected to instances of role reversal or role elimination, especially biographical material about women who have been recognized for achievements outside their homes. Most tellingly, the parents objected to exposure of their children to other religions without some disclaimer that the other religions were wrong and that the parents' Fundamentalist views were correct.

In ruling against the parents, the Sixth Circuit found that "to the plaintiffs there is but one acceptable view—the Biblical view, as they interpret the Bible," and that they "view every human situation and decision, whether related to personal belief and conduct or to public policy and programs, from a theological or religious perspective."[79] For a school system to avoid conflict with their beliefs, the court continued, the curriculum would have to be tailored to the principles of the parents' religious beliefs, something that the Supreme Court had said would violate the Establishment Clause in the case that struck down Arkansas's anti-evolution statute, *Epperson* v. *Arkansas*.[80] Instead, the court found that mere exposure to ideas, even on a repeated basis, cannot constitute a violation of the religious-freedom rights of a child or parent without some form of "compulsion to affirm or deny a religious belief or to engage or refrain from engaging in a practice forbidden or required in the exercise of a plaintiff's religion."[81]

Although attempts by parents to impose their religious outlooks on the school have been rebuffed, the law is a little more unsettled when students are responsible for the attempt. A majority of courts, including the U.S. Supreme Court, appear to hold that the issue should be treated no differently whether the progenitors are parents or students. One federal appeals court, however, has permitted students a small amount of leeway here. Because it is inconsistent with other decisions, it should not be relied upon in determining student rights.

In *Jones* v. *Clear Creek Independent School District,* the Fifth Circuit found no constitutional infirmity in a procedure that permitted high-school students to vote to have a nonsectarian, nonproselytizing prayer to solemnize their graduation ceremony.[82] The *Jones* court found that the purpose of the procedure permitting prayer was not religious, but merely one of solemnizing an important event. It also said that students would not have the impression that government is endorsing religion because they will have participated in an election to decide whether a prayer would be offered.[83]

The case cannot be reconciled with the U.S. Supreme Court's decision in *Lee* v. *Weisman,* where the Court held that the practice of public-school graduation prayers violates the First Amendment's Establishment Clause because it amounts to compelled attendance and participation in a formal religious exercise.[84] The Court noted that graduation is an event that is under the control of public officials and that student attendance is, in a real sense, obligatory, even if formally unnecessary to receive a diploma. The Court explicitly rejected arguments (1) that students could freely give up their right to participate in the graduation ceremony to avoid the religious exercise; (2) that the prayers were brief and thus unobjectionable; and (3) that graduation was more meaningful with a religious acknowledgment as a solemnization of the event because the official involvement amounted to support or endorsement for religion.[85]

Like the graduation prayer held unconstitutional in *Lee,* the electoral procedure approved by the *Jones* court fails constitutional muster because it has as its object "a prayer to be used in a formal religious exercise which students, for all practical purposes, are obliged to attend."[86] It thus puts "school-age children who object[] in an untenable position" and is inconsistent with the Court's "heightened concerns with protecting freedom of conscience from subtle coercive pressure in the elementary and secondary public schools."[87] The *Lee* Court noted that "peer pressure, on attending students to stand as a group or, at least, maintain respectful silence during the Invocation and Benediction . . . , though subtle and indirect, can be as real as any overt compulsion."[88] Thus, the Court concluded that the high school student who objects will be left with "a reasonable perception that she is being forced by the State to pray in a manner her conscience will not allow."[89] The intervention of a student election, or the conduct of the prayer by a fellow student, changes none of these peer pressures or messages of exclusion for the student whose rights of conscience are violated.

In fact, the electoral procedure that the *Jones* court found a saving grace was emphatically rejected by the Supreme Court in *Lee:* "While in some societies the wishes of the majority might prevail, the Establishment Clause of the First Amendment is addressed to this contingency and rejects [it]. The Constitution forbids the State to exact religious conformity from a student as the price of attending her own graduation."[90]

The nonsectarian nature of the prayers also does not change the constitutional analysis either. For government officials to insist on a nonsectarian format impermissibly "direct[s] and control[s] the content of the prayers."[91] Nonetheless, the religious character of what is intended and being performed remains.[92]

The bottom line is that under *Jones,* just like in *Lee,* a graduating senior has the "reasonable perception that she is being forced by the State to pray" at her graduation.[93] Rather than offer a novel way around *Lee*'s prohibition on graduation prayer, student-led prayer resulting from a student election presents similar constitutional problems. Those problems have been recognized by other federal courts that have declined the invitation to follow the Fifth Circuit.[94]

Still, the government has no power to prevent those who wish to pray in that manner from doing so—on their own. Even a school valedictorian, speaking without prompting, direction, or approval of school officials, can offer a prayer at graduation without violating the Establishment Clause or the *Lee* Court's admonitions, as a voluntary exercise of free-speech rights in a limited public forum.

Conclusion

Although the First Amendment rights of minors are not coextensive with those of adults, there are substantial limitations on government authority to restrict youthful speech or minors' access to ideas or images. One aspect of the different treatment of adults and minors is that material can be "obscene for minors" that is not obscene for adults. Still, to be "obscene for minors," the material must be obscene for the reasonable seventeen-year-old.

A fundamental obstacle to government regulations that limit access is that the restrictions may not have the spillover effect of limiting adult access to the materials, nor can they generally overrule parental choices about the kinds of materials they would permit their children to read or view. Such regulations must also be sensitive to the greater maturity and constitutionally protected rights of older minors to have access to material that might be more problematic for younger children. Meanwhile, children's expressive rights remain substantial and cannot be regulated in traditional public fora like the streets and parks in the same manner that they can in the context of the school environment.

In schools, officials have countervailing authority over student expressive rights to avoid disruption or the violation of the rights of others. That authority has often been exercised, with court approval, over vulgarity, profanity, and indecency. It may not be exercised, however, in a narrowly partisan or ideological manner.

It is within the school's curriculum or with respect to those school activities that appear to bear the school's imprimatur that official discretion is at its apex. Thus, student expression, textbooks, and other matters that would otherwise be immune from school censorship may be regulated to further the school's educational mission or for legitimate pedagogical reasons. Here, too, a school's authority may not be exercised with political objectives in mind. That authority cannot be exercised, either, to advance religion. Thus, laws or rules that are either anti-evolution or pro-creationism will be struck down, as will attempts by parents or even a majority of students to use the instrumentality of the public school to further their religious views. Most importantly, the courts have recognized that schools and school libraries should serve a goal of open inquiry and further the exploration of ideas, an objective that is palpably consistent with the philosophy underlying the First Amendment. For that reason, any removal of school library books will receive such heightened judicial scrutiny that the removal is unlikely to survive the constitutional objection.

NOTES

1. *Kingsley Pictures Corp.* v. *Regents,* 360 U.S. 684, 688 (1959).

2. *Prince* v. *Massachusetts,* 321 U.S. 158, 170 (1944).

3. *Ginsberg* v. *New York,* 390 U.S. 629, 639–40 (1968).

4. *Sable Communications, Inc.* v. *FCC,* 492 U.S. 115, 126 (1989).

5. *Ginsberg* v. *New York,* 390 U.S. 629, 639–40 (1968).

6. *FCC* v. *Pacifica Found.,* 438 U.S. 726 (1978).

7. *Bethel School Dist. No. 403* v. *Fraser,* 478 U.S. 675 (1986).

8. *Sable Communications, Inc.* v. *FCC,* 492 U.S. 115, 126 (1989).

9. *Butler* v. *Michigan,* 352 U.S. 380, 383 (1957).

10. *Id.*

11. *Reno* v. *ACLU,* 117 S.Ct. 2329 (1997).

12. *Erznoznik* v. *City of Jacksonville,* 422 U.S. 205 (1975).

13. *Id.* at 213–14.

14. *Bolger* v. *Youngs Drug Products Corp.,* 463 U.S. 60, 74 (1983)

15. *Id.* at 75 n. 30 (quoting *Erznoznik* v. *City of Jacksonville,* 422 U.S. 205, 212 (1975)).

16. *Id.*

17. *Id.* at 74–75.

18. *Reno* v. *ACLU,* 117 S.Ct. 2329, 2348 (1997).

19. *Id.* at 2348.

20. *Id.*

21. *American Booksellers v. Webb,* 919 F.2d 1493, 1504–05 (11th Cir. 1990) *cert. denied,* 500 U.S. 942 (1991) (relying on *Pope v. Illinois,* 481 U.S. 497 (1987)).

22. *Tinker v. Des Moines School Dist.,* 393 U.S. 503, 506, 511 (1969).

23. *Id.* at 513.

24. *Id.* at 508.

25. *Id.* at 508–09 (citation omitted).

26. *Erznoznik v. City of Jacksonville,* 422 U.S. 205, 213–14 (1975).

27. *Id.* at 214.

28. *Island Trees Union Free School District No. 26 v. Pico,* 457 U.S. 853 (1982).

29. *Id.* at 853.

30. *Id.* at 870 (plurality op.).

31. *Id.* at 871 (plurality op.).

32. *Id.* (plurality op.).

33. *Id.* (plurality op.).

34. *Id.* at 874 (plurality op.).

35. *Id.* at 879 (opinion of Blackmun, J.).

36. *Id.* at 868 (plurality op.) (footnote and citation omitted).

37. *Id.* at 869 (citing *Right to Read Defense Comm. v. School Comm.,* 454 F. Supp. 703, 715 (D. Mass. 1978)).

38. *Id.*

39. *Case v. Unified School Dist. No. 233,* 908 F. Supp. 864 (D. Kan. 1995).

40. *Id.* at 875–76.

41. *Hazelwood School Dist. v. Kuhlmeier,* 484 U.S. 260 (1988).

42. *Id.* at 266 (citations omitted).

43. *Id.* (citation omitted).

44. *Id.* at 271 (footnote omitted).

45. *Id.*

46. *Id.*

47. *Id.* at 272.

48. *Id.* at 273 (footnote omitted).

49. *Virgil v. School Board,* 862 F.2d 1517, 1525 (11th 1989).

50. *Hazelwood School Dist. v. Kuhlmeier,* 484 U.S. 260, 267 (1988).

51. *See, e.g., Mass. Gen. Laws Ann. Ch. 71,* sec. 82 (West 1982, Supp. 1994).

52. *See, e.g., Desilets v. Clearview Reg. Bd. of Educ.,* No. C-23-90 (NJ Super. Ct. Law Div. May 7, 1991), *aff'd on other grounds,* 630 A.2d 333 (NJ Super. Ct. A.D. 1993), aff'd, 647 A.2d 150 (NJ 1994); *Barcik v. Kubiaczyk,* 912 P.2d 408 (Or. App. 1996).

53. *Seyfried v. Walton,* 668 F.2d 213 (3rd Cir. 1981).

54. *Bethel School Dist. No. 403 v. Fraser,* 478 U.S. 675 (1986).

55. *Bystrom v. Fridley High School,* 822 F.2d 747 (8th Cir. 1987).

56. *Burch v. Barker,* 861 F.2d 1149 (9th Cir. 1987).

57. *Pratt v. Independent School Dist. No. 831,* 670 F.2d 771 (8th Cir. 1982).

58. *Id.* at 773.

59. *Thomas v. Board of Education,* 607 F.2d 1043, 1049 (2d Cir. 1979), *cert. denied,* 444 U.S. 1081 (1980).

60. *Id.* at 1050.

61. *Ambach v. Norwick,* 441 U.S. 68, 77 (1979).

62. *Island Trees Union Free School District No. 26 v. Pico,* 457 U.S. 853, 864 (1982) (plurality op.) (citation omitted).

63. *See Abington Township v. Schempp,* 374 U.S. 203 (1963).

64. *Epperson v. Arkansas,* 393 U.S. 97, 98–99 (1968).

65. *Island Trees Union Free School District No. 26 v. Pico,* 457 U.S. 853, 864 (1982).

66. *Epperson v. Arkansas,* 393 U.S. 97, 104 (1968).

67. *Id.* (quoting *Keyishian v. Board of Regents,* 385 U.S. 589, 603 (1967)).

68. *Id.* at 103.

69. *Id.* at 103–04.

70. *Id.* at 107.

71. *Id.* at 103.

72. *Edwards v. Aguillard,* 482, U.S. 578, 587 (1987).

73. *Id.* at 593.

74. *Id.* at 594.

75. *Id.* at 596.

76. *Smith v. Board of School Comm'rs,* 827 F.2d 684 (11th Cir. 1987).

77. *Id.* at 690.

78. *Id.* at 692.

79. *Mozert v. Hawkins County Board of Educ.,* 827 F.2d 1058, 1064 (6th Cir. 1987), *cert. denied,* 484 U.S. 1066 (1988).

80. *Epperson v. Arkansas,* 393 U.S. 97, 106 (1968).

81. *Mozert v. Hawkins County Board of Educ.,* 827 F.2d 1058, 1069 (6th Cir. 1987), *cert. denied,* 484 U.S. 1066 (1988).

82. *Jones v. Clear Creek Independent School Dist.*, 977 F.2d 963 (5th Cir. 1992), *cert. denied*, 508 U.S. 967 (1993).

83. *Id.* at 969.

84. *Lee* v. *Weisman*, 505 U.S. 577 (1992).

85. *Id.* at 593–95.

86. *Id.* at 589.

87. *Id.* at 590, 592.

88. *Id.* at 593.

89. *Id.*

90. *Id.* at 596.

91. *Id.* at 588.

92. *See Wallace* v. *Jaffree*, 472 U.S. 38 (1985) (holding that Alabama's moment-of-silence law was religiously motivated, anticipated that such a moment would be used for prayer, and thus was unconstitutional).

93. *Lee* v. *Weisman*, 505 U.S. 577, 593 (1992).

94. *See, e.g., Harris* v. *Joint School Dist. No. 241*, 41 F.3d 447 (9th Cir. 1994).

CHAPTER 9

Cyberspace—
The Last Frontier

The wild and revolutionary nature of cyberspace raises anew the wide variety of First Amendment issues that have plagued all previous forms of communication. The many still-unanswered free-speech questions as well as many seemingly settled issues are likely to be reexamined by the courts in the context of the information superhighway. None of this is entirely unexpected. Long ago, Supreme Court Justice Robert Jackson observed that discrete media forms "have differing natures, values, abuses, and dangers. Each, in my view, is a law unto itself."[1]

Modern cases have made Jackson's sentiment a feature of free-speech jurisprudence. In upholding the constitutionality of the Fairness Doctrine—which once required broadcasters to air programming on controversial issues, ensure that all responsible viewpoints had access to airwaves, and grant a "right of reply" to those who had been personally attacked in a broadcast—the Court noted that "differences in the characteristics of new media justify differences in the First Amendment standards applied to them."[2] Those differences account for why such a "right of reply" could be validly attached to broadcasting but would amount to an unconstitutional invasion into the editorial function if applied to newspapers, according to the Court.[3]

The case law thus establishes that "[e]ach medium of expression, of course, must be assessed for First Amendment purposes by standards suited to it, for each may present its own problems."[4] In this regard, the law works by apt analogy. Does the medium in question more resemble broadcasting than print? An affirmative answer leads to one form of analysis; a negative one leads to a different form with potentially contradictory results.

The Communications Decency Act

For cyberspace, the analogy issue was the brooding omnipresence as Congress overwhelmingly enacted the Communications Decency Act (CDA) as part of its overhaul of telecommunications law in 1996. The CDA criminalized the online transmission of "any comment, request, suggestion, proposal, image or other communication which is . . . indecent" to a person known to be under the age of eighteen, as well as the display of "patently offensive" material "in a manner available to" a person under eighteen. One could avoid violating the act through "good faith, reasonable, effective and appropriate actions" to restrict minor access or by requiring a valid proof of age to obtain access. Supporters of the CDA claimed that the Internet was a form of electronic communication no different from broadcasting. Because the Court had permitted the FCC to regulate broadcast indecency to protect young minds,[5] they contended Internet indecency should be well within the government's regulatory authority.

The principal sponsor of the legislation, Senator James Exon (D-Nebraska), claimed that if "an individual were distributing pornographic photos, cartoons, videos, and stories to children, or if someone were posting lewd photographs on lampposts and telephone poles for all to see, or if children were welcome to enter and browse adult book stores and triple X rated video arcades, there would be a public outrage [sufficient] . . . that most people, under those circumstances, would immediately call the police to arrest and charge any person responsible for such offenses." Because, to him, such activity could clearly be criminalized, Senator Exon saw no constitutional impediment to exacting criminal penalties when the same activities could take place "in America's electronic neighborhood . . . via a child's computer."

In the debate before the vote on the CDA, he continued: "[I]t is no exaggeration to say that the most disgusting, repulsive pornography is only a few clicks away from any child with a computer. I am not talking just about *Playboy* and *Penthouse* magazines. By comparison, those magazines pale in offensiveness with the other things that are readily available. I am talking about the most hardcore, perverse types of pornography, photos, and stories featuring torture, child abuse, and bestiality."[6]

The effect of the CDA was enormously broad. Rather than incorporate a "harmful to minors" standard, it utilized the much more vague and subjective terms of *indecency* and *patently offensive*. Ironically, the material it would cover was so broad that the U.S. Supreme Court case that CDA supporters relied upon to support the act's constitutionality was made illegal to post on the Internet by the CDA itself. The Court's opinion in that case, *FCC v. Pacifica Foundation,* ran afoul of the CDA because it reprints, as an appendix, a George Carlin monologue that the Court adjudged to be indecent and subject to prohibition under the Federal Communication Commission's broadcast regulations.[7] This kind of breadth placed public libraries that provided patrons with access to the World Wide Web in jeopardy of criminal prosecution.

Two sets of plaintiffs immediately challenged the constitutionality of the CDA's indecency and patently offensive prohibitions. No challenge was made to the act's anti-obscenity provisions, because obscenity was already illegal in cyberspace and falls outside the First Amendment's protections. The first plaintiff coalition, led by the American Civil Liberties Union, included some cyberspace public interest groups, several AIDS education groups, Planned Parenthood, and others whose communications could run afoul of the act. The second, led by the American Library Association and the Freedom to Read Foundation, included major online companies (such as America Online, Prodigy, and Microsoft), booksellers, publishers, journalists, and other citizens groups. The two cases were consolidated into one.

During the trial in a federal courtroom in Philadelphia, government witnesses made some curious statements about how they intended to implement the CDA. Howard Schmidt, a federal agent who specialized in computer crimes, said that the Justice Department would not prosecute an anti-AIDS Internet site that used a graphic illustration of an erect penis to demonstrate proper condom use, but would prosecute the online display of the *Vanity Fair* magazine cover featuring actress Demi Moore, nude and pregnant, even though the image was displayed on newsstands and in newspaper advertisements. The critical difference, Schmidt explained, was that the first site was clearly educational, while the other was merely "fun."

A specially convened three-judge federal court struck down the act. Of particular significance among the three separate opinions, Judge Stewart Dalzell wrote that "the Internet may fairly be regarded as a never-ending worldwide conversation. The Government may not, through the CDA, interrupt that conversation. As the most participatory form of mass speech yet developed, the Internet deserves the highest protection from governmental intrusion."[8] He went on to criticize the government's attempt to justify the CDA's intrusion on adult speech by asserting a child-protection rationale for being "as dangerous as it is compelling. Laws regulating speech for the protection of children have no limiting principle, and a well-intentioned law restricting protected speech on the basis of its content is, nevertheless, state-sponsored censorship."[9]

The U.S. Supreme Court subsequently reached similar conclusions. Conceding "the legitimacy and importance of the congressional goal of protecting children from harmful materials"[10] and recognizing that sexual expression on the Internet ranged from "the modestly titillating to the hardest-core,"[11] the Court nonetheless found the act violated the First Amendment.

In doing so, the Court rejected a number of analogies that the government offered in defense of the CDA. The statute, it concluded, was not like an "obscene for minors" law, was not like the prohibition on broadcast indecency, and was not another form of zoning regulation, concentrating similar businesses in a single location. In fact, the CDA covered a far greater range of communications than these types of laws, with potentially unsettling results for free speech in the twenty-first century.

In the case that upheld "obscene for minors" laws, the Court had noted a saving grace of the law was that it still permitted parents to purchase and show their children the magazines prohibited for sale directly to minors.[12] In doing so, the government properly conceded that parental choices should usually take precedence. The CDA, on the other hand, treated parental consent or participation in permitting their child to access indecent or patently offensive Internet messages as though it were a criminal act. In fact, the *Reno* Court observed that, under the CDA, "a parent who sent his 17-year-old college freshman information on birth control via e-mail could be incarcerated even though neither he, his child, nor anyone in their home community, found the material 'indecent' or 'patently offensive,' if the college town's community thought otherwise."[13]

Another difference was that the "obscene for minors" statute the Court upheld, though not the CDA, was limited to commercial transactions.[14] As a result, the CDA covered a wide variety of free government-generated material and private communications available on the Web that were not subject to harmful-to-minors regulation. A third distinction between the two laws was that "obscene for minors" laws, but not the CDA, exempted from its coverage material found to have "redeeming social importance for minors."[15] Even material otherwise considered obscene becomes protected speech when it has serious literary, artistic, political, or scientific value. How, the Court wondered, could indecent or offensive material be accorded less protection than obscene material? Finally, the harmful-to-minors law the Court upheld covered persons under the age of seventeen, while the CDA included those under eighteen, adding a full year of coverage of those on the cusp of adulthood.[16] As the Court later noted, it is "clear that the strength of the Government's interest in protecting minors is not equally strong throughout" adolescence.[17]

The Court also rejected analogy to the *Pacifica* case, where the FCC's regulation of indecent broadcasts was upheld. Unlike that regulation, the Court said the CDA's "broad categorical prohibitions are not limited to particular times and are not dependent on any evaluation by an agency familiar with the unique characteristics of the Internet."[18] Courts have traditionally deferred to expert agency evaluations; here no agency with a long history of familiarity was involved because of the novelty of the Internet. Second, the FCC rule at issue in *Pacifica* was not a criminal prohibition; the CDA was. Thus, the stakes were raised because punishment could include imprisonment, and a more careful evaluation of the competing First Amendment issues was in order.

Finally, the *Pacifica* decision rested substantially on the FCC rule's application "to a medium which as a matter of history had 'received the most limited First Amendment protection,' in part, because warnings could not adequately protect the listener from unexpected program content."[19] In so declaring, the Court was referencing its finding in *Pacifica* that one could be assaulted by surprise by a string of expletives simply by turning on the radio or television set, thereby justifying a time-sensitive regulation.[20] In contrast, no such experience could occur on the Internet because, as the District Court found, communication over the Internet "requires a series of affirmative steps more deliberate and directed than merely turning a dial."[21] To the extent that a child-protection justification entered into the equation, the District Court had held, and the Supreme Court accepted, that a "child requires some sophistication and some ability to read to retrieve material and thereby to use the Internet unattended."[22] The Court also noted that, unlike television, there was no spectrum scarcity that required a traffic-cop-like government presence on the Internet, where expressive access is potentially universal.

The Supreme Court also rejected the notion that the CDA was no different than a zoning ordinance that kept adult bookstores and movie theaters out of residential areas. Such zoning laws are aimed at secondary

effects, the attraction of criminal elements to a neighborhood or a diminu-
tion of property values, and are not aimed at speech that is deemed undesirable or problematic. The CDA, however, was applicable to the "entire
universe of cyberspace" and constituted a content-specific blanket restriction on speech, the Court said.[23]

In deciding that communication over the Internet should receive the
highest level of constitutional protection available, strict scrutiny, the
Court firmly anchored this "dynamic, multifaceted category of communication" with content "as diverse as human thought" in an eighteenth-
century context that would have been familiar to those who framed the
First Amendment:

> Through the use of chat rooms, any person with a phone line can become a
> town crier with a voice that resonates farther than it could from any soapbox.
> Through the use of Web pages, mail exploders, and newsgroups, the same in-
> dividual can become a pamphleteer.[24]

The Court found that the CDA violated the First Amendment because it was not narrowly tailored to protect minors from potentially
harmful materials and instead "suppresses a large amount of speech that
adults have a constitutional right to receive and to address to one another."[25] Among speech the Court recognized could fall within the
CDA's prohibitions were "a serious discussion about birth control practices, homosexuality, the First Amendment issues raised by the Appendix to our *Pacifica* opinion, or the consequences of prison rape,"[26] as
well as "artistic images that include nude subjects, and arguably the
card catalog of the Carnegie Library."[27] The Court concluded that the
CDA "unquestionably silences some speakers whose messages would be
entitled to constitutional protection."[28]

One way that the CDA silenced protected speech was by imposing a
technologically infeasible or prohibitively expensive requirement that
speakers verify the age of all who attempt to access the allegedly indecent or patently offensive message. The requirement imposed a significant prior restraint on speech, which can occur when compliance is
practically impossible or added expense is incurred. On the other hand,
at the receiving end, the Court noted, parents wishing to control their
children's access to such material have a reasonably effective means of
doing so through filtering software installed on their home computers.[29]

If the CDA was really intended to assist parents in bringing up their
children, it would have shown greater solicitude for the parenting

decisions of those who want their children to see some of the sites or receive some of the messages that the act made criminal. Instead, a parent who permitted a seventeen-year-old to obtain Internet information from a site "she, in her parental judgment, deems appropriate could face a lengthy prison term."[30] So would "a parent who sent his 17-year-old college freshman information on birth control via e-mail."[31]

Finally, the Court rejected the government's last three arguments, designed to save the CDA. First, the government argued that there are adequate alternative channels for indecent communications. The Court derided this argument as the "equivalent to arguing that a statute could ban leaflets on certain subjects as long as individuals are free to publish books."[32] Since 1939, the Court has said "one is not to have the exercise of his liberty of expression in appropriate places abridged on the plea that it may be exercised in some other place."[33]

Second, the government argued that the CDA is relatively narrow because it only applied when there was knowledge of receipt by a specific person under the age of eighteen. In rejecting that argument, the Court said, even if true, it would permit an opponent of such speech to enter a chat room and "inform the would-be discoursers that his 17-year-old child . . . would be present."[34] Such a situation would constitute a "heckler's veto," whereby a single dissenter could silence otherwise protected speech, a result the First Amendment does not permit.

Finally, the government argued that the CDA contained an implicit exception for those Internet communications that have redeeming social value, a position the Court found unsupported by the statute's language or the legislative record.

The Court concluded that the "interest in encouraging freedom of expression in a democratic society outweighs any theoretical but unproven benefit of censorship."[35]

Relying on the *Reno* decision, a federal court has also invalidated a state CDA that used a harmful-to-minors standard as a violation of the Constitution's Commerce Clause.[36] That clause stands as a bar against a state's attempt to regulate conduct outside the state's borders and against burdens on interstate commerce, an area that falls within the exclusive authority of the federal government. Similarly, another federal court struck down a state law that made it a crime to use an online pseudonym or create unauthorized links to sites with trade names or logos.[37]

In response to the Court's decision in *Reno,* Congress subsequently enacted the Child Online Protection Act (COPA), a bar on commercial

Internet expression that is "harmful to minors." The limitation to commercial expression and the harmful-to-minors standard was an attempt to fit within the rubric of the *Reno* decision. Nonetheless, a federal trial court issued a preliminary injunction stopping the government from enforcing COPA upon determining that the plaintiffs were likely to succeed on the merits and that COPA "imposes a burden on speech that is protected for adults."[38] The case is still pending as this book is being written.

What *Reno* and its progeny teach are that laws or practices that attempt to limit Internet access out of a concern for juvenile innocence

1. cannot adversely affect adult access to the same material,
2. must respect the rights of access of older minors who are near-adults,
3. must respect the rights of parents who choose to permit their children to access sites that others might deem appropriate only for more mature individuals,
4. cannot rely on a defense that the access that is denied might be had in other fora, and
5. must be evaluated for constitutional purposes in the same highly free-speech protective manner that restrictions on access to newspapers and books are.

That last aspect of the case is likely to be the most significant aspect of the *Reno* decision. It strongly suggests that public libraries treat the Internet no differently than their policies on books.

Workplace Issues

Although Internet speech is evaluated under standards of strict scrutiny, restrictions on government-employee access to the Internet on the job may be susceptible to further restrictions, according to a recent decision by the Fourth Circuit. The issue arose after the state of Virginia passed a law that prohibited state employees from using state-owned or leased computers to access sexually explicit Internet sites without prior agency approval. The state justified the law on the grounds that it was necessary to maintain operational efficiency and to avoid the creation of a sexually hostile work environment. Several state university professors challenged the statute as an unconstitutional interference with academic freedom. They claimed that their positions necessitated research into sexual themes in art, literature, history, and philosophy, and other topics of current interest such as sexual crimes and diseases.

The professors won their case at the trial level because a federal judge found the law discriminated against sexual content when other content could be at least as distracting to employees or hold the same potential to harass others. That decision was reversed by the Fourth Circuit, which found the statute to be a legitimate exercise of government authority. Crucially, the court found that the "challenged aspect of the Act does not regulate the speech of the citizenry in general, but rather the speech of state employees in their capacity as employees."[39] In so saying, the court determined that the state could restrict employees from accessing or engaging in expression that is part of their work for the government, even when it could not similarly restrict a member of the public. One exception to this general rule that the court recognized was that the state could not restrict the employee with respect to expression on matters of public concern.

Applying the decision literally to public libraries in the states of Maryland, Virginia, West Virginia, and the Carolinas, where the case has precedential effect, laws may be passed that generally restrict on-duty public-library employees in their Internet access on nonideological grounds, even as members of the public access the same Internet sites that are off-limits to those librarians. Because libraries are limited public forums, such a content-based restriction on a member of the public cannot be effectuated. Head librarians in Virginia, where such a law exists, may still give permission for legitimate employee needs of access, such as a librarian assisting a patron in obtaining access to an employee-forbidden site.

In this case, the state had provided two basic justifications for the law, even though a moral objection probably motivated the legislature to enact the law in the first place. First, Virginia asserted that its interest in operational efficiency was an attempt to prevent employees from pursuing amusement in the form of voyeurism on "company" time. As was discussed in chapter 7, on workplace rights, operational efficiency can sometimes be used to defeat an employee's claim of right to speak out on the job as to a matter of public concern. Second, it claimed that the law advanced the state's anti-sexual-harassment policies. The Fourth Circuit did not address this rationale, finding it unnecessary to explore the state's justifications for the law.

The trial court did, however. It found the state's anti-harassment claim to be more pretext than real. It noted that the law only targeted sexually explicit Web addresses but did not include within its prohibitions material demeaning or offensive to women that was not sexually explicit, nor Internet material that was racially, ethnically, or religiously harassing.[40] Instead, the targeting of sexually explicit sites, the court said, was a form of content discrimination forbidden by the First Amendment. At the same time, the statute overbroadly covered materials that could not constitute sexual harassment. Instead, the broad prohibition interfered with "countless work-related endeavors by state employees dealing with sexuality and the human body."[41] Importantly, the court, citing other judicial decisions declared, "[T]he mere presence of sexually explicit materials in the workplace does not foster a hostile work environment or otherwise violate gender discrimination laws."[42]

This determination by an overruled trial court does not have the standing of precedent but does provide some persuasive authority for how a court might examine the issue.

A second case, decided by the same judge, involved a constitutional challenge to a public library's adoption of a filtering system on all of its Internet access terminals. The library system attempted to justify its filtering policy as a means to prevent sexual harassment of employees. The court rejected that rationale, noting that the library had the burden of showing the justification was "'real, not merely conjectural and that the regulation will in fact alleviate these harms in a direct and material way."[43] The court also noted with approval another federal court's declaration that merely "alleging the need to avoid sexual harassment is not enough . . . the defendant[] must show that the threat of disruption is actual, material, and substantial."[44] The evidence showed only three isolated instances of possible harassment in public libraries anywhere in the nation. On that basis, the court found it unreasonable to consider the problem a real one.[45]

Finally, the court held that the policy was not the least-restrictive means to advance the library system's interest in preventing sexual harassment. The installation of "privacy screens," which the evidence had shown worked well at other libraries, was an adequate means by which free-speech rights could be preserved without imposing the images viewed on others.[46]

These two decisions appear to be in line with the developing law of sexual harassment. Although a public library has an obligation to prevent sexual harassment of its employees, there also is a First Amendment right on the part of patrons to access the full range of protected First Amendment speech once a library undertakes to provide Internet service. As a limited public forum, the public library has no more authority to prevent a patron from accessing pornography on the Internet in the name of an anti-harassment policy than it does to prevent other patrons from reading *Playboy, Mein Kampf,* or hate literature in the main reading room.

It must, however, take steps to prevent an employee from feeling the brunt of a patron's repeated attention that is obviously an attempt to use Internet images to harass the employee. Courts have found that it is possible for a customer to engage in sexual harassment of employees that an employer is obligated to prevent.[47] Still, libraries may stand in a different status than most employers. In a case involving a store that sold, among other things, adult magazines, the court found that anti-harassment laws would violate the First Amendment if they required the removal of adult materials in a store in that business.[48] By the same token, if a public library were required to eliminate access to sexually expressive materials that are fully protected by the First Amendment, the underlying anti-harassment law would trench upon free-speech rights.

Nonetheless, in such circumstances where a patron attempts to harass an employee, prudent policy would call for an explicit, written, and well-articulated and publicized anti-harassment policy and the assignment, if possible, of another employee to Internet assistance to whom such images did not have the same severe offensive impact. By this action, the offending patron's objective is defeated. Moreover, it would not be a violation of the patron's First Amendment rights if the anti-harassment policy treated a patron's continued and pervasive attempts at harassing an employee to be grounds for the forfeiture of Internet privileges for a defined period of time.

Filtering and the First Amendment

Internet access has now reached an estimated 73 percent saturation point in public libraries, with continued rapid growth expected. Its arrival has produced cries of outrage from some people who think the mere availability of access to be the equivalent of a porn shop taking up residence in the library. "It is one thing to allow X-rated movie theaters and bookstores to peddle their smut to adults who pay for it themselves," wrote syndicated columnist and former Reagan administration official Linda Chavez, "but it is quite another to force taxpayers to provide the same material and worse in a county building open to persons of all ages."[49]

One organization, relying on unconfirmed patron and staff complaints, internal memos, e-mail messages, or incident reports about patrons accessing pornographic or sexually explicit material on public Internet terminals, as well as press accounts and librarian discussions, claims that it has documented 503 incidents of pornography access in public libraries, of which 231 involved adults accessing sexual material. Going by the name Filtering Facts, the group is an opponent of access to sexually expressive materials in public libraries and of the American Library Association's (ALA) policies on intellectual freedom. Among the incidents it claims to have documented were twenty instances of adults accessing child pornography, which, if true, would constitute a crime. It also claimed 195 instances of children accessing pornography. In releasing its report, Filtering Facts president David Burt accused the ALA, by virtue of its policy favoring the use of privacy screens around Internet terminals, of wanting "public libraries to literally create peep show booths for children, except there's no slot for quarters because taxpayers have already paid the quarter."[50]

Along with politicians who see a cost-free moral issue on which to take a public stand and who realize that officeholders are rarely penalized for opposing free speech, sincerely concerned parents have heard these reports and have pressed libraries to install filtering software. Such software blocks access to Internet sites, often based on a database of sites and a preset list of words deemed likely to be found on sites deemed problematic by the programmer. Critics have accused those who market such software of incorporating political biases into the programming.

One popular filtering program, Cybersitter, claims to block 95 percent of all "objectionable" content, while also admitting that it "sometimes" blocks unobjectionable sites as well because its blacklist of offensive words cannot be context-sensitive. Among the nonsexual sites Cybersitter has blocked is the home page of the feminist National Organization for Woman. Another program, Surfwatch, provides access-blocking ability in five areas of potential concern: drugs, alcohol, and tobacco; gambling; sexually explicit images or text; violence; and hate speech. It also claims to be capable of blocking the use of chat rooms. Surfwatch boasts a 90 to 95 percent success capability in blocking explicit sites, but it has also been known to block any triple-X site, including the home page for Super Bowl XXXI.

Cyber Patrol's blocking programming covers violence, profanity, nudity, sex, "gross depictions," intolerance, satanic/cult, drugs/drug culture, militant/extremist, sex education, questionable/illegal material, gambling, and alcohol and tobacco.[51] A 1997 report accused Cyber Patrol of blocking sites based on the sponsor's liberal politics, including the Internet free-speech group, the Electronic Frontier Foundation; Planned Parenthood; an animal rights group; and feminist groups. Its sensitivities were so great that even personal ads were enough to cause a site to be blocked. Even though it has since been refined, Cyber Patrol continues to block the news-group-laden site Deja News, because the site's archive of messages includes some Cyber Patrol considers too sexual in nature. X-Stop, yet another filtering software, claims to have achieved an astonishing 99 percent success rate in blocking hard-core porn sites, yet testers have found that it also blocks the Web addresses for Godiva chocolates, *Redbook* magazine, and medical and gay sites that have nothing to do with hard-core sex.

Down the road, a new system is being developed. The Platform for Internet Content Selection (PICS) is an industry-developed system that will be capable of providing filtering in the future. The system depends upon the self-rating of Web sites that would be encoded onto the sites themselves. Internet browsers would be capable of reading the rating and providing or denying access depending on the settings activated by the user. For those Web sites that do not engage in voluntary ratings, the industry would develop default ratings based on sexual and violent content.

Despite the flaws in the current generation of filters, such software has found a foothold, sometimes by force of statute, in public libraries. The ALA Office for Information Technology Policy has estimated that 14.6 percent of the public libraries offering Internet access use filtering software. This number is consistent with several statewide surveys. Other libraries, though, permit uninhibited access, sometimes with a posted warning, along the lines of

> The Internet is an unregulated medium. It offers access to a wealth of material that is personally, professionally, and culturally enriching. It also enables access to material that may be offensive, disturbing, and/or illegal.

Such a policy of unimpeded access in Livermore, California, prompted an unsuccessful lawsuit by a parent. After discovering that her twelve-year-old son had, on several occasions, downloaded images of naked women at the public library and later printed the pictures at a relative's house, this woman filed suit with the help of a politically conservative legal group. They sought to force the city to cease operating computers from which children may access harmful material. A state court judge dismissed the lawsuit as being without merit; the Constitution provides no grounds to force a library to filter.[52]

It is likely, however, that the Constitution does provide grounds to challenge a public library's policy that places filters on its Internet access terminals. Filtering all terminals, out of a concern for children, amounts to "an unnecessarily broad suppression of speech addressed to adults."[53]

So far, only one court has addressed the issue, but its analysis is in line with basic First Amendment principles and is likely to be followed by other courts. The trustees of the Loudoun County, Virginia, public libraries had adopted a "Policy on Internet Sexual Harassment," which required all library computers to be outfitted with site-blocking software capable of impeding access to child pornography, obscenity, and material that is harmful to minors. Under the policy, computers would be located in full view of library staff for oversight purposes. Furthermore, the library would not provide e-mail, chat rooms, or pornography. Anyone accessing pornography and refusing to stop would be referred to the police. To effectuate the policy, the library purchased X-Stop filtering software. In addition to blocking the types of sites anticipated by the policy, X-Stop also inhibited access to sites deemed permissible by the policy, such as the Safer Sex Page, Books for Gay and Lesbian Teens/Youth, and the Renaissance Transgender Association.

The policy allowed a patron to ask that particular sites be unblocked by filing a written request that included her or his name, the site, and the reason for seeking access. A librarian would then review the request and determine whether to unblock the site manually.

A group of residents sued in federal court to challenge the constitutionality of the policy. The court struck down the policy as a violation of First Amendment rights.[54] Noting that the library board's expert, David Burt of Filtering Facts, admitted that "[f]iltering cannot be rightly compared to 'selection,' since it involves an active, rather than passive exclusion of certain types of content," the court reaffirmed its earlier ruling that the board's action is "appropriately characterized as a removal decision" and should be viewed as a content-based restriction, deserving of strict scrutiny.[55]

In further finding that the library was a limited public forum, it noted that the library board had repeatedly indicated that the library's "primary objective" was to provide people with unrestricted "access to all avenues of ideas," regardless of age, race, religion, origin, background, or views.[56] As such, strict-scrutiny analysis applied, unless the restrictions could be viewed as a time, place, or manner regulation, a position the board unsuccessfully pressed on the court.

In rejecting filtering as a time, place, or manner restriction, the court relied on the U.S. Supreme Court's rulings that neither "content-based blanket restrictions on speech" nor the kinds of "secondary effects" that justify zoning regulations can be based on the subject or viewpoint of any speech.[57]

Having determined that strict scrutiny applied, the court found little evidence that a real problem existed from unfiltered Internet access. As the library's expert, Burt was able to point to only four incidents throughout the country:

1. a complaint that in another Virginia county a boy had allegedly accessed pornography, which was resolved by the library through the installation of privacy screens to protect the sensibilities of offended patrons;
2. a newspaper report from Los Angeles County, California, that use of X-rated chat rooms, personal ads, and sex sites forced those seeking to do research on the Internet to wait in line;
3. an experience in Orange County, Florida, that people were using library computers for pornography, causing the adoption of a filtering policy there; and
4. two instances of children accessing pornography in an Austin, Texas, library.

Without any instances of harassing or hostile environment complaints and insufficient evidence to demonstrate a substantial disruption of the library, the court ruled that the board had failed to show that its policy was reasonably necessary to effectuate a real government interest.

Finally, even if a compelling government interest was at stake, the court ruled that less restrictive means of achieving legitimate ends were available:

> First, the installation of privacy screens is a much less restrictive alternative that would further [the board's] interest in preventing the development of a sexually hostile environment. Second, there is undisputed evidence in the record that charging library staff with casual monitoring of Internet use is neither extremely intrusive nor a change from other library policies. [Testimony had established there were] no problems with the library staff being responsible for "'shooing' people away from sites we know are objectionable, just as

we always have with prepubescent boys giggling over gynecological pictures in medical books." . . . Third, filtering software could be installed on only some Internet terminals and minors could be limited to using those terminals. Alternately, the library could install filtering software that could be turned off when an adult is using the terminal. While we find that all of these alternatives are less restrictive than the Policy, we do not find that any of them would necessarily be constitutional if implemented. That question is not before us.[58]

In so ruling, the judge, who had trained as a librarian before her career in the law, was merely noting a variety of means that were available as more free-speech friendly solutions to the supposed problem. In doing so, she expressed no advisory opinion on whether any or all of these were capable of meeting constitutional objections. As we will see later in this chapter, several of them face considerable constitutional opposition.

In addition to failing to meet the requirements of strict scrutiny, the Loudoun policy was found "overinclusive" because it limited "all patrons, adult and juvenile, to material deemed fit for juveniles."[59] Finally, the court found that the policy contained inadequate standards for restricting access, as well as inadequate safeguards to ensure prompt judicial review of overly zealous restrictions. In fact, the use of X-Stop was ruled standardless. X-Stop blocks some 80,000 Internet sites, of which the library staff had reviewed about 172. By entrusting initial blocking decisions to a private vendor who does not share the criteria it uses to block sites, the library failed to meet the first requirement of legitimate restraints on access: adequate standards.

The court did not discuss the constitutional implications of delegating decisions on how to implement the government's interest to a third party. In other areas of law, however, it is well-established that the third party must adopt constitutionally valid standards if it is to be utilized as a stand-in for the government itself. None of the forms of filtering software meet those standards. They are primarily utilized in the home by parents, who do not have to comply with constitutional requirements, and are designed to reach material that parents consider to be troubling forms of expression for their children, even if permissible under the First Amendment.

Moreover, by forcing people to petition to have sites unblocked, the policy had a "severe chilling effect" by making people publicly declare their desire to see something that someone had deemed inappropriate.[60] Even if the requirement did not intimidate patrons, it resulted in an impermissible delay in the exercise of First Amendment freedoms, the court ruled.[61] The court's decision on this issue is also well rooted in the U.S. Supreme Court's jurisprudence. In 1965, the Court invalidated a law that required people to tell the post office in writing that they were willing to receive "communist political propaganda" in the mail. The Court found that the requirement would have attached a stigma to the requesting individual and thus would have a deterrent effect on people's willingness to acknowledge that they want such material "because it requires an official act (*viz.,* returning the reply card) as a limitation on the unfettered exercise of the addressee's First Amendment rights."[62] The same might be said for any requirement that a minor file a parental permission form before receiving access to unfiltered Internet access. In certain circumstances, the U.S. Supreme Court has recognized that minors may have a right of access to information without seeking parental permission or giving a parent notice.[63]

Similarly, the Court also invalidated a more recent law that required cable television operators to segregate and block indecent programming unless the customer wrote to request its reception as being too restrictive and " 'sacrificing' important First Amendment interests for too 'speculative a gain.' "[64]

The "Tap on the Shoulder" and Other Policing of Patron Use

The court's decision in this case, known as *Mainstream Loudoun,* will likely guide other courts facing similar issues. Unlike the issue of selection versus censorship, where considerations of limited funds provides librarians with greater discretion in selecting which books to purchase, full Internet access costs no more than limited Internet access. Because cost considerations are removed from the equation, a more straightforward First Amendment analysis necessarily attends. That is why some of the less restrictive alternatives noted by the court also run into constitutional problems.

For example, "shooing" people away from objectionable sites—sometimes known as the "tap on the shoulder" approach—fails to establish adequate and knowable standards for restricting Internet access and invests too much discretion in a public official. It is clear that offensiveness is not a basis for restricting First Amendment rights.[65] It is equally clear that other people's reactions to the expression accessed are not a content-neutral justification for restricting speech.[66] Thus, with strict scrutiny being the appropriate level of First Amendment analysis, only sites that constitute a form of unprotected speech or that otherwise would not be permitted in the books or other materials in the library because of compelling state interests could be restricted in this fashion. Even so, privacy screens or polarized covers that permit only the person in front of the terminal to see the content provide a less restrictive means to accomplish that interest.

A further problem with investing some official with authority to "shoo" or "tap" is that it gives considerable discretion to the librarian. Without "explicit standards for those who [must] apply them . . . [a librarian is] impermissibly [invested with] an ad hoc and subjective basis [for exclusion], with the attendant dangers of arbitrary and discriminatory application."[67]

The *Mainstream Loudoun* court also suggested the possibility that minors could be limited to using filtered terminals and librarians could turn off the filters when an adult is using the terminal. These approaches are equally problematic, however. As noted in chapter 8, children have substantial First Amendment rights. Even harmful-to-minors laws must permit distribution to youth of those materials that "have a serious literary, artistic, political or scientific value for a legitimate minority of normal, older adolescents."[68] Nudity alone is not enough to justify a bar on minors' access.[69] Where these overinclusive filters prevent them from accessing material that they have a free-speech right to see, those rights are violated.

Just as untenable, the one-size-fits-all nature of the filters improperly and unconstitutionally restricts the near-adult of age seventeen to the same sites deemed appropriate to the six-year-old.[70] Filters cannot be sufficiently age-sensitive to adapt to the full range of ages that use the library. Finally, the requirement that an adult ask a librarian to turn off the filter imposes the same kind of potentially chilling effect and stigma that was described earlier. The Constitution appears to require that the "off" position be the default setting for any filter.

Conclusion

The U.S. Supreme Court has concluded that cyberspace receives the highest level of protection that the First Amendment affords. As a result, the same considerations that apply to printed words and images apply as well to the electronic word and the digital image. Any policy on Internet access that a public library adopts cannot adversely affect adult access to protected speech, must respect the rights of access of both older minors and younger minors who have a right to access protected speech and some speech that parents could find troubling but have serious value for youth, and must respect the rights of parents who choose to permit their children to access sites that others might deem appropriate only for more mature individuals. Most importantly, such policies should be content and viewpoint neutral in all respects.

Although many parents will be concerned that little Johnny could use a library terminal to access nude images, the First Amendment does not permit a public library to enforce that parent's sensibilities. As part of the process of obtaining a child's library card, most libraries require a parent to take responsibility for the child's reading materials. This disclaimer of responsibility puts parents on notice that the library staff does not act in the place of the parent while the child is at the library (a legal concept known as *in loco parentis*). Such disclaimers should, wisely, indicate that this responsibility applies as well to Internet usage at the library.

In fact, a library's Internet policies should be easily accessible for all and posted in conspicuous locations in the library. In addition, to assist parents concerned about sites their children might visit, a library would be prudent to offer a list of recommended sites, such as the "great sites" compilation posted by the American Library Association and found at http://www.ala.org/parentspage/greatsites.

It is also advisable to make use of other devices that will help minimize offense to patrons or employees. Privacy and polarized screens will ensure that patrons accessing material that have the potential to offend will not impose their Internet choices on others. The information superhighway is a boon to the idea of access to knowledge. It ought not be stymied out of a concern for the dark alleys and seedy neighborhoods that are also present.

NOTES

1. *Kovacs v. Cooper*, 336 U.S. 77, 97 (1949) (Jackson, J., concurring).

2. *Red Lion Broadcasting Co. v. FCC*, 395 U.S. 367, 386 (1969).

3. *Miami Herald Publishing Co. v. Tornillo*, 418 U.S. 241 (1974).

4. *Southeastern Promotions, Ltd. v. Conrad*, 420 U.S. 546, 557 (1975) (citing *Joseph Burstyn, Inc. v. Wilson*, 343 U.S. 495, 503 (1952)).

5. *FCC v. Pacifica Found.*, 438 U.S. 726 (1978).

6. Cong. Rec., 104th Cong., at S8330 (Remarks of Sen. Exon) (June 14, 1995).

7. *FCC* v. *Pacifica Found.*, 438 U.S. 726 (1978).

8. *ACLU* v. *Reno*, 929 F. Supp. 824, 883 (E.D. Pa. 1996) (Dalzell, J.), *aff'd*, 117 S.Ct. 2329 (1997).

9. *Id.* at 882.

10. *Reno* v. *ACLU*, 117 S.Ct. 2329, 2334 (1997).

11. *Id.* at 2336 (footnote omitted).

12. *Ginsberg* v. *New York*, 390 U.S. 629, 639 (1968).

13. *Reno* v. *ACLU*, 117 S.Ct. 2329, 2348 (1997).

14. *Id.* at 2341.

15. *Id.* (quoting *Ginsberg* v. *New York*, 390 U.S. 629, 646 (1968)).

16. *Id.*

17. *Id.* at 2348.

18. *Id.* at 2342.

19. *Id.* (citation omitted).

20. *FCC* v. *Pacifica Found.*, 438 U.S. 726, 750 (1978).

21. *Reno* v. *ACLU*, 117 S.Ct. 2329, 2336 (1997) (citation omitted).

22. *Id.*

23. *Id.* at 2342.

24. *Id.* at 2344.

25. *Id.* at 2346.

26. *Id.* at 2344.

27. *Id.* at 2348.

28. *Id.* at 2346.

29. *Id.* at 2347.

30. *Id.* at 2348.

31. *Id.*

32. *Id.* at 2348–49.

33. *Id.* at 2349 (quoting *Schneider* v. *State*, 308 U.S. 147, 163 (1939)).

34. *Id.*

35. *Id.* at 2351.

36. *American Library Association* v. *Pataki*, 969 F. Supp. 160 (S.D. N.Y. 1997).

37. *ACLU* v. *Miller*, 977 F. Supp. 1228 (N.D. Ga. 1997).

38. *ACLU* v. *Reno*, 31 F. Supp.2d 473 (E.D. Pa. 1999).

39. *Urofsky* v. *Gilmore*, 1999 WL 61952, at 4 (4th Cir. Feb. 10, 1999).

40. *Urofsky* v. *Allen*, 995 F. Supp. 634, 640 (E.D. Va. 1998) *rvd on other grounds, sub. nom., Urofsky* v. *Gilmore*, 1999 WL 61952 (4th Cir. Feb. 10, 1999).

41. *Id.*

42. *Id.* at 640 (footnote omitted).

43. *Mainstream Loudoun* v. *Board of Trustees,* 24 F. Supp.2d 552, 565 (E.D. Va. 1998) (quoting *Turner Broadcasting Sys., Inc.* v. *FCC,* 512 U.S. 622, 664 (1994)).

44. *Id.* (quoting *Johnson* v. *County of Los Angeles Fire Dep't,* 865 F. Supp. 1430, 1439 (C.D. Cal. 1994)).

45. *Id.* at 566.

46. *Id.* at 567.

47. *See, e.g., Lockard* v. *Pizza Hut, Inc.,* 162 F.3d 1062 (10th Cir. 1998).

48. *Stanley* v. *The Lawson Co.,* 993 F. Supp. 1084, 1089 (N.D. Ohio 1997).

49. www.filteringfacts.org (Aug. 16, 1999).

50. *Id.*

51. www.cyberpatrol.com/cp_block.htm (Aug. 16, 1999).

52. *Kathleen R.* v. *City of Livermore,* VO152664 (Alameda Cty. Super. Ct. Jan. 14, 1999).

53. *Reno* v. *ACLU,* 117 S.Ct. 2329, 2346 (1997).

54. *Mainstream Loudoun* v. *Board of Trustees,* 24 F. Supp.2d 552 (E.D. Va. 1998).

55. *Id.* at 561 (reaffirming *Mainstream Loudoun* v. *Board of Trustees,* 2 F. Supp.2d 783, 794–95 (E.D. Va. 1998).

56. *Id.* at 563.

57. *Id.* at 563–64 (relying upon *Reno* v. *ACLU,* 117 S.Ct. 2329, 2342 (1997) and *Boos* v. *Barry,* 485 U.S. 312, 321 (1988)).

58. *Id.* at 567.

59. *Id.*

60. *Id.* at 570 n. 22

61. *Id.*

62. *Lamont* v. *Postmaster General,* 381 U.S. 301, 304 (1965).

63. *See Lambert* v. *Wicklund,* 117 S.Ct. 1169 (1997).

64. *Denver Area Educational Telecommun. Consortium* v. *FCC,* 518 U.S. 727, 760 (1996) (citation omitted).

65. *See, e.g., Street* v. *New York,* 394 U.S. 576, 592 (1969).

66. *Boos* v. *Barry,* 485 U.S. 312, 321 (1988).

67. *Grayned* v. *City of Rockford,* 408 U.S. 104, 108–09 (1972).

68. *American Booksellers Ass'n* v. *Virginia,* 882 F.2d 125, 127 (4th Cir. 1989) (citation omitted).

69. *Erznoznik* v. *City of Jacksonville,* 422 U.S. 205, 212–14 (1975).

70. *See Reno* v. *ACLU,* 117 S.Ct. 2329, 2348 (1997) (finding the government's interest in restricting access to Internet sites to diminish as minors age and develop).

The *Library Bill of Rights* and Its Interpretations

The *Library Bill of Rights*

The American Library Association affirms that all libraries are forums for information and ideas, and that the following basic policies should guide their services.

I. Books and other library resources should be provided for the interest, information, and enlightenment of all people of the community the library serves. Materials should not be excluded because of the origin, background, or views of those contributing to their creation.

II. Libraries should provide materials and information presenting all points of view on current and historical issues. Materials should not be proscribed or removed because of partisan or doctrinal disapproval.

III. Libraries should challenge censorship in the fulfillment of their responsibility to provide information and enlightenment.

IV. Libraries should cooperate with all persons and groups concerned with resisting abridgment of free expression and free access to ideas.

V. A person's right to use a library should not be denied or abridged because of origin, age, background, or views.

VI. Libraries which make exhibit spaces and meeting rooms available to the public they serve should make such facilities available on an equitable basis, regardless of the beliefs or affiliations of individuals or groups requesting their use.

Adopted June 18, 1948. Amended by the ALA Council, February 2, 1961; June 27, 1967; and January 23, 1980; reaffirmed January 23, 1996.

Access for Children and Young People to Videotapes and Other Nonprint Formats

An Interpretation
of the *Library Bill of Rights*

Library collections of videotapes, motion pictures, and other nonprint formats raise a number of intellectual freedom issues, especially regarding minors.

The interests of young people, like those of adults, are not limited by subject, theme, or level of sophistication. Librarians have a responsibility to ensure young people have access to materials and services that reflect diversity sufficient to meet their needs.

To guide librarians and others in resolving these issues, the American Library Association provides the following guidelines.

Article V of the *Library Bill of Rights* says, "A person's right to use a library should not be denied or abridged because of origin, age, background, or views."

ALA's Free Access to Libraries for Minors: An Interpretation of the *Library Bill of Rights* states:

> The "right to use a library" includes free access to, and unrestricted use of, all the services, materials, and facilities the library has to offer. Every restriction on access to, and use of, library resources, based solely on the chronological age, educational level, or legal emancipation of users violates Article V.
>
> . . . [P]arents—and only parents—have the right and the responsibility to restrict the access of their children—and only their children—to library resources. Parents or legal guardians who do not want their children to have access to certain library services, materials, or facilities should so advise their children. Librarians and governing bodies cannot assume the role of parents or the functions of parental authority in the private relationship between parent and child. Librarians and governing bodies have a public and professional obligation to provide equal access to all library resources for all library users.

Policies which set minimum age limits for access to videotapes and/or other audiovisual materials and equipment, with or without parental permission, abridge library use for minors. Further, age limits based on the cost of the materials are unacceptable. Unless directly and specifically prohibited by law from circulating certain motion pictures and video productions to minors, librarians should apply the same standards to circulation of these materials as are applied to books and other materials.

Recognizing that libraries cannot act *in loco parentis,* ALA acknowledges and supports the exercise by parents of their responsibility to guide their own children's reading and viewing. Published reviews of films and videotapes and/or reference works which provide information about the content, subject matter, and recommended audiences can be made available in conjunction with nonprint collections to assist parents in guiding their children without implicating the library in censorship. This material may include information provided by video producers and distributors, promotional material on videotape packaging, and Motion

Picture Association of America (MPAA) ratings *if they are included on the tape or in the packaging by the original publisher* and/or if they appear in review sources or reference works included in the library's collection. Marking out or removing ratings information from videotape packages constitutes expurgation or censorship.

MPAA and other rating services are private advisory codes and have no legal standing*. For the library to add such ratings to the materials if they are not already there, to post a list of such ratings with a collection, or to attempt to enforce such ratings through circulation policies or other procedures constitutes labeling, "an attempt to prejudice attitudes" about the material, and is unacceptable. The application of locally generated ratings schemes intended to provide content warnings to library users is also inconsistent with the *Library Bill of Rights*.

---

*For information on case law, please contact the ALA Office for Intellectual Freedom.

See also "Statement on Labeling" and "Expurgation of Library Materials," Interpretations of the Library Bill of Rights.

Adopted June 28, 1989, by the ALA Council; the quotation from "Free Access to Libraries for Minors" was changed after Council adopted the July 3, 1991, revision of that Interpretation.

Access to Electronic Information, Services and Networks

An Interpretation
of the *Library Bill of Rights*

The world is in the midst of an electronic communications revolution. Based on its constitutional, ethical, and historical heritage, American librarianship is uniquely positioned to address the broad range of information issues being raised in this revolution. In particular, librarians address intellectual freedom from a strong ethical base and an abiding commitment to the preservation of the individual's rights.

Freedom of expression is an inalienable human right and the foundation for self-government. Freedom of expression encompasses the freedom of speech and the corollary right to receive information. These rights extend to minors as well as adults. Libraries and librarians exist to facilitate the exercise of these rights by selecting, producing, providing access to, identifying, retrieving, organizing, providing instruction in the use of, and preserving recorded expression regardless of the format or technology.

The American Library Association expresses these basic principles of librarianship in its *Code of Ethics* and in the *Library Bill of Rights* and its Interpretations. These serve to guide librarians and library governing bodies in addressing issues of intellectual freedom that arise when the library provides access to electronic information, services, and networks.

Issues arising from the still-developing technology of computer-mediated information generation, distribution, and retrieval need to be approached and regularly reviewed from a context of constitutional principles and ALA policies so that fundamental and traditional tenets of librarianship are not swept away.

Electronic information flows across boundaries and barriers despite attempts by individuals, governments, and private entities to channel or control it. Even so, many people, for reasons of technology, infrastructure, or socio-economic status, do not have access to electronic information.

In making decisions about how to offer access to electronic information, each library should consider its mission, goals, objectives, cooperative agreements, and the needs of the entire community it serves.

THE RIGHTS OF USERS

All library system and network policies, procedures, or regulations relating to electronic resources and services should be scrutinized for potential violation of user rights. User policies should be developed according to the policies and guidelines established by the American Library Association, including "Guidelines for the Development and Implementation of Policies, Regulations and Procedures Affecting Access to Library Materials, Services and Facilities."

Users should not be restricted or denied access for expressing or receiving constitutionally protected speech. Users' access should not be changed without due process, including, but not limited to, formal notice and a means of appeal.

Although electronic systems may include distinct property rights and security concerns, such elements may not be be employed as a subterfuge to deny users' access to information. Users have the right to be free of unreasonable limitations or conditions set by libraries, librarians, system administrators, vendors, network service providers, or others. Contracts, agreements, and licenses entered into by libraries on behalf of their users should not violate this right. Users also have a right to information, training, and assistance necessary to operate the hardware and software provided by the library.

Users have both the right of confidentiality and the right of privacy. The library should uphold these rights by policy, procedure, and practice. Users should be advised, however, that because security is technically difficult to achieve, electronic transactions and files could become public.

The rights of users who are minors shall in no way be abridged.[1]

EQUITY OF ACCESS

Electronic information, services, and networks provided directly or indirectly by the library should be equally, readily, and equitably accessible to all library users. American Library Association policies oppose the charging of user fees for the provision of information services by all libraries and information services that receive their major support from public funds (50.3; 53.1.14; 60.1; 61.1). It should be the goal of all libraries to develop policies concerning access to electronic resources in light of "Economic Barriers to Information Access: An Interpretation of the *Library Bill of Rights*" and "Guidelines for the Development and Implementation of Policies, Regulations and Procedures Affecting Access to Library Materials, Services and Facilities."

INFORMATION RESOURCES AND ACCESS

Providing connections to global information, services, and networks is not the same as selecting and purchasing material for a library collection. Determining the accuracy or authenticity of electronic information may present special problems. Some information accessed electronically may not meet a library's selection or collection development policy. It is, therefore, left to each user to determine what is appropriate. Parents and legal guardians who are concerned about their children's use of electronic resources should provide guidance to their own children.

Libraries and librarians should not deny or limit access to information available via electronic resources because of its allegedly controversial content or because of the librarian's personal beliefs or fear of confrontation. Information retrieved or utilized electronically should be considered constitutionally protected unless determined otherwise by a court with appropriate jurisdiction.

Libraries, acting within their mission and objectives, must support access to information on all subjects that serve the needs or interests of each user, regardless of the user's age or the content of the material. Libraries have an obligation to provide access to government information available in electronic format. Libraries and librarians should not deny access to information solely on the grounds that it is perceived to lack value.

In order to prevent the loss of information, and to preserve the cultural record, libraries may need to expand their selection or collection development policies to ensure preservation, in appropriate formats, of information obtained electronically.

Electronic resources provide unprecedented opportunities to expand the scope of information available to users. Libraries and librarians should provide access to information presenting all points of view. The provision of access does not imply sponsorship or endorsement. These principles pertain to electronic resources no less than they do to the more traditional sources of information in libraries.[2]

---

1. See "Free Access to Libraries for Minors"; "Access to Resources and Services in the School Library Media Program"; and "Access for Children and Young People to Videotapes and Other Nonprint Formats."

2. See "Diversity in Collection Development."

Adopted by the ALA Council, January 24, 1996.

Access to Library Resources and Services regardless of Gender or Sexual Orientation

An Interpretation
of the *Library Bill of Rights*

American libraries exist and function within the context of a body of laws derived from the United States Constitution and the First Amendment. The *Library Bill of Rights* embodies the basic policies which guide libraries in the provision of services, materials, and programs.

In the preamble to its *Library Bill of Rights,* the American Library Association affirms that *all* [emphasis added] libraries are forums for information and ideas. This concept of *forum* and its accompanying principle of *inclusiveness* pervade all six Articles of the *Library Bill of Rights.*

The American Library Association stringently and unequivocally maintains that libraries and librarians have an obligation to resist efforts that systematically exclude materials dealing with any subject matter, including gender, homosexuality, bisexuality, lesbianism, heterosexuality, gay lifestyles, or any facet of sexual orientation:

- Article I of the *Library Bill of Rights* states that "Materials should not be excluded because of the origin, background, or views of those contributing to their creation." The Association affirms that books and other materials coming from gay presses, gay, lesbian, or bisexual authors or other creators, and materials dealing with gay lifestyles are protected by the *Library Bill of Rights.* Librarians are obligated by the *Library Bill of Rights* to endeavor to select materials without regard to the gender or sexual orientation of their creators by using the criteria identified in their written, approved selection policies. (ALA policy 53.1.5).

- Article II maintains that "Libraries should provide materials and information presenting all points of view on current and historical issues. Materials should not be proscribed or removed because of partisan or doctrinal disapproval." Library services, materials, and programs representing diverse points of view on gender or sexual orientation should be considered for purchase and inclusion in library collections and programs. (ALA policies 53.1.1, 53.1.9, and 53.1.11). The Association affirms that attempts to proscribe or remove materials dealing with gay or lesbian life without regard to the written, approved selection policy violate this tenet and constitute censorship.

- Articles III and IV mandate that libraries "challenge censorship" and cooperate with those "resisting abridgement of free expression and free access to ideas."

- Article V holds that "A person's right to use a library should not be denied or abridged because of origin, age, background, or views." In the *Library Bill of Rights* and all its Interpretations, it is intended that: "origin" encompasses all the characteristics of individuals that are inherent in the circumstances of their birth; "age" encompasses all the characteristics of individuals that are inherent in their levels of development and maturity; "background" encompasses all the characteristics of individuals that are a result of their life experiences; and "views" encompasses all the opinions and beliefs held and expressed by individuals.

  Therefore, Article V of the *Library Bill of Rights* mandates that library services, materials, and programs be available to all members of the community the library serves, without regard to gender or sexual orientation.

- Article VI maintains that "Libraries which make exhibit spaces and meeting rooms available to the public they serve should make such facilities available on an equitable basis, regardless of the beliefs or affiliations of individuals or groups requesting their use." This protection extends to all groups and members of the community the library serves, without regard to gender or sexual orientation.

The American Library Association holds that any attempt, be it legal or extra-legal, to regulate or suppress library services, materials, or programs must be resisted in order that protected expression is not abridged. Librarians have a professional obligation to ensure that all library users have free and equal access to the entire range of library services, materials, and programs. Therefore, the Association strongly opposes any effort to limit access to information and ideas. The Association also encourages librarians to proactively support the First Amendment rights of all library users, including gays, lesbians, and bisexuals.

Adopted by the ALA Council, June 30, 1993.

Access to Resources and Services in the School Library Media Program

An Interpretation
of the *Library Bill of Rights*

The school library media program plays a unique role in promoting intellectual freedom. It serves as a point of voluntary access to information and ideas and as a learning laboratory for students as they acquire critical thinking and problem solving skills needed in a pluralistic society. Although the educational level and program of the school necessarily shapes the resources and services of a school library media program, the principles of the *Library Bill of Rights* apply equally to all libraries, including school library media programs.

School library media professionals assume a leadership role in promoting the principles of intellectual freedom within the school by providing resources and services that create and sustain an atmosphere of free inquiry. School library media professionals work closely with teachers to integrate instructional activities in classroom units designed to equip students to locate, evaluate, and use a broad range of ideas effectively. Through resources, programming, and educational processes, students and teachers experience the free and robust debate characteristic of a democratic society.

School library media professionals cooperate with other individuals in building collections of resources appropriate to the developmental and maturity levels of students. These collections provide resources which support the curriculum and are consistent with the philosophy, goals, and objectives of the school district. Resources in school library media collections represent diverse points of view on current as well as historical issues.

While English is, by history and tradition, the customary language of the United States, the languages in use in any given community may vary. Schools serving communities in which other languages are used make efforts to accommodate the needs of students for whom English is a second language. To support these efforts, and to ensure equal access to resources and services, the school library media program provides resources which reflect the linguistic pluralism of the community.

Members of the school community involved in the collection development process employ educational criteria to select resources unfettered by their personal, political, social, or religious views. Students and educators served by the school library media program have access to resources and services free of constraints resulting from personal, partisan, or doctrinal disapproval. School library media professionals resist efforts by individuals to define what is appropriate for all students or teachers to read, view, or hear.

Major barriers between students and resources include: imposing age or grade level restrictions on the use of resources, limiting the use of interlibrary loan and access to electronic information, charging fees for information in specific formats, requiring permissions from parents or teachers, establishing restricted shelves or closed collections, and labeling. Policies, procedures, and rules related to the use of resources and services support free and open access to information.

The school board adopts policies that guarantee students access to a broad range of ideas. These include policies on collection development and procedures for the review of resources about which concerns have been raised. Such policies, developed by persons in the school community, provide for a timely and fair hearing and assure that procedures are applied equitably to all expressions of concern. School library media professionals implement district policies and procedures in the school.

Adopted July 2, 1986; amended January 10, 1990, by the ALA Council.

—————————

Challenged Materials

An Interpretation
of the *Library Bill of Rights*

The American Library Association declares as a matter of firm principle that it is the responsibility of every library to have a clearly defined materials selection policy in written form which reflects the *Library Bill of Rights,* and which is approved by the appropriate governing authority.

Challenged materials which meet the criteria for selection in the materials selection policy of the library should not be removed under any legal or extra-legal pressure. The *Library Bill of Rights* states in Article I that "Materials should not be excluded because of the origin, background, or views of those contributing to their creation," and in Article II, that "Materials should not be proscribed or removed because of partisan or doctrinal disapproval." Freedom of expression is protected by the Constitution of the United States, but constitutionally protected expression is often separated from unprotected expression only by a dim and uncertain line. The Constitution requires a procedure designed to focus searchingly on challenged expression before it can be suppressed. An adversary hearing is a part of this procedure.

Therefore, any attempt, be it legal or extra-legal, to regulate or suppress materials in libraries must be closely scrutinized to the end that protected expression is not abridged.

Adopted June 25, 1971; amended July 1, 1981; amended January 10, 1990, by the ALA Council.

Diversity in Collection Development

An Interpretation
of the *Library Bill of Rights*

Throughout history, the focus of censorship has fluctuated from generation to generation. Books and other materials have not been selected or have been removed from library collections for many reasons, among which are prejudicial language and ideas, political content, economic theory, social philosophies, religious beliefs, sexual forms of expression, and other topics of a potentially controversial nature.

Some examples of censorship may include removing or not selecting materials because they are considered by some as racist or sexist; not purchasing conservative religious materials; not selecting materials about or by minorities because it is thought these groups or interests are not represented in a community; or not providing information on or materials from non-mainstream political entities.

Librarians may seek to increase user awareness of materials on various social concerns by many means, including, but not limited to, issuing bibliographies and presenting exhibits and programs.

Librarians have a professional responsibility to be inclusive, not exclusive, in collection development and in the provision of interlibrary loan. Access to all materials legally obtainable should be assured to the user, and policies should not unjustly exclude materials even if they are offensive to the librarian or the user. Collection development should reflect the philosophy inherent in Article II of the *Library Bill of Rights:* "Libraries should provide materials and information presenting all points of view on current and historical issues. Materials should not be proscribed or removed because of partisan or doctrinal disapproval." A balanced collection reflects a diversity of materials, not an equality of numbers. Collection development responsibilities include selecting materials in the languages in common use in the community which the library serves. Collection development and the selection of materials should be done according to professional standards and established selection and review procedures.

There are many complex facets to any issue, and variations of context in which issues may be expressed, discussed, or interpreted. Librarians have a professional responsibility to be fair, just, and equitable and to give all library users equal protection in guarding against violation of the library patron's right to read, view, or listen to materials and resources protected by the First Amendment, no matter what the viewpoint of the author, creator, or selector. Librarians have an obligation to protect library collections from removal of materials based on personal bias or prejudice, and to select and support the access to materials on all subjects that meet, as closely as possible, the needs and interests of all persons in the community which the library serves. This includes materials that reflect political, economic, religious, social, minority, and sexual issues.

Intellectual freedom, the essence of equitable library services, provides for free access to all expressions of ideas through which any and all sides of a question, cause, or movement may be explored. Toleration is meaningless without tolerance for what some may consider detestable. Librarians cannot justly permit their own preferences to limit their degree of tolerance in collection development, because freedom is indivisible.

Adopted July 14, 1982; amended January 10, 1990, by the ALA Council.

Economic Barriers to Information Access

An Interpretation
of the *Library Bill of Rights*

A democracy presupposes an informed citizenry. The First Amendment mandates the right of all persons to free expression, and the corollary right to receive the constitutionally protected expression of others. The publicly supported library provides free and equal access to information for all people of the community the library serves. While the roles, goals and objectives of publicly supported libraries may differ, they share this common mission.

The library's essential mission must remain the first consideration for librarians and governing bodies faced with economic pressures and competition for funding.

In support of this mission, the American Library Association has enumerated certain principles of library services in the *Library Bill of Rights*.

Principles Governing Fines, Fees, and User Charges

Article I of the *Library Bill of Rights* states:

> "Books and other library resources should be provided for the interest, information, and enlightenment of all people of the community the library serves."

Article V of the *Library Bill of Rights* states:

> "A person's right to use a library should not be denied or abridged because of origin, age, background, or views."

The American Library Association opposes the charging of user fees for the provision of information by all libraries and information services that receive their major support from public funds. All information resources that are provided directly or indirectly by the library, regardless of technology, format, or methods of delivery, should be readily, equally, and equitably accessible to all library users.

Libraries that adhere to these principles systematically monitor their programs of service for potential barriers to access and strive to eliminate such barriers when they occur. All library policies and procedures, particularly those involving fines, fees, or other user charges, should be scrutinized for potential barriers to access. All services should be designed and implemented with care, so as not to infringe on or interfere with the provision or delivery of information and resources for all users. Services should be re-evaluated on a regular basis to ensure that the library's basic mission remains uncompromised.

Librarians and governing bodies should look for alternative models and methods of library administration that minimize distinctions among users based on their economic status or financial condition. They should resist the temptation to impose user fees to alleviate financial pressures, at long-term cost to institutional integrity and public confidence in libraries.

Library services that involve the provision of information, regardless of format, technology, or method of delivery, should be made available to all library users on an equal and equitable basis. Charging fees for the use of library collections, services, programs, or facilities that were purchased with public funds raises barriers to access. Such fees effectively abridge or deny access for some members of the community because they reinforce distinctions among users based on their ability and willingness to pay.

PRINCIPLES GOVERNING CONDITIONS OF FUNDING

Article II of the *Library Bill of Rights* states:

> "Materials should not be proscribed or removed because of partisan or doctrinal disapproval."

Article III of the *Library Bill of Rights* states:

> "Libraries should challenge censorship in the fulfillment of their responsibility to provide information and enlightenment."

Article IV of the *Library Bill of Rights* states:

> "Libraries should cooperate with all persons and groups concerned with resisting abridgment of free expression and free access to ideas."

The American Library Association opposes any legislative or regulatory attempt to impose content restrictions on library resources, or to limit user access to information, as a condition of funding for publicly supported libraries and information services.

The First Amendment guarantee of freedom of expression is violated when the right to receive that expression is subject to arbitrary restrictions based on content.

Librarians and governing bodies should examine carefully any terms or conditions attached to library funding and should oppose attempts to limit through such conditions full and equal access to information because of content. This principle applies equally to private gifts or bequests and to public funds. In particular, librarians and governing bodies have an obligation to reject such restrictions when the effect of the restriction is to limit equal and equitable access to information.

Librarians and governing bodies should cooperate with all efforts to create a community consensus that publicly supported libraries require funding unfettered by restrictions. Such a consensus supports the library mission to provide the free and unrestricted exchange of information and ideas necessary to a functioning democracy.

The Association's historic position in this regard is stated clearly in a number of Association policies: 50.4, "Free Access to Information"; 50.9, "Financing of Libraries"; 51.2, "Equal Access to Library Service"; 51.3, "Intellectual Freedom"; 53, "Intellectual Freedom Policies"; 59.1, "Policy Objectives"; and 60, "Library Services for the Poor."

Adopted by the ALA Council, June 30, 1993.

Evaluating Library Collections

An Interpretation
of the *Library Bill of Rights*

The continuous review of library materials is necessary as a means of maintaining an active library collection of current interest to users. In the process, materials may be added and physically deteriorated or obsolete materials may be replaced or removed in accordance with the collection maintenance policy of a given library and the needs of the community it serves. Continued evaluation is closely related to the goals and responsibilities of libraries and is a valuable tool of collection development. This procedure is not to be used as a convenient means to remove materials presumed to be controversial or disapproved of by segments of the community. Such abuse of the evaluation function violates the principles of intellectual freedom and is in opposition to the Preamble and Articles I and II of the *Library Bill of Rights,* which state:

> The American Library Association affirms that all libraries are forums for information and ideas, and that the following basic policies should guide their services.
>
> I. Books and other library resources should be provided for the interest, information, and enlightenment of all people of the community the library serves. Materials should not be excluded because of the origin, background, or views of those contributing to their creation.
>
> II. Libraries should provide materials and information presenting all points of view on current and historical issues. Materials should not be proscribed or removed because of partisan or doctrinal disapproval.

The American Library Association opposes such "silent censorship" and strongly urges that libraries adopt guidelines setting forth the positive purposes and principles of evaluation of materials in library collections.

Adopted February 2, 1973; amended July 1, 1981, by the ALA Council.

Exhibit Spaces and Bulletin Boards

An Interpretation
of the *Library Bill of Rights*

Libraries often provide exhibit spaces and bulletin boards. The uses made of these spaces should conform to the *Library Bill of Rights:* Article I states, "Materials should not be excluded because of the origin, background, or views of those contributing to their creation." Article II states, "Materials should not be proscribed or removed because of partisan or doctrinal disapproval." Article VI maintains that exhibit space should be made available "on an equitable basis, regardless of the beliefs or affiliations of individuals or groups requesting their use."

In developing library exhibits, staff members should endeavor to present a broad spectrum of opinion and a variety of viewpoints. Libraries should not shrink from developing exhibits because of controversial content or because of the beliefs or affiliations of those whose work is represented. Just as libraries do not endorse the viewpoints of those whose works are represented in their collections, libraries also do not endorse the beliefs or viewpoints of topics which may be the subject of library exhibits.

Exhibit areas often are made available for use by community groups. Libraries should formulate a written policy for the use of these exhibit areas to assure that space is provided on an equitable basis to all groups which request it.

Written policies for exhibit space use should be stated in inclusive rather than exclusive terms. For example, a policy that the library's exhibit space is open "to organizations engaged in educational, cultural, intellectual, or charitable activities" is an inclusive statement of the limited uses of the exhibit space. This defined limitation would permit religious groups to use the exhibit space because they engage in intellectual activities, but would exclude most commercial uses of the exhibit space.

A publicly supported library may limit use of its exhibit space to strictly "library-related" activities, provided that the limitation is clearly circumscribed and is viewpoint neutral.

Libraries may include in this policy rules regarding the time, place, and manner of use of the exhibit space, so long as the rules are content-neutral and are applied in the same manner to all groups wishing to use the space. A library may wish to limit access to exhibit space to groups within the community served by the library. This practice is acceptable provided that the same rules and regulations apply to everyone, and that exclusion is not made on the basis of the doctrinal, religious, or political beliefs of the potential users.

The library should not censor or remove an exhibit because some members of the community may disagree with its content. Those who object to the content of any exhibit held at the library should be able to submit their complaint and/or their own exhibit proposal to be judged according to the policies established by the library.

Libraries may wish to post a permanent notice near the exhibit area stating that the library does not advocate or endorse the viewpoints of exhibits or exhibitors.

Libraries which make bulletin boards available to public groups for posting notices of public interest should develop criteria for the use of these spaces based on the same considerations as those outlined above. Libraries may wish to develop criteria regarding the size of material to be displayed, the length of time materials may remain on the bulletin board, the frequency with which material may be posted for the same group, and the geographic area from which notices will be accepted.

Adopted July 2, 1991, by the ALA Council.

Expurgation of Library Materials

An Interpretation
of the *Library Bill of Rights*

Expurgating library materials is a violation of the *Library Bill of Rights*. Expurgation as defined by this Interpretation includes any deletion, excision, alteration, editing, or obliteration of any part(s) of books or other library resources by the library, its agent, or its parent institution (if any). By such expurgation, the library is in effect denying access to the complete work and the entire spectrum of ideas that the work intended to express. Such action stands in violation of Articles I, II, and III of the *Library Bill of Rights,* which state that "Materials should not be excluded because of the origin, background, or views of those contributing to their creation," that "Materials should not be proscribed or removed because of partisan or doctrinal disapproval," and that "Libraries should challenge censorship in the fulfillment of their responsibility to provide information and enlightenment."

The act of expurgation has serious implications. It involves a determination that it is necessary to restrict access to the complete work. This is censorship. When a work is expurgated, under the assumption that certain portions of that work would be harmful to minors, the situation is no less serious.

Expurgation of any books or other library resources imposes a restriction, without regard to the rights and desires of all library users, by limiting access to ideas and information.

Further, expurgation without written permission from the holder of the copyright on the material may violate the copyright provisions of the United States Code.

Adopted February 2, 1973; amended July 1, 1981; amended January 10, 1990, by the ALA Council.

Free Access to Libraries for Minors

An Interpretation
of the *Library Bill of Rights*

Library policies and procedures which effectively deny minors equal access to all library resources available to other users violate the *Library Bill of Rights*. The American Library Association opposes all attempts to restrict access to library services, materials, and facilities based on the age of library users.

Article V of the *Library Bill of Rights* states, "A person's right to use a library should not be denied or abridged because of origin, age, background, or views." The "right to use a library" includes free access to, and unrestricted use of, all the services, materials, and facilities the library has to offer. Every restriction on access to, and use of, library resources, based solely on the chronological age, educational level, or legal emancipation of users violates Article V.

Libraries are charged with the mission of developing resources to meet the diverse information needs and interests of the communities they serve. Services, materials, and facilities which fulfill the needs and interests of library users at different stages in their personal development are a necessary part of library resources. The needs and interests of each library user, and resources appropriate to meet those needs and interests, must be determined on an individual basis. Librarians cannot predict what resources will best fulfill the needs and interests of any individual user based on a single criterion such as chronological age, level of education, or legal emancipation.

The selection and development of library resources should not be diluted because of minors having the same access to library resources as adult users. Institutional self-censorship diminishes the credibility of the library in the community, and restricts access for all library users.

Librarians and governing bodies should not resort to age restrictions on access to library resources in an effort to avoid actual or anticipated objections from parents or anyone else. The mission, goals, and objectives of libraries do not authorize librarians or governing bodies to assume, abrogate, or overrule the rights and responsibilities of parents or legal guardians. Librarians and governing bodies should maintain that parents—and only parents—have the right and the responsibility to restrict the access of their children—and only their children—to library resources. Parents or legal guardians who do not want their children to have access to certain library services, materials or facilities, should so advise their children. Librarians and governing bodies cannot assume the role of parents or the functions of parental authority in the private relationship between parent and child. Librarians and governing bodies have a public and professional obligation to provide equal access to all library resources for all library users.

Librarians have a professional commitment to ensure that all members of the community they serve have free and equal access to the entire range of library resources regardless of content, approach, format, or amount of detail. This principle of library service applies equally to all users, minors as well as adults. Librarians and governing bodies must uphold this principle in order to provide adequate and effective service to minors.

Adopted June 30, 1972; amended July 1, 1981; July 3, 1991, by the ALA Council.

Library-Initiated Programs as a Resource

An Interpretation
of the *Library Bill of Rights*

Library-initiated programs support the mission of the library by providing users with additional opportunities for information, education, and recreation. Article I of the *Library Bill of Rights* states: "Books and other library resources should be provided for the interest, information, and enlightenment of all people of the community the library serves."

Library-initiated programs take advantage of library staff expertise, collections, services, and facilities to increase access to information and information resources. Library-initiated programs introduce users and potential users to the resources of the library and to the library's primary function as a facilitator of information access. The library may participate in cooperative or joint programs with other agencies, organizations, institutions, or individuals as part of its own effort to address information needs and to facilitate information access in the community the library serves.

Library-initiated programs on site and in other locations include, but are not limited to, speeches, community forums, discussion groups, demonstrations, displays, and live or media presentations.

Libraries serving multilingual or multicultural communities make efforts to accommodate the information needs of those for whom English is a second language. Library-initiated programs across language and cultural barriers introduce otherwise unserved populations to the resources of the library and provide access to information.

Library-initiated programs "should not be proscribed or removed (or canceled) because of partisan or doctrinal disapproval" of the contents of the program or the views expressed by the participants, as stated in Article II of the *Library Bill of Rights*. Library sponsorship of a program does not constitute an endorsement of the content of the program or the views expressed by the participants, any more than the purchase of material for the library collection constitutes an endorsement of the contents of the material or the views of its creator.

Library-initiated programs are a library resource, and as such, are developed in accordance with written guidelines, as approved and adopted by the library's policy-making body. These guidelines include an endorsement of the *Library Bill of Rights* and set forth the library's commitment to free and open access to information and ideas for all users.

Library staff select topics, speakers and resource materials for library-initiated programs based on the interests and information needs of the community. Topics, speakers and resource materials are not excluded from library-initiated programs because of possible controversy. Concerns, questions or complaints about library-initiated program[s] are handled according to the same written policy and procedures which govern reconsiderations of other library resources.

Library-initiated programs are offered free of charge and are open to all. Article V of the *Library Bill of Rights* states: "A person's right to use a library should not be denied or abridged because of origin, age, background, or views."

The "right to use a library" encompasses all of the resources the library offers, including the right to attend library-initiated programs. Libraries do not deny or abridge access to library resources, including library-initiated programs, based on an individual's economic background and ability to pay.

Adopted January 27, 1982. Amended June 26, 1990, by the ALA Council.

Meeting Rooms

An Interpretation
of the *Library Bill of Rights*

Many libraries provide meeting rooms for individuals and groups as part of a program of service. Article VI of the *Library Bill of Rights* states that such facilities should be made available to the public served by the given library "on an equitable basis, regardless of the beliefs or affiliations of individuals or groups requesting their use."

Libraries maintaining meeting room facilities should develop and publish policy statements governing use. These statements can properly define time, place, or manner of use; such qualifications should not pertain to the content of a meeting or to the beliefs or affiliations of the sponsors. These statements should be made available in any commonly used language within the community served.

If meeting rooms in libraries supported by public funds are made available to the general public for nonlibrary sponsored events, the library may not exclude any group based on the subject matter to be discussed or based on the ideas that the group advocates. For example, if a library allows charities and sports clubs to discuss their activities in library meeting rooms, then the library should not exclude partisan political or religious groups from discussing their activities in the same facilities. If a library opens its meeting rooms to a wide variety of civic organizations, then the library may not deny access to a religious organization. Libraries may wish to post a permanent notice near the meeting room stating that the library does not advocate or endorse the viewpoints of meetings or meeting room users.

Written policies for meeting room use should be stated in inclusive rather than exclusive terms. For example, a policy that the library's facilities are open "to organizations engaged in educational, cultural, intellectual, or charitable activities" is an inclusive statement of the limited uses to which the facilities may be put. This defined limitation would permit religious groups to use the facilities because they engage in intellectual activities, but would exclude most commercial uses of the facility.

A publicly supported library may limit use of its meeting rooms to strictly "library-related" activities, provided that the limitation is clearly circumscribed and is viewpoint neutral.

Written policies may include limitations on frequency of use, and whether or not meetings held in library meeting rooms must be open to the public. If state and local laws permit private as well as public sessions of meetings in libraries, libraries may choose to offer both options. The same standard should be applicable to all.

If meetings are open to the public, libraries should include in their meeting room policy statement a section which addresses admission fees. If admission fees are permitted, libraries shall seek to make it possible that these fees do not limit access to individuals who may be unable to pay, but who wish to attend the meeting. Article V of the *Library Bill of Rights* states that "a person's right to use a library should not be denied or abridged because of origin, age, background, or views." It is inconsistent with Article V to restrict indirectly access to library meeting rooms based on an individual's or group's ability to pay for that access.

Adopted July 2, 1991, by the ALA Council.

Restricted Access to Library Materials

An Interpretation
of the *Library Bill of Rights*

Libraries are a traditional forum for the open exchange of information. Attempts to restrict access to library materials violate the basic tenets of the *Library Bill of Rights.*

Historically, attempts have been made to limit access by relegating materials into segregated collections. These attempts are in violation of established policy. Such collections are often referred to by a variety of names, including "closed shelf," "locked case," "adults only," "restricted shelf," or "high demand." Access to some materials also may require a monetary fee or financial deposit. In any situation which restricts access to certain materials, a barrier is placed between the patron and those materials. That barrier may be age related, linguistic, economic, or psychological in nature.

Because materials placed in restricted collections often deal with controversial, unusual, or "sensitive" subjects, having to ask a librarian or circulation clerk for them may be embarrassing or inhibiting for patrons desiring the materials. Needing to ask for materials may pose a language barrier or a staff service barrier. Because restricted collections often are composed of materials which some library patrons consider "objectionable," the potential users may be predisposed to think of the materials as "objectionable" and, therefore, are reluctant to ask for them.

Barriers between the materials and the patron which are psychological, or are affected by language skills, are nonetheless limitations on access to information. Even when a title is listed in the catalog with a reference to its restricted status, a barrier is placed between the patron and the publication. (See also "Statement on Labeling.")

There may be, however, countervailing factors to establish policies to protect library materials—specifically, for reasons of physical preservation including protection from theft or mutilation. Any such policies must be carefully formulated and administered with extreme attention to the principles of intellectual freedom. This caution is also in keeping with ALA policies, such as "Evaluating Library Collections," "Free Access to Libraries for Minors," and the "Preservation Policy."

Finally, in keeping with the "Joint Statement on Access" of the American Library Association and Society of American Archivists, restrictions that result from donor agreements or contracts for special collections materials must be similarly circumscribed. Permanent exclusions are not acceptable. The overriding impetus must be to work for free and unfettered access to all documentary heritage.

Adopted February 2, 1973; amended July 1, 1981; July 3, 1991, by the ALA Council.

Statement on Labeling

An Interpretation
of the *Library Bill of Rights*

Labeling is the practice of describing or designating materials by affixing a prejudicial label and/or segregating them by a prejudicial system. The American Library Association opposes these means of predisposing people's attitudes toward library materials for the following reasons:

1. Labeling is an attempt to prejudice attitudes and as such, it is a censor's tool.
2. Some find it easy and even proper, according to their ethics, to establish criteria for judging publications as objectionable. However, injustice and ignorance rather than justice and enlightenment result from such practices, and the American Library Association opposes the establishment of such criteria.
3. Libraries do not advocate the ideas found in their collections. The presence of books and other resources in a library does not indicate endorsement of their contents by the library.

A variety of private organizations promulgate rating systems and/or review materials as a means of advising either their members or the general public concerning their opinions of the contents and suitability or appropriate age for use of certain books, films, recordings, or other materials. For the library to adopt or enforce any of these private systems, to attach such ratings to library materials, to include them in bibliographic records, library catalogs, or other finding aids, or otherwise to endorse them would violate the *Library Bill of Rights*.

While some attempts have been made to adopt these systems into law, the constitutionality of such measures is extremely questionable. If such legislation is passed which applies within a library's jurisdiction, the library should seek competent legal advice concerning its applicability to library operations.

Publishers, industry groups, and distributors sometimes add ratings to material or include them as part of their packaging. Librarians should not endorse such practices. However, removing or obliterating such ratings—if placed there by or with permission of the copyright holder—could constitute expurgation, which is also unacceptable.

The American Library Association opposes efforts which aim at closing any path to knowledge. This statement, however, does not exclude the adoption of organizational schemes designed as directional aids or to facilitate access to materials.

Adopted July 13, 1951; amended June 25, 1971; July 1, 1981; June 26, 1990, by the ALA Council.

The Universal Right to Free Expression

An Interpretation
of the *Library Bill of Rights*

Freedom of expression is an inalienable human right and the foundation for self-government. Freedom of expression encompasses the freedoms of speech, press, religion, assembly, and association, and the corollary right to receive information.

The American Library Association endorses this principle, which is also set forth in the Universal Declaration of Human Rights, adopted by the United Nations General Assembly. The Preamble of this document states that ". . . recognition of the inherent dignity and of the equal and inalienable rights of all members of the human family is the foundation of freedom, justice, and peace in the world . . ." and ". . . the advent of a world in which human beings shall enjoy freedom of speech and belief and freedom from fear and want has been proclaimed as the highest aspiration of the common people. . . ."

Article 18 of this document states:

> Everyone has the right to freedom of thought, conscience, and religion; this right includes freedom to change his religion or belief, and freedom, either alone or in community with others and in public or private, to manifest his religion or belief in teaching, practice, worship, and observance.

Article 19 states:

> Everyone has the right to freedom of opinion and expression; this right includes freedom to hold opinions without interference and to seek, receive and impart information and ideas through any media regardless of frontiers.

Article 20 states:

> 1. Everyone has the right to freedom of peaceful assembly and association.
> 2. No one may be compelled to belong to an association.

We affirm our belief that these are inalienable rights of every person, regardless of origin, age, background, or views. We embody our professional commitment to these principles in the *Library Bill of Rights* and *Code of Ethics,* as adopted by the American Library Association.

We maintain that these are universal principles and should be applied by libraries and librarians throughout the world. The American Library Association's policy on International Relations reflects these objectives: ". . . to encourage the exchange, dissemination, and access to information and the unrestricted flow of library materials in all formats throughout the world."

We know that censorship, ignorance, and limitations on the free flow of information are the tools of tyranny and oppression. We believe that ideas and information topple the walls of hate and fear and build bridges of cooperation and understanding far more effectively than weapons and armies.

The American Library Association is unswerving in its commitment to human rights and intellectual freedom; the two are inseparably linked and inextricably entwined. Freedom of opinion and expression is not derived from or dependent on any form of government or political power. This right is inherent in every individual. It cannot be surrendered, nor can it be denied. True justice comes from the exercise of this right.

We recognize the power of information and ideas to inspire justice, to restore freedom and dignity to the oppressed, and to change the hearts and minds of the oppressors.

Courageous men and women, in difficult and dangerous circumstances throughout human history, have demonstrated that freedom lives in the human heart and cries out for justice even in the face of threats, enslavement, imprisonment, torture, exile, and death. We draw inspiration from their example. They challenge us to remain steadfast in our most basic professional responsibility to promote and defend the right of free expression.

There is no good censorship. Any effort to restrict free expression and the free flow of information aids the oppressor. Fighting oppression with censorship is self-defeating.

Threats to the freedom of expression of any person anywhere are threats to the freedom of all people everywhere. Violations of human rights and the right of free expression have been recorded in virtually every country and society across the globe.

In response to these violations, we affirm these principles:

> The American Library Association opposes any use of governmental prerogative that leads to the intimidation of individuals which prevents them from exercising their rights to hold opinions without interference, and to seek, receive, and impart information and ideas. We urge libraries and librarians everywhere to resist such abuse of governmental power, and to support those against whom such governmental power has been employed.

> The American Library Association condemns any governmental effort to involve libraries and librarians in restrictions on the right of any individual to hold opinions without interference, and to seek, receive, and impart information and ideas. Such restrictions pervert the function of the library and violate the professional responsibilities of librarians.

> The American Library Association rejects censorship in any form. Any action which denies the inalienable human rights of individuals only damages the will to resist oppression, strengthens the hand of the oppressor, and undermines the cause of justice.

> The American Library Association will not abrogate these principles. We believe that censorship corrupts the cause of justice, and contributes to the demise of freedom.

Adopted by the ALA Council, January 16, 1991.

Guidelines for the Development and Implementation of Policies, Regulations and Procedures Affecting Access to Library Materials, Services and Facilities

INTRODUCTION

Publicly supported libraries exist within the context of a body of law derived from the United States Constitution and appropriate state constitutions, defined by statute, and implemented by regulations, policies and procedures established by their governing bodies and administrations. These regulations, policies and procedures establish the mission of the library, define its functions, services and operations and ascertain the rights and responsibilities of the clientele served by the library.

Publicly supported library service is based upon the First Amendment right of free expression. The publicly supported library provides free and equal access to information for all people of the community it serves. Thus, publicly supported libraries are governmental agencies designated as limited public forums for access to information. Libraries that make meeting rooms, exhibit spaces and/or bulletin boards available for public use are also designated as limited public forums for the exchange of information.

Many libraries adopt administrative policies and procedures regulating the organization and use of library materials, services and facilities. These policies and procedures affect access and may have the effect of restricting, denying or creating barriers to access to the library as a public forum, including the library's resources, facilities and services. Library policies and procedures that impinge upon First Amendment rights are subject to a higher standard of review than may be required in the policies of other public services and facilities.

Policies, procedures or regulations that may result in denying, restricting or creating physical or economic barriers to access to the library's public forum must be based on a compelling government interest. However, library governing authorities may place reasonable and narrowly drawn restrictions on the time, place or manner of access to library resources, services or facilities, provided that such restrictions are not based upon arbitrary distinctions between individuals or classes of individuals.

The American Library Association has adopted the *Library Bill of Rights* and Interpretations of the *Library Bill of Rights* to provide library governing authorities, librarians and other library staff and library users with guidelines on how constitutional principles apply to libraries in the United States of America.

The American Library Association's Intellectual Freedom Committee recommends that publicly supported libraries use the following guidelines, based on constitutional principles, to develop policies, regulations and procedures.

GUIDELINES

All library policies, regulations and procedures should be carefully examined to determine if they may result in denying, restricting or creating barriers to access. If they may result in such restrictions, they:

1. should be developed and implemented within the legal framework that applies to the library. This includes: the United States Constitution, including the First and Fourteenth Amendments, due process and equal treatment under the law; the applicable state constitution; federal and state civil rights legislation; all other applicable federal, state and local legislation; and applicable case law;
2. should cite statutes or ordinances upon which the authority to make that policy is based, when appropriate;
3. should be developed and implemented within the framework of the *Library Bill of Rights* and its Interpretations;
4. should be based upon the library's mission and objectives;
5. should only impose restrictions on the access to, or use of library resources, services or facilities when those restrictions are necessary to achieve the library's mission and objectives;

6. should narrowly tailor prohibitions or restrictions, in the rare instances when they are required, so they are not more restrictive than needed to serve their objectives;
7. should attempt to balance competing interests and avoid favoring the majority at the expense of individual rights, or allowing individual users' rights to interfere materially with the majority's rights to free and equal access to library resources, services and facilities;
8. should avoid arbitrary distinctions between individuals or classes of users, and should not have the effect of denying or abridging a person's right to use library resources, services, or facilities based upon arbitrary distinctions such as origin, age, background or views;

> In the *Library Bill of Rights* and all of its Interpretations, it is intended that: "origin" encompasses all the characteristics of individuals that are inherent in the circumstances of their birth; "age" encompasses all the characteristics of individuals that are inherent in their levels of development and maturity; "background" encompasses all the characteristics of individuals that are a result of their life experiences; and "views" encompasses all the opinions and beliefs held and expressed by individuals;

9. should not target specific users or groups of users based upon an assumption or expectation that such users might engage in behavior that will materially interfere with the achievement of substantial library objectives;
10. must be clearly stated so that a reasonably intelligent person will have fair warning of what is expected;
11. must provide a means of appeal;
12. must be reviewed regularly by the library's governing authority and by its legal counsel;
13. must be communicated clearly and made available in an effective manner to all library users;
14. must be enforced evenhandedly, and not in a manner intended to benefit or disfavor any person or group in an arbitrary or capricious manner;

> Libraries should develop an ongoing staff training program designed to foster the understanding of the legal framework and principles underlying library policies and to assist staff

in gaining the skill and ability to respond to potentially difficult circumstances in a timely, direct and open manner. This program should include training to develop empathy and understanding of the social and economic problems of some library users;

15. should, if reasonably possible, provide adequate alternative means of access to information for those whose behavior results in the denial or restriction of access to any library resource, service or facility.

Adopted June 28, 1994, by the ALA Intellectual Freedom Committee.

Guidelines and Considerations for Developing a Public Library Internet Use Policy

Intellectual Freedom's Meaning and Scope

Libraries are *the* information source in our society. They link individuals with the knowledge, information, literature, and other resources people seek. It is never libraries' role to keep individuals from what other people have to say.

By providing information and ideas across the spectrum of social and political thought, and making these ideas and information available and accessible to anyone who wants or needs them, libraries allow individuals to exercise their First Amendment right to seek and receive all types of information, from all points of view. Materials in any given library cover the spectrum of human thought, some of which people may consider to be untrue, offensive, or even dangerous.

In the vast amount of information on the Internet, there are some materials—often loosely called "pornography"—that parents, or adults generally, do not want children to see. A very small fraction of those sexually explicit materials is actually obscenity or child pornography, materials not constitutionally protected. The rest fall within the overwhelming majority of materials on the Internet protected by the First Amendment.

Obscenity and child pornography are illegal. Federal and state statutes, the latter varying slightly depending on the jurisdiction, proscribe such materials. The U.S. Supreme Court has settled most questions about what obscenity and child pornography statutes are constitutionally sound.

According to the Court:

> *Obscenity* must be determined using a three-part test. To be obscene, (1) the average person, applying contemporary community standards, must find that the work, taken as a whole, appeals to prurient interests; (2) the work must depict or describe, in a patently offensive way, sexual conduct as specified in the applicable statutes; and (3) the work, taken as a whole, must lack serious literary, artistic, political, or scientific value.
>
> *Child pornography* may be determined using a slightly less rigorous test. To be child pornography, the work must involve depictions of sexual conduct specified in the applicable statutes and use images of children below a specified age.

Many states and some localities have "harmful to minors" laws. These laws regulate free speech with respect to minors, typically forbidding the display or dissemination of certain sexually explicit materials to children, as further specified in the laws.

According to the U.S. Supreme Court:

> Materials *"harmful to minors"* include descriptions or representations of nudity, sexual conduct, or sexual excitement that appeal to the prurient, shameful, or morbid interest of minors; are patently offensive to prevailing standards in the adult community as a whole with respect to what is suitable material for minors; and lack serious literary, artistic, political, or scientific value for minors.

Knowing what materials are actually obscenity or child pornography is difficult, as is knowing, when minors are involved, what materials are actually "harmful to minors." The applicable statutes and laws, together with the written decisions of courts that have applied them in actual cases, are the only official guides. Libraries and librarians are *not* in a position to make those decisions for library users or for citizens generally. Only courts have constitutional authority to determine, in accordance with due process, what materials are obscenity, child pornography, or "harmful to minors."

Obscenity and child pornography statutes apply to materials on the Internet; such materials are currently being regulated there. The applicability of particular "harmful to minors" laws to materials on the Internet is unsettled, however. Because of the uncertainty, various federal and state legislative proposals are pending specifically to "protect" children from sexually explicit materials on the Internet.

INTELLECTUAL FREEDOM'S FIRST AMENDMENT FOUNDATIONS

Courts have held that the public library is a "limited public forum." "Limited" means it is a place for access to free and open communication, subject to reasonable restrictions as to the time, place, and manner for doing so. As with any public forum the government has opened for people to use for communication, the First Amendment protects people's right to use the forum without the government interfering with what is communicated there. This is the very essence of the Constitution's guarantee of freedom of speech.

In a public forum, the government is prohibited from exercising discrimination with respect to the *content* of communication, unless the government demonstrates that the restriction is necessary to achieve a "compelling" government interest and there is no less restrictive alternative for achieving that interest. This means public libraries cannot exclude books about abortion just because they discuss the subject of abortion. That would be discrimination with respect to *content*. Books can be selected on the basis of content-neutral criteria such as the quality of the writing, their position on best-seller lists, the presence or absence of other materials in the collection related to certain time periods or historical figures, and the like; they can be deselected on the basis of wear and tear, the availability of more current materials, and similar criteria. Libraries, however, cannot deliberately suppress the record of human thought on a particular subject or topic.

Filtering and other means to block content on the Internet are mechanisms that allow discrimination with respect to the *content* of communication. Filters are notoriously inept at doing what computer software engineers have designed them to do—typically, block "hard-core pornography" and other "offensive" sites on the Internet. But even at their hypothetical best, mechanisms to screen and block content on the Internet exclude far more than just obscenity and child pornography. They exclude a wide range of sexually explicit materials protected under the Constitution. For instance, materials that depict homosexual relations, variations on conventional heterosexuality, and even nudity and heterosexual relations channeled toward reproduction and family life represent distinct subjects or topics. Their suppression is discrimination with respect to the *content* of communication.

Filtering and other means to block content on the Internet only can be utilized if the government—in this case, the public library—can demonstrate both that the need is compelling and that the method chosen to achieve the purpose is the least restrictive method possible. The lawsuit brought by the American Library Association—*American Library Ass'n v. United States Department of Justice,* consolidated with and decided by the U.S. Supreme Court under the name of *Reno v. American Civil Liberties Union*—invalidated the provisions of the Communications Decency Act of 1996 that criminalized "indecent" and "patently offensive" electronic communication. The Court did so on the ground that those provisions, suppressing speech addressed to adults, reduced the entire population only to what is fit for children. It recognized "the governmental interest in protecting children from harmful materials," but found that less restrictive means were available to achieve that interest. In the context of limiting or avoiding children's exposure to possibly "harmful" materials on library computers with Internet access, less restrictive means than the use of filters are available.

It is well documented that filtering software is over-inclusive, blocking not only sites that may have sexual content, strong language, or unconventional ideas considered harmful or offensive—but also sites having no controversial content whatsoever. Filters are known to have blocked webpages of the Religious Society of Friends (Quakers), the American Association of University Women, the Banned Books page at Carnegie Mellon University, the AIDS Quilt site, the Fileroom Project censorship database, and even the conservative Heritage Foundation. The fact that the site covering the recent Mars exploration was blocked by certain software because the URL contained "mar*sex*pl" shows how crude the filtering technology truly is. Over-inclusive blocking violates the First Amendment rights of youth and children, as well as adults, to access constitutionally protected materials.

Adults cannot be reduced to the level of what is fit for children, and the public library, therefore, cannot restrict them to Internet-access computers with filtering software. Young adults and children also have First Amendment rights, although such rights are variable, depending on the age of the minor and other factors, including maturity, not yet settled in the law. Even though minors' First Amendment rights are not as extensive as those of adults, the public library cannot restrict them solely to computers with filtering software. Libraries favor parents' control of their children's use of the Internet. Only unfiltered Internet access accommodates both parental control and sensitive recognition of the First Amendment rights of young people.

Librarians and the strength of their commitment to professional standards and values assure that, at least through the public library, the least restrictive means available to achieve the government's interest in protecting children will be implemented.

SPECIFIC INTERNET USE POLICY PROVISIONS

The position of the American Library Association is set forth in several documents adopted by the Council, its governing body. The *Interpretation* of the *Library Bill of Rights* entitled *Access to Electronic Information, Services, and Networks* calls for free and unfettered access to the Internet for any library user, regardless of age. The *Resolution on the Use of Filtering Software in Libraries* and the *Statement on Library Use of Filtering Software* reiterate the U.S. Supreme Court's declaration in *Reno v. American Civil Liberties Union* that the Internet is a forum of free expression deserving full constitutional protection. The *Resolution* and *Statement* condemn as a violation of the *Library Bill of Rights* any use of filtering software by libraries that blocks access to constitutionally protected speech.

Consistent with these policies, which collectively embody the library profession's understanding of First Amendment constraints on library Internet use, the Intellectual Freedom Committee offers guidelines to public libraries, as follows:

- Adopt a comprehensive, written Internet use policy that, among other things, sets forth reasonable time, place, and manner restrictions. Expressly prohibit any use of library equipment to access material that is obscene, child pornography, or "harmful to minors" (consistent with any applicable state or local law).

- Communicate the relevant policies for use of Internet-access computers to all library users, and include the parents of children who may use the library without direct parental supervision. Do so in a clear and conspicuous manner sufficient to alert library users that filtering software is not utilized.

- Post notices at all Internet-access computers that use of library equipment to access the illegal materials specified in the Internet use policy is prohibited.

- Offer a variety of programs, at convenient times, to educate library users, including parents and children, on the use of the Internet. Publicize them widely.

- Offer library users recommended Internet sites. For youth and children, especially, offer them, according to age group, direct links to sites with educational and other types of material best suited to their typical needs and interests (*e.g.,* the American Library Association's 700+ *Great Sites for Kids and the Adults Who Care about Them* and its Internet guide for young adults, *TEENHoopla*).

Answers to Objections

Various metaphors have been offered, both by opponents of free and open access in libraries, as well as proponents, to explain the use of the Internet in libraries and the impact of filtering software. Two metaphors offered by opponents and the arguments built around them deserve close examination:

> *The "selection" metaphor.* Filtering Internet resources is tantamount to selecting materials in a library. Since libraries, opponents of unfettered Internet access say, are not constrained to select any particular materials for their collections, filtering is constitutionally unobjectionable.

This metaphor is faulty. Filtering the Internet is not selecting materials. The only selection decisions involved in use of the Internet in libraries are those as to whether, for instance, the World Wide Web will be offered with other tools based on special Internet protocols, *e.g., ftp* (file transfer protocol) or *telenet*. Selecting the World Wide Web for the library means selecting the entire resource, just as selecting *Time* means selecting the entire magazine. A library cannot select *Time* and then decide to redact or rip out the pages constituting the "American Scene" feature or the "Washington Diary." That would be censorship. It is the same with the World Wide Web. It is not an accident of terminology that the Web consists of a vast number of web*pages* and that browser software permits the user to *bookmark* those that are interesting or useful.

The "interlibrary loan" metaphor. Internet access is tantamount to interlibrary loan service. Typing a website URL into a browser's location entry box and pressing the <Enter> key amounts to an interlibrary loan request that the library, opponents of unfettered access say, is free to deny.

This metaphor is faulty, too. Far more frequently than typing and entering URLs, surfers of the World Wide Web click on hot links for automatic access to the webpages they wish to see. More significantly, absent financial constraints, any public library true to its function as a public forum makes available to users any constitutionally protected material, whether that means locating the material within the library itself or obtaining it elsewhere through interlibrary loan.

As articulated by the U.S. Supreme Court in the American Library Association case culminating in *Reno v. American Civil Liberties Union,* the Internet represents a vast library. It is a virtual library already present within any public library that selects Internet access. The fundamental First Amendment question is: given the free availability of a near-infinite range of content on the Internet, can the library ever deliberately deprive a library user of the constitutionally protected materials he or she seeks? The emphatic answer of the librarian informed by principles of intellectual freedom is: *absolutely not.*

But what about obscenity and child pornography, as well as, when minors are involved, materials "harmful to minors"?

- As for obscenity and child pornography, prosecutors and police have adequate tools to enforce criminal laws. Libraries are not a component of law enforcement efforts naturally directed toward the source, *i.e.,* the publishers, of such material.

- As for materials "harmful to minors," it is true that, in *some* jurisdictions, libraries that choose not to utilize filtering or other means to block content on the Internet may find themselves in a "bind"; under some circumstances, they may be subject to liability under "harmful to minors" laws.

Libraries should be cautioned that laws differ from state to state, and they should seek advice on laws applicable in their jurisdiction from counsel versed in First Amendment principles. In particular, they should determine whether any "harmful to minors" law applies to materials available at the library, either through Internet access or otherwise.

They should specifically inquire whether they are expressly exempt from the particular "harmful to minors" laws in their jurisdiction, as libraries frequently are.

Moreover, libraries should be aware that the legal framework and context of regulation is rapidly changing; federal, state, and local governments have begun to legislate specifically in the area of library Internet use. Libraries should actively oppose proposed legislation that exposes them to new liabilities and negatively impacts intellectual freedom. As always, they should be vigilant about new regulations of free speech.

Adopted by the ALA Intellectual Freedom Committee June 1998.

Dealing with Concerns about Library Resources

As with any public service, libraries receive complaints and expressions of concern. One of the librarian's responsibilities is to handle these complaints in a respectful and fair manner. The complaints that librarians often worry about most are those dealing with library resources or free access policies. The key to successfully handling these complaints is to be sure the library staff and the governing authorities are all knowledgeable about the complaint procedures and their implementation. As normal operating procedure each library should:

1. *Maintain a materials selection policy.* It should be in written form and approved by the appropriate governing authority. It should apply to all library materials equally.
2. *Maintain a library service policy.* This should cover registration policies, programming and services in the library that involve access issues.
3. *Maintain a clearly defined method for handling complaints.* The complaint must be filed in writing and the complainant must be properly identified before action is taken. A decision should be deferred until fully considered by appropriate administrative authority. (A sample form is attached.) The process should be followed, whether the complaint originates internally or externally.
4. *Maintain in-service training.* Conduct periodic in-service training to acquaint staff, administration, and the governing authority with the materials selection policy and library service policy and procedures for handling complaints.

5. *Maintain lines of communication with civic, religious, educational, and political bodies of the community.* Library board and staff participation in local civic organizations and presentations to these organizations should emphasize the library's selection process and intellectual freedom principles.

6. *Maintain a vigorous public information program on behalf of intellectual freedom.* Newspapers, radio, and television should be informed of policies governing resource selection and use, and of any special activities pertaining to intellectual freedom.

7. *Maintain familiarity with any local municipal and state legislation pertaining to intellectual freedom and First Amendment rights.* Following these practices will not preclude receiving complaints from pressure groups or individuals but should provide a base from which to operate when these concerns are expressed. When a complaint is made, follow one or more of the steps listed below:

   a. Listen calmly and courteously to the complaint. Remember the person has a right to express a concern. Use of good communication skills helps many people understand the need for diversity in library collections and the use of library resources. In the event the person is not satisfied, advise the complainant of the library policy and procedures for handling library resource statements of concern. If a person does fill out a form about their concern, make sure a prompt written reply related to the concern is sent.

   b. It is essential to notify the administration and/or the governing authority (library board, etc.) of the complaint and assure them that the library's procedures are being followed. Present full, written information giving the nature of the complaint and identifying the source.

   c. When appropriate, seek the support of the local media. Freedom to read and freedom of the press go hand in hand.

   d. When appropriate, inform local civic organizations of the facts and enlist their support. Meet negative pressure with positive pressure.

   e. Assert the principles of the *Library Bill of Rights* as a professional responsibility. Laws governing obscenity, subversive material and other questionable matter are subject to interpretation by courts. Library materials found to meet the standards set in the materials selection policy should not be removed from public access until after an adversary hearing resulting in a final judicial determination.

f. Contact the ALA Office for Intellectual Freedom and your state intellectual freedom committee to inform them of the complaint and to enlist their support and the assistance of other agencies.

The principles and procedures discussed above apply to all kinds of resource related complaints or attempts to censor and are supported by groups such as the National Education Association, the American Civil Liberties Union and the National Council of Teachers of English, as well as the American Library Association. While the practices provide positive means for preparing for and meeting pressure group complaints, they serve the more general purpose of supporting the *Library Bill of Rights,* particularly Article 3 which states that "Libraries should challenge censorship in the fulfillment of the responsibility to provide information and enlightenment."

Revised January 12, 1983, by the Intellectual Freedom Committee.

Conducting a
Challenge Hearing

Challenges to materials only occasionally reach the stage of a full-blown administrative hearing; often they are resolved at an earlier step in the challenge resolution process. When a hearing is necessary, however, certain important do's and don'ts should be observed. A number of battles have been lost because the challenge hearing has been poorly organized. Even though procedures have been followed to the letter up to this point, the handling of the challenge hearing may be the weak link in the process.

The challenge process begins when someone objects to materials in a library collection. At this point, providing an explanation of selection procedures, a copy of the selection policy, or a copy of the reconsideration or complaint form will often terminate the problem (see figure 1). Most complainants never return the reconsideration form because he or she sees the logic of the selection process which emphasizes intellectual freedom and due process. The complainant tends to be satisfied in registering a concern and knowing the library is taking the concern seriously.

There are a few, however, who wish to follow through on the procedures established in the selection policy for handling complaints and approved by the governing authority. To activate the reconsideration procedure, a complaint should be in writing. In fact, the written and approved selection policy should state that anonymous phone calls, rumors, or voiced concerns are not honored; action occurs only when the reconsideration or complaint form has been returned. The reconsideration committee, comprised of representatives of all library users and the librarian, should accomplish the following steps:

FIGURE 1   Sample Request for Reconsideration of Library Resources

[This is where you identify who in your own structure has authorized use of this form—Director, Board of Trustees, Board of Education, etc.—and to whom to return the form.]

Example: The school board of Mainstream County, U.S.A., has delegated the responsibility for selection and evaluation of library/educational resources to the school library media specialist/curriculum committee, and has established reconsideration procedures to address concerns about those resources. Completion of this form is the first step in those procedures. If you wish to request reconsideration of school or library resources, please return the completed form to the Coordinator of Library Media Resources, Mainstream School Dist., 1 Mainstream Plaza, Anytown, U.S.A.

Name _____   Date _____

Address _____

City _____ State ____ Zip _____ Phone _____

Do you represent self _____ Organization _____

1. Resource on which you are commenting:

   _____ Book   _____ Textbook _____ Video _____ Display

   _____ Magazine   _____ Library Program _____ Audio Recording

   _____ Newspaper _____ Electronic information/network (please specify)

   _____ Other   _____

   Title _____

   Author/Producer _____

2. What brought this resource to your attention?

3. Have you examined the entire resource?

4. What concerns you about the resource? (use other side or additional pages if necessary)

5. Are there resource(s) you suggest to provide additional information and/or other viewpoints on this topic?

Revised by the American Library Association
Intellectual Freedom Committee
June 27, 1995

1. Read, view or listen to the challenged material in its entirety;
2. Review the selection process and the criteria for selection;
3. Check reviews and recommended lists to determine recommendations by the experts and critics;
4. Meet to discuss the challenge; and
5. Make a recommendation to the administrator on retention, replacement, or removal.

The complainant should be notified of the committee's decision. At the same time, the procedure for appealing the decision, if the complainant disagrees with it, also should be provided. The appeal level may be a school board, a board of trustees or a city or county board of commissioners or council. (The selection policy should clearly identify the chain of command.) The appeal also must be in writing in order for the chair of the governing authority to place it on the agenda for the next meeting. The librarian should follow up on this step to make certain the presiding officer is aware of the policies and procedures which should be followed, including open meetings law and the agenda. Normally, the board conducts a challenge hearing which provides the forum for the complainant to air his or her objections to the title in the collection and the recommendation of the reconsideration committee.

A hearing on challenged material is serious and often lengthy. Such a hearing may be the only item on the agenda; indeed, best results are most often achieved this way.

Never attempt to stage a hearing quietly. The entire community should be aware of the meeting and what has transpired up to this point. The hearing should be announced well in advance. Publicity is very important to assure good attendance at the meeting. Make the time and place very clear. Indicate in an announcement or news release that an open hearing is being held and that the public is invited. Try to obtain full coverage by the local press, radio and television. Prepare a news release for each of these groups to make certain they have the facts correct. Deliver copies of the media center's or library's selection policies to them, along with a coy of the *Library Bill of Rights*. These policies, of course, should include procedures for handling complaints.

Decide in advance on a length of time for the entire hearing. Have a definite beginning and ending time. Guard against overlong meetings when decisions may be made by small groups in the late hours. This has spelled disaster in some instances.

Attempt to estimate in advance the size of the gathering for the hearing. Make certain the meeting place is large enough to prevent postponing the meeting or changing locations at the last minute. A late site change may result in losing part of the group attending. There have also been situations in which one faction arrived early, securing the choice front seats. To preclude this, the room can be divided, with people favoring retention of the material on one side, opponents of the material on the other.

Seek help and advice from your state intellectual freedom committee, local and state colleges and universities, educational groups, teachers' professional organizations, coalitions and the ALA Office for Intellectual Freedom. Many of the non-library groups have committees on intellectual freedom, freedom of speech, and/or academic freedom. Even when representatives from these groups are not present at the hearing, solicited resolutions in written form sometimes help in supporting your philosophy.

Make arrangements in advance to tape proceedings and keep minutes. Announce at the hearing where and when these will be available to the general public. They should be accessible as soon as possible after the hearing.

Solicit people who will be willing to speak in support of the freedom to read, view and listen. This pool of speakers should be contacted well in advance of the hearing. In fact, many librarians have lists of persons they have contacted previously and who are library supporters. The best spokespersons in hearings tend to be attorneys, ministers, people from the news media, educators, and, of course, librarians. Response to persons from the local community is usually more favorable than to people brought in from outside. Student speakers are also effective. They speak from the heart and do not have any vested interest other than maintaining their freedom of choice guaranteed by the Constitution.

As people arrive for the hearing, they should be given a copy of the selection policy. The policy should include the following elements, among others: a statement of the philosophy of materials selection, a statement that the governing board is legally responsible for selection of materials, a statement detailing the delegation of this responsibility to the professional library personnel, criteria for selection of materials, procedures for implementing the criteria, and a section on procedures for handling challenged materials. If the *Library Bill of Rights* is not a formal part of the policy, it should be duplicated and distributed as well.

One or more persons should be stationed at the entrance to sign in people wishing to speak. Request that they identify the side on which they will be speaking. If at all possible, attempt to have the same number of speakers on both sides. They should be allowed to speak in the order they signed in. Limit each speaker to a specific amount of time, i.e., three or four minutes, and appoint a timekeeper in advance. No participant should be allowed to speak a second time until everyone registered has been heard once. It is extremely important to adhere strictly both to the time limits and to the order of the speakers.

All members of your advisory board, your reconsideration committee and governing board should already be well-schooled in intellectual freedom principles and procedures. It is the responsibility of the librarian to accomplish this to ensure their support when a challenge hearing is necessary. All those selected to testify should be reminded they are defending a principle more than an individual title. The actual title in question should play a secondary role. It is very difficult to disagree with the freedom to read, view and listen in a democratic society.

Begin the hearing on time. The chair of the governing board should preside as at any other business meeting. After calling the meeting to order, he or she should review the procedures to be followed at the meeting, even though the procedures for handling complaints are in the selection policy. The board should delay its decision until a later date and this should be announced at the beginning of the hearing. The meeting is simply to hear all sides of the issue.

Through the whole process, it is crucial to follow the traditional advice of remaining calm. Remember to practice what you preach and ensure due process. Listen carefully and courteously to everyone. By using good communication skills, you will help people understand your logic in ensuring diversity in library collections.

Keep your governing authority up-to-date on all events and incidents. Examine your personal philosophy of intellectual freedom on a regular basis. Meet all negative pressure with positive pressures, such as emphasizing intellectual freedom rather than the perils of censorship.

By following this advice, you will be able to conduct a successful challenge hearing and improve your image in the process.

Policy on Confidentiality
of Library Records

The Council of the American Library Association strongly recommends that the responsible officers of each library, cooperative system, and consortium in the United States:

1. Formally adopt a policy which specifically recognizes its circulation records and other records identifying the name of library users to be confidential in nature.*
2. Advise all librarians and library employees that such records shall not be made available to any agency of state, federal, or local government except pursuant to such process, order, or subpoena as may be authorized under the authority of, and pursuant to, federal, state, or local law relating to civil, criminal, or administrative discovery procedures or legislative investigative power.
3. Resist the issuance or enforcement of any such process, order, or subpoena until such time as a proper showing of good cause has been made in a court of competent jurisdiction.**

---

*Note: See also ALA "Code of Ethics," point III: "We protect each library user's right to privacy and confidentiality with respect to information sought or received and materials consulted, borrowed, acquired or transmitted."

**Note: Point 3, above, means that upon receipt of such process, order, or subpoena, the library's officers will consult with their legal counsel to determine if such process, order, or subpoena is in proper form and if there is a showing of good cause for its issuance; if the process, order, or subpoena is not in proper form or if good cause has not been shown, they will insist that such defects be cured.

Adopted January 20, 1971; revised July 4, 1975, and July 2, 1986, by the ALA Council.

Policy concerning Confidentiality of Personally Identifiable Information about Library Users

The ethical responsibilities of librarians, as well as statutes in most states and the District of Columbia, protect the privacy of library users. Confidentiality extends to "information sought or received, and materials consulted, borrowed or acquired," and includes database search records, reference interviews, circulation records, interlibrary loan records, and other personally identifiable uses of library materials, facilities, or services.

The First Amendment's guarantee of freedom of speech and of the press requires that the corresponding rights to hear what is spoken and read what is written be preserved, free from fear of government intrusion, intimidation, or reprisal. The American Library Association reaffirms its opposition to "any use of government prerogatives which lead to the intimidation of the individual or the citizenry from the exercise of free expression . . . [and] encourages resistance to such abuse of government power . . ." (ALA Policy 53.4). In seeking access or in the pursuit of information, confidentiality is the primary means of providing the privacy that will free the individual from fear of intimidation or retaliation.

Libraries are one of the great bulwarks of democracy. They are living embodiments of the First Amendment because their collections include voices of dissent as well assent. Libraries are impartial resources providing information on all points of view, available to all persons regardless of age, race, religion, national origin, social or political views, economic status, or any other characteristic. The role of libraries as such a resource must not be compromised by an erosion of the privacy rights of library users.

The American Library Association regularly receives reports of visits by agents of federal, state, and local law enforcement agencies to libraries, where it is alleged they have asked for personally identifiable information about library users. These visits, whether under the rubric of simply informing libraries of agency concerns or for some other reason, reflect an insensitivity to the legal and ethical bases for confidentiality, and the role it plays in the preservation of First Amendment rights, rights also extended to foreign nationals while in the United States. The government's interest in library use reflects a dangerous and fallacious equation of what a person reads with what that person believes or how that person is likely to behave. Such a presumption can and does threaten the freedom of access to information. It also is a threat to a crucial aspect of First Amendment rights: that freedom of speech and of the press include the freedom to hold, disseminate, and receive unpopular, minority, "extreme," or even "dangerous" ideas.

The American Library Association recognizes that, under limited circumstances, access to certain information might be restricted due to a legitimate "national security" concern. However, there has been no showing of a plausible probability that national security will be compromised by any use made of *unclassified* information available in libraries. Thus, the right of access to this information by individuals, including foreign nationals, must be recognized as part of the librarian's legal and ethical responsibility to protect the confidentiality of the library user.

The American Library Association also recognizes that law enforcement agencies and officers may occasionally believe that library records contain information which would be helpful to the investigation of criminal activity. If there is a reasonable basis to believe such records are *necessary* to the progress of an investigation or prosecution, the American judicial system provides the mechanism for seeking release of such confidential records: the issuance of a court order, following a showing of *good cause* based on *specific facts,* by a court of competent jurisdiction.

Adopted July 2, 1991, by the ALA Council.

GLOSSARY

Below are definitions of some of the terms used in the Guidelines to assist in understanding the applicable standards:

Arbitrary distinctions   inappropriate categorizations of persons, classes of persons, conduct, or things based upon criteria irrelevant to the purpose for which the distinctions are made. For example, a rule intended to regulate the length of time an item may be borrowed should not be based on an irrelevant consideration (arbitrary distinction) such as a personal characteristic of the borrower (height or age).

Compelling government interest   a term often used by courts when assessing the burden of government regulation or action upon a fundamental right such as freedom of speech. For such a rule to withstand constitutional challenge, the government must show more than a merely important reason—the reason for the rule must be *compelling*—so important that it outweighs even the most valued and basic freedom it negatively impacts.

Limited public forum   a public place designated by the government, or established through tradition, as a place dedicated to a particular type of expression. As in a public forum, only reasonable time, place and manner restrictions on speech within the scope of the designated purpose of the forum may be imposed. The government may exclude entire categories of speech which do not fall within the designated purpose of the forum, but may not discriminate against particular viewpoints on subjects appropriate to the forum.

Materially interfere a term used by courts to describe the necessary level of intrusion, inconvenience or disruption of an accepted or protected activity caused by certain conduct in order to justify regulation of that conduct. A material interference is much more than mere annoyance—it must be an *actual obstacle* to the exercise of a right.

Substantial objectives goals related to the fundamental mission of a government institution, and not merely incidental to the performance of that mission. Providing free and unrestricted access to a broad selection of materials representing various points of view is a substantial objective of a public library. Having spotless white carpeting is not.

INDEX

The letter *n* refers to notes. Notes appear
at the end of the chapter.

Robert S. Peck is Senior Director for Legal Affairs and Policy Research for the Association of Trial Lawyers of America. Peck is president of the Freedom to Read Foundation, and he chairs the national Lawyers for Libraries project. He also serves on the First Amendment Advisory Council of the Media Institute. A prolific author in the area of constitutional law, his books include *The Bill of Rights and the Politics of Interpretation* (1992). He also teaches legal ethics and constitutional law at American University in Washington, D.C.